THE GREEKS

ANTONY ANDREWES

was born in 1910, in Tavistock, Devon, England, and was educated at Winchester College, Winchester (1923–9), and at New College, Oxford (1929–33). He was a Fellow of Pembroke College, Oxford (1933–46), and of New College, Oxford (1946–53), in Ancient History, and has been Wykeham Professor of Ancient History at Oxford since 1953. Professor Andrewes was awarded the M.B.E. (Mil.) in 1944, and elected a Fellow of the British Academy in 1957. From 1962 to 1965 he was President of the Society for the Promotion of Hellenic Studies in London. He is the author of *The Greek Tyrants* (1956), and with Russell Meiggs brought out the second edition of Hill's *Sources for Greek History, B.C. 478–411* (1951). He is married and has two daughters.

THE GREEKS

by

ANTONY ANDREWES

Wykeham Professor of Ancient History
in the University of Oxford

W · W · NORTON & COMPANY

New York · London

W. W. Norton & Company, Inc., 500 Fifth Avenue, New York, N.Y. 10110
W. W. Norton & Company Ltd., 37 Great Russell Street, London WC1B 3NU

Books That Live
The Norton imprint on a book means that in the publisher's
estimation it is a book not for a single season but for the years.
W. W. Norton & Company, Inc.

Library of Congress Cataloging in Publication Data
Andrewes, Antony, 1919–
The Greeks.
(The Norton library)
Bibliography: p.
Includes index.
1. Civilization, Greek. I. Title.
DF78.A5   1978   938   77-18938

ISBN 0-393-00877-0

6 7 8 9 0

Acknowledgements

My thanks are due to many friends and colleagues for help given at one time or another with the subjects covered in this book. They could not all be named, but I must mention my special obligation to Russell Meiggs, without whose encouragement this book would probably never have got started at all; to Moses Finley, who gave time and trouble on the most generous scale to reading and discussing various drafts, and saved me from many errors of fact and logic; and to Martin Robertson, who also read the typescript. It would have been a much worse book without this friendly help; the remaining errors are all my own.

A. A.

Author's foreword

The scope of this book needs some preliminary definition. The people whom we call the Greeks called themselves 'Hellenes', as their descendants do today, and their primary geographical base was roughly that of modern Hellas, the Greek peninsula and the islands of the Aegean Sea. But, for most of the time we are here considering, 'Hellenes' would tend to exclude many mountain tribes in the north and north-west of the peninsula, while it would certainly include the 'East Greek' settlements on the western coast of Turkey, the 'West Greek' cities of South Italy and Sicily, and all the colonies scattered round the shores of the Mediterranean and the Black Sea.

Though prehistory must claim some attention, my main concern is with the civilisation which emerged into literacy before the end of the eighth century, fought off the Persian invasion of 480 B.C., tore itself apart in the long Peloponnesian War between Athens and Sparta in the late fifth century, and was overpowered by Macedon in the latter part of the fourth century. Here we conventionally distinguish an 'archaic' period, ending about 500 B.C., and a 'classical' period, covering the fifth century and most of the fourth: the period which runs from Alexander's death in 323 to the final Roman conquest is distinguished as 'Hellenistic'. Like the conventional chopping-up of English or European history into centuries, this is a shorthand convenient for historians and does not mark points of sudden and total change. Still, classical Greece as a whole is perceptibly different from archaic Greece as a whole. If a line has to be drawn somewhere, the reform of Cleisthenes at Athens in 507 makes a good landmark, or the wars with Persia that culminated in the invasion of 480.

The prehistoric Greeks of the Mycenaean age (Chapter 2) are relevant to the extent that legends about this resplendent time (c. 1600–1200) lived on in more or less distorted form, and that its real or imagined princes were the actors in that heroic age to which all Greeks looked back. The 'dark age' which followed the collapse of the Mycenaean kingdoms is still more relevant, for this was the formative period in which the institutions of archaic Greece took shape. It is dark in the sense that for over four centuries Greece was wholly illiterate, so that no contemporary record survives and many of the inquiries pursued in this book run out into blank query at the earlier end, frustrated by our ignorance of what went on in the dark age. These are large subjects, especially the Mycenaean age where fresh discovery and new interpretation may radically change the picture while a book is printing. I have not attempted even a complete sketch, but have concentrated mainly on the two sources which best reveal the state of society in their time: for the Mycenaean age, the documents in the script called 'Linear B', deciphered as Greek by Michael Ventris in 1952; for the dark age, the poems of Homer, which tell two stories of the heroic age, but the social background implied by these poems seems to belong to a later time, when Greece had settled down from its troubles and migrations.

No detailed narrative of the archaic and classical periods is attempted here. The main events are covered in the list of dates at the end, and in Chapter 4 I have tried to characterise the main periods and turning-points of political history. Thereafter (Chapters 5–12) various aspects of Greek society are treated, one by one, over the whole course of its history down to the Macedonian conquest. There is no systematic discussion of art or literature, though I hope that no reader of these pages can conclude that I think these subjects unimportant; and I am not competent to discuss the technical virtues of Greek philosophy. Nor is there much about the apparatus of daily life. These subjects have their handbooks; I have rather been concerned to try to define the basic and distinctive features of Greek society, attending particularly to those factors which an English or American reader might find unfamiliar. Professional scholars will find that I have neglected what they regard as important, or dilated on things they regard as peripheral. But in such matters choice can only be subjective, and the criterion must be what oneself finds distinctive or significant.

The decision to stop at Alexander's conquest of the East was a great deal more uneasy. The life of the older Greek cities continued after this, and Hellenistic studies rightly claim increasing attention from today's historians. It is indeed precisely in the social and economic field that the much fuller documentation of the Hellenistic world makes its study so rewarding, as Rostovtzeff magnificently showed.[1]

1. *Social and Economic History of the Hellenistic World* (1941).

Foreword

But while this society is eminently worth study, either for its own sake or as a stage in a larger process, its background and much of its values were substantially different from those of classical Greece. This book is about the original Greek contribution. To do justice to the Hellenistic world—supposing that I were capable of that—would require a full exposition of its quite different framework, a matter not to be crammed into a summary epilogue,[1] and full exposition would crowd out the elbow-room needed by the main theme, which even as it is may seem sketchily treated. The question is, whether this later period throws enough light on the earlier to justify the compression that would be demanded, and in my judgment it does not.

A.A.

1. V. Ehrenberg devotes almost half of *The Greek State* (1960) to the Hellenistic world.

Contents

Maps

The plates have been omitted from the paperback edition.

THE GREEKS

CHAPTER I

Geography and climate

THE CLEAR ATMOSPHERE of Greece, the firm outlines and the colour of the landscape, combine to tell the traveller from north or west that he has entered a different world; and he will be struck, especially if he arrives in summer, by the bareness of the land. Its ancient civilisation developed mainly in the south and east, a land of limestone mountains, almost rainless in the height of summer, where the winter-sown crops ripen early and very few rivers have running water all the year round. The mountains dominate everywhere, and the deeply indented coast keeps most districts in close touch with the sea. It is a poor land, and not even the richest of its ancient inhabitants led a very luxurious life, but it is also a land in which a full life can be led on rather slender resources; and the climate does not keep people in their houses, but brings them out into the sight and company of their neighbours. Geography and climate do not by themselves account for the manifold achievement of the ancient Greeks, but they determined some of the ways in which their civilisation grew. An examination of Greek society must begin with the physical facts.

*

To start with the peninsula itself, northern Greece is divided by the high chain of Pindus, running north and south. To the west of this, the subsidiary ranges mostly follow the same line; in the northern part of the west coast they border the sea, leaving few cultivable plains and fewer harbours. The roomier east, on the other hand, is cut up by transverse ranges running roughly east and west, so that the Thessalian plain is divided from Macedon, Boeotia from Thessaly, Attica from Boeotia. To the south of this, two great arms of the sea, the Corinthian and Saronic Gulfs, almost meet to make the Peloponnese an island but are separated by the narrow Isthmus of Corinth. In the Peloponnese,

the main mountain ranges are again aligned north and south, tailing off
into long barren promontories. The ranges of Euboea and Attica,
however, continue south-eastwards into the Aegean Sea, where their
crests appear as islands, and curve round to the east to join up with the
ranges of western Asia Minor.

This coastal strip of what is now western Turkey, and the great
offshore islands which still belong to Greece, are physically very like
the Greek homeland on the opposite shore of the Aegean, but with a
kinder climate, especially in the central section called Ionia. This was
a tempting area for Greek settlement, which extended a certain distance
up the main river valleys. But when one climbs to the central plateau
of Anatolia one reaches a different and less hospitable world, which
was early subject to Greek influence, but not to systematic settlement
till after Alexander's conquests. To the north of the Aegean, the coast
of Thrace, though considerably bleaker, was also country of a familiar
type. It attracted Greek colonists, but they made little impression on
the inland tribes in the Thracian mountains. To the south, the long
high island of Crete shuts the Aegean off from the open sea towards
Africa, and Carpathos and Rhodes partly close the gap between Crete
and Asia Minor. These again were natural places for Greeks to settle.

Greece itself is deeply penetrated by the sea, and there were sailors in
the Aegean already in Neolithic times. Of course, not all mainland
Greeks knew or loved the sea. The coastal regions were very short of
ships' timber already in the classical period. Navigation was a doubtful and dangerous business, especially in a world which did not know
the compass, and it was mainly confined to the summer when the
winds in the Aegean are regular and steady. But for very many Greeks
the sea was an essential element of life, never far out of mind as it was
seldom long out of sight. Their poets at all times rejoiced in the sight
of a fine ship, and even Hesiod (of whom more below), though he
hated to leave the land, still felt obliged to include a section on sailing
in the poem of instruction which he composed for farmers. The
Greeks were inevitably led out into the Aegean.

The mountains of southern and eastern Greece are not impenetrable
obstacles. They have often been made responsible for the characteristic
development of ancient Greek politics, the growth of jealously independent city-states and the reluctance of Greek to unite with Greek;
and it is surely true that without these barriers it would have been
easier for Greece to coalesce into a single political unit. But the not

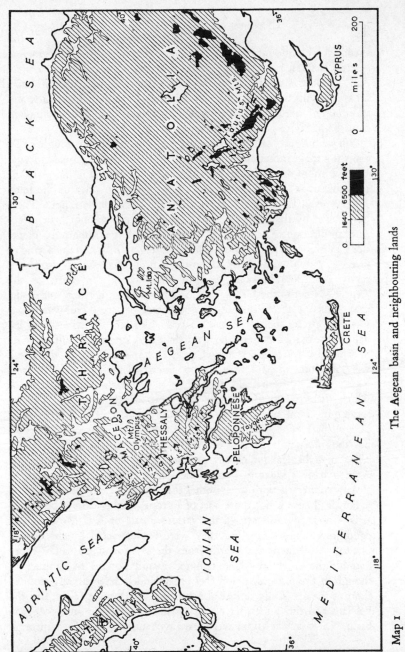

Map I

The Aegean basin and neighbouring lands

inconsiderable mountains of the Peloponnese were little hindrance to
Spartan armies, much less to peaceful travel. Communications were
easy between Corinth, Megara, Attica and Boeotia. Of the main
areas of civilised Greek life, only Thessaly lay somewhat apart, and
the ring of high mountains which surrounds the Thessalian plain
must be partly responsible for that.

But as one proceeds northwards, the obstacles grow tougher. To
cross the main mountain chain of northern Greece from east to west
is much more of an undertaking than to cross the Peloponnese in the
same direction, and the northern edges of Greece towards the main
Balkan peninsula are guarded by still more formidable ranges. These
have never by themselves deterred invasion from the north or piecemeal infiltration, when other conditions encouraged such movement,
but they are some impediment to regular travel. In fact, in the period of
Greece's growth and power, the mountaineers of the north were only
rarely and sporadically tempted to descend on the coasts of the
Aegean. Nor did the Greeks of that time show much interest in the
mountaineers, except further east, in Thrace, where there were silver
mines to attract them. For the classical Athenian, the tribes who inhabited the main mountain mass, north of the Corinthian Gulf and west
of Thessaly, were imperfectly Greek, and the Balkans to the north
were an unknown and alien region. Even when these uncouth areas
were tamed by Rome and opened up to civilisation, the great roads
which traversed them ran east and west across the top of Greece,
leaving it on one side, an appendix to the continental mass and not an
integral part of it. The map may seem to attach Greece to Europe,
but the inhabitants have never felt quite sure of the connection. A
relief map brings out clearly the factors which tend to make the
Aegean basin a separate geographical unit, whose shores are more
closely connected with one another than with the world outside.

For, if Greece is not quite part of Europe, neither does it belong to
Asia. Greek colonists settled the various coasts of Asia Minor where
conditions suited them, but they were less attracted by the central
plateau. Movement westwards from the Anatolian plateau is more
natural; the coast has often tempted inland powers to conquer it,
though in the historic period these mainlanders have usually stopped
short at the sea. Only universal conquerors with wider aims, like the
Persians and the Turks, have tried to incorporate the whole Aegean
basin. Nor was Asia Minor ever the main channel of peaceful communi-

cation with the east. Some impulses were transmitted from one people to another over the land mass; men and armies have traversed the plateau when they needed to; but at all normal times the sea is very much the easier route from the Aegean to Syria. This sea passage, however, involves leaving the closed basin of the Aegean and sailing past less hospitable shores or across the open sea, and that called for more confidence. Geography does not in the same way bind Syria and Greece together, and the Greek cities of Cyprus were never integral members of the Greek community in the way that Rhodes was. The passage into the Black Sea, with its strong currents, was another obstacle, and the Black Sea itself could be forbidding enough, as could also the open sea to the west of Greece in the direction of Italy and Sicily.

In this sense, the Aegean basin forms a naturally separate unit, which helps to account for the fact that the east and south of the Greek mainland were always more important than the west and north, and contributed more to the common civilisation of the Hellenes. On the west side of the peninsula, the climate is damper and the winters warmer, with richer vegetation. Messenia in the south-west Peloponnese and Elis in the north-west are fertile areas capable of supporting a dense population; further north the coast had a fringe of fully Greek cities, most of them prosperous enough, and the offshore islands are still more attractive, especially Corcyra (Corfu). But these states played a less active role, and were not the leaders even in the colonisation of Italy and Sicily, for which their position might seem to have marked them out.

The outer Greek world of the colonies, extending from the Black Sea coasts in the north-east to Marseilles and the Spanish coast in the west, and including Cyrenaica on the north coast of Africa, was more diverse in structure and in climate, but settlement spread widely wherever conditions were not too different from those of the homeland, or the country was not already thickly occupied by peoples well enough organised to resist. The rest of this chapter deals with the Greek homeland, the peninsula and the Aegean basin, for it was in this area that Greek civilisation was formed. It must be remembered that some of the statements which follow, about climate and agriculture, could not be applied without modification to the whole of the colonial area.

*

The climate of Greece as a whole is of the type called Mediterranean, though the proximity of the larger land-masses of the Balkans and Asia Minor, and winds from the cooler waters of the Black Sea, to some extent modify this. Athens and the south-east have a higher summer temperature, and three months or more with no rain except an occasional storm, basically from mid-June to mid-September. During the summer, the vegetation largely dries up. Greece is a windy land at all times, and in July and August the weather of the Aegean is dominated by a regular wind blowing from north or north-east, the 'Etesian' wind of the ancients, which cools the islands but discourages trees. Other seasons are subject to sudden variations of the type familiar in Atlantic countries. Serious rain commonly begins in October, with a maximum in December, but the weather may continue warm through November, the sea slowing up the seasonal change of temperature. Even the winter is only moderately cold at sea-level; snow seldom lies for more than an hour or two in the plain of Attica. Spring is capricious enough: though March will have some warm days, it is still basically winter. In April and May the weather settles down, with a rising temperature and a sudden rush of flowers and even grass; in the lowlands, the crops will be ripe before the end of May.

Western Greece gets more rain in winter, having a slightly different system of winds, and those with a westerly component have moisture to shed when they reach the land and the mountains. The summer shows the same general character as in the east, though the rainless period is shorter. The conspicuous climatic difference comes when one climbs into the mountains, where the annual rainfall may rise higher than the average for central and northern Europe, and the summer temperature is less extreme. On the peaks, patches of snow last into June, and below them one finds running water at the height of summer; there are large woods of oak and other trees below the pine belt; anywhere above 3,000 feet there is summer pasture for sheep and goats—whereas in the burnt-up plains trees are an occasional oasis and water is drawn mainly from wells. Some states had both climates at their disposal, as Sparta with her fertile river-plain lying immediately below the heights of Taygetus; but the territory of Athens and Corinth was for practical purposes altogether lowland, whereas many Arcadian states were wholly in the highland zone and their style of life differed accordingly.

The low annual rainfall of the south-east means that a comparatively slight variation from the normal may have serious consequences. Besides, a proportion of this rain comes in sudden storms which are more destructive than helpful. Most Greek rivers, when they flow at all, carry a large amount of visible silt down to the plains or out to sea, and the erosion of soil at the higher levels can be clearly seen. No quantitative estimate can be made of the amount of arable land that has been lost in this way, but certainly some has. Some traces remain of older terracing of ground which is not now cultivable. Plato in an imaginative passage of the *Critias* pictures an earlier Attica where the hills were deep in earth, whereas in his day only rock remained, the bones of the land laid bare: he also claims thick woods for this vanished age. There had certainly been some loss here. Greece used much wood for fuel and for construction, and may have used more in the earliest times before temples were built of stone. The felling of timber inevitably means further denudation, and in these climatic conditions it is very hard to replant effectively, even when there is the will to attempt it. Goats have a very destructive taste for young shoots. Plato exaggerates, and one may reasonably doubt if more than a quarter of the area of Greece could ever have borne any kind of crop, but this and other passages of ancient literature show clearly that climatic conditions in the centuries B.C. were in general what they are now, and human activity had like effects. But the soil of the plains is in general very fertile, and the warm climate and the sun bring crops on quickly.

*

Agriculture in such a country and climate (pl. 10, 11) is still a laborious business, though in a different way from the agriculture of wetter climates. The farmer's basic problem was that he had too much moisture in the autumn and winter and too little in the summer. The remedy, as in American dry farming, was a constant working of the soil, to pulverise it and help it retain its moisture. The early Boeotian poet, Hesiod, in his *Works and Days*, a poem of moral admonition and practical advice to his brother and his fellow-farmers, gives us a calendar of farming life which is extremely useful, for no systematic treatise on agriculture happens to be preserved from the following centuries. After Hesiod, we must rely on passing mention of agricultural detail in other sorts of literature. Normally, a crop would be taken from a field only in alternate years. The fallow would be turned over with the plough in spring, and had to be kept clean thereafter;

it might be ploughed again in the summer. The main ploughing and the sowing came in the autumn, the recommended time being October, though one might take a chance and leave it as late as the winter solstice. Care had still to be taken to see that the seed was not waterlogged, or exposed through the soil being washed away. Wheat was the main cereal crop, though some soils were considered more suitable for barley, as parts of the plain of Attica. The early-ripening grain must be reaped in the lowlands in May. Having no hay to think about, Hesiod could then allow himself and his men a cheerful holiday in June before they started winnowing the grain in July; then another brief rest till the main grape harvest in September, and in October the round began again.

The Greeks seem to have made little advance on the primitive techniques with which they began. There is not, indeed, much technical information from the earlier stages of the Greek civilisation, for Hesiod was more concerned to rebuke the lazy and unthrifty than to impart knowledge about tools or procedure. But he does describe in some detail his ox-drawn plough, a comparatively simple machine, which had a separate share, share-beam and ploughbeam, though he still recommends the farmer to have in reserve a more primitive implement, made from a single piece of wood. In either case, the share might have a metal tip, or shoe, but this is not mentioned by Hesiod, whose mind was wholly on the virtues of different kinds of wood. Sowing was done entirely by hand, a delicate art; reaping, with a one-handed sickle. Threshing was simpler, the grain being trodden out, mainly by oxen, in the open air on those circular paved threshing-floors which are still a conspicuous feature of the Greek countryside, the wind blowing the chaff away. There was some slight progress towards a rotation of crops, and considerable interest in varieties of seed. Otherwise, there was no important innovation after the introduction of the metal-tipped ploughshare, in the time before our literature begins.

Except for some swampy areas in Boeotia and Thessaly, there was no pasture in the plains in summer, nor could the ordinary farmer afford to give up to other uses land which might yield a crop. Horses therefore, much as upper-class Greeks delighted in them, were for the rich, for racing and up to a point for war. Cavalry formed only a small proportion of the classical city's fighting force and were not always very efficient, except in Thessaly and to some extent in Boeotia. Mules were important for transport (and might be harnessed to the plough, though oxen were more normal), but few roads capable of wheeled traffic crossed the mountains from one plain to another. Even on the plain, unmetalled tracks sink deep into mud in winter, so pack transport was normal, as it remained till very recent years, with the result that transport by sea was apt to be preferred where possible. Oxen were essential for ploughing, but there was little pasture for cattle. For milk and cheese, ancient Greece relied mainly on the goat: after Homer, there is not much mention of sheep's milk, which is extensively drunk in modern Greece, and the sheep seem to have been kept primarily for wool and secondarily for meat. Both sheep and goats were reared in large numbers. So far as possible, they were relegated to the hills in summer, though long-distance seasonal migration to high mountain pasture seems to have been practised less than in medieval or modern times. But anywhere in Greece the limestone ridges of which the land is mainly composed grow in their jagged perforations a scrub vegetation, which provides some nourishment for goats and some firewood, but serves no other economic purpose. Driving the animals uphill deprived the plain of one of its few possible sources of manure, but burning and ploughing in weeds were some substitute.

The place which butter takes in our diet was filled mainly by olive oil. The olive, with its long roots and narrow leaves, is well adapted to absorb the maximum moisture from the soil and lose as little as possible in the heat of summer. A grain crop can very often be grown between the trees. Its oil, used for cooking and light and for other purposes, was one of the few Greek products whose surplus might be exported for profit, and the return from the land planted with olives was proportionately greater, so that when foreign cereals began to be imported in quantity it was natural to extend the culture of the olive at the expense of home-grown cereals. Another important competitor for land was the vine, grown low in small bushes whose leaves protect the soil from the summer sun. The vine will grow, in a favourable aspect, at a fair height, but the olive is confined to the plains and lower slopes. No doubt then, as today, mountain areas like Arcadia, which were short of arable land, exchanged meat and cheese for the oil and cereals grown at lower levels.

Greece lives on bread to an extent which surprises present-day northerners, and spring was a hungry time till the harvest was ripe, especially before the introduction of maize provided a fresh resource.

Meat was for feast days and other special occasions; public sacrifice meant a full meal for the poor man, the god being content with fat and bones, burnt on his altar. Fish was a larger item, not only fresh but dried, and some of it imported from afar: eggs and vegetables also played their part: but the essential items were bread, olives, milk, with fruit in season and honey to provide sugar. In that warm climate, the human body requires less stoking than it does in the colder north. The physical stamina and resilience of the Greek are supported on a diet which an Englishman or an American would find exiguous. The Greeks rejoiced in wine too, but in ancient times it was thought dissolute to drink it neat—five parts of water to two of wine are cited as a respectable proportion. The mental breakdown of a powerful Spartan king was attributed to his having learnt from Scythian envoys the habit of drinking wine unmixed. The god Dionysus was gratefully honoured for having taught mankind the proper use of the grape, and so was the goddess Demeter who gave them grain. These were the basic gifts.

Statistics of population are unprocurable; for the earlier periods, and over much of the country, there is not even much material for guessing. Clearly, it was easy for the population to outrun the limited resources of Greek agriculture, and overcrowding must have been at least part of the cause of the colonising movement of the eighth and seventh centuries. By the classical period, Greece was importing grain from three main areas: Sicily and South Italy, where the fertile plains were occupied by Greek colonists; South Russia, where there was a border of Greek colonies and depots—but these lands were not occupied in depth, and those who wished to succeed in this branch of the trade had to court the favour of native princes; and Egypt, where the Greeks had little more than a single foothold in the trading colony of Naucratis, though they more effectively occupied Cyrenaica along the African coast to the west.

*

After food, the most serious shortage was always of metal. Greece had some valuable silver mines: Laurium in the promontory southeast of Athens, where the discovery of a new vein early in the fifth century was an important element in the growth of Athens' power; the island of Siphnos, further south, which prospered greatly in the archaic period, but then the sea flooded the mines; most important of

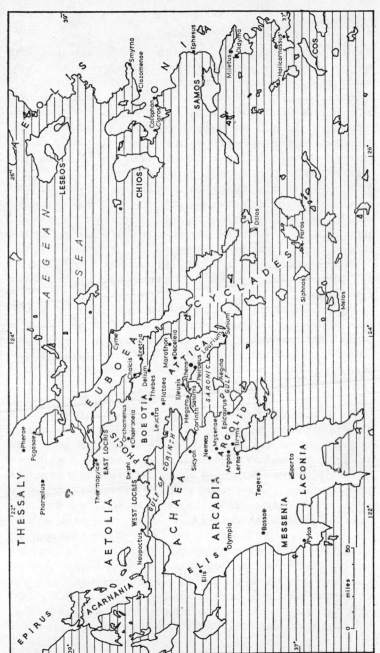

Map 2   Greece and the Aegean

all, the Thracian mining area, east of the river Strymon (producing gold as well as silver), for which several states contended with the native inhabitants from the sixth century onwards. There were only sporadic deposits of iron or copper, the most important being again in the north, in Macedon and Thrace. Next in importance were Euboea and Laconia, but though Laconian iron had later a high reputation this does not appear very early. In any case, most of this iron occurred in forms which were not easily dealt with by ancient techniques of smelting, and a high percentage of the metal was lost. Copper was imported from Cyprus, but the tin which was needed for the alloy, bronze, was always in short supply. Indeed, it is not at all clear where the Bronze Age civilisations of the Mediterranean got this necessary metal. Iron was found in the north-east of Asia Minor and up into modern Armenia, and the earliest supply for Greece probably came from this direction, when the Hittites lost their control of it. Later, but still early, the Greeks found another source among the Etrurians of central Italy.

Shipbuilding materials form a third conspicuous need. The importance of shipping needs no further stress, but timber was not to be found within easy reach of the sea and had mostly to be imported, from Macedon or Thrace or the famous pine-woods of Mount Ida near Troy. Nor could Greece provide her own pitch, sail-cloth, or ropes.

*

The social effects of the climate must not be forgotten. For most of the year, the Greek could work and eat and talk in the open air, somewhat scantily clad, seeking the shade rather than the sun; and this had a large effect on his way of life. Farming left some time to spare, even for the industrious Hesiod, and the ancient Greek spent most of it talking with his fellow-farmers, as his successor does today in the village café. The townsman felt the same need, which was satisfied by those colonnades which adorned Greek cities, giving shade or shelter for conversation—the Greek word for these porches, *stoa*, gave the Stoic philosophers their name. Winter did not check the gregarious impulse: Hesiod, who is eloquent on the cold of his upland home, characteristically stresses the need for the farmer to work in his own house, not lounge and talk in the smithy—and that is a clear enough indication of the way in which most men spent the cold season.

Consequently, the Greek lived a very public life. The pressure of the community on the individual was greater than it is in climates where man must shelter indoors for most of his leisure time. It was harder to hide from disapproval, more essential to display what might earn praise. The immediate spoken word was dominant: oratory was decisive in politics, written pamphlets a secondary growth: poetry was for recitation and not for silent reading, except perhaps for a sophisticated minority after the classical period. In a civilisation where so much depends on immediate impact, and where the individual has not much time to brood on his course of action, he must be alert and active; and he easily develops that touchy pride which is still noticeable today. The northerner, perhaps exaggerating the contrast, is apt to regard the Greek as volatile and irresponsible. One may doubt if in the long run the Greek is really less reasonable, but it is true that the climate imposes a difference of rhythm and idiom, and we must take account of that.

CHAPTER 2

Mycenaean Greece

THE PREHISTORY OF Greece includes a Palaeolithic period whose
remains have only recently come to light, and a long Neolithic period
for which the evidence has again been greatly increased in recent
years. The following Bronze Age is somewhat artificially divided,
according to its styles of pottery, into three main phases, for mainland
Greece called Early, Middle and Late Helladic, with subdivisions of
varying complexity.[1] Middle Helladic began *c.* 1900, and it gave way,
some time after 1600, to Late Helladic, the phase called Mycenaean
after the famous citadel where its remains were first uncovered. That
civilisation suffered violent blows around 1200, and collapsed into an
illiterate 'dark age', which saw the establishment of the full Iron Age.
The early phases of this are again distinguished in terms of their pottery,
Protogeometric and Geometric.

*

The translation of the archaeological record into historical terms is
a tricky and disputable business. In this long span of time there was no
doubt much coming and going, conquest and migration. A great upheaval at the end of the Bronze Age is clearly attested and dated, for
the migrant peoples tried to break their way into Egypt and were
repulsed by Rameses III about 1190; and we can be sure there were
other such movements earlier. But important cultural changes, of the
kind which have led archaeologists to divide the Bronze Age up into
its periods, need not always result from migration or conquest; con-

1. Cretan archaeology has three 'Minoan' periods, the culture of the Aegean
islands three 'Cycladic' periods, both similarly subdivided. The divisions into
periods do not coincide with those of Helladic. In this chapter, the term Minoan
is occasionally used to distinguish the Bronze Age civilisation of Crete, but the
detailed classification is not here relevant.

versely, there might be conquest without any very marked break in culture. Where the symptoms are extensive—desertion or destruction of the old habitation sites, new styles of building or dress, change in burial customs, and the like—one may fairly infer a substantial change of population, probably effected by force. Even so, one must not just forget the earlier population, which is more likely to have been submerged than obliterated or completely expelled, so that it might reassert itself or make a significant contribution at a later stage.

Where the evidence consists only of such material remains as can physically survive many centuries of burial—pottery, easily broken but almost impossible to destroy, is liable to take a disproportionate share of our attention—the interpreter must be very circumspect. Something can be inferred from the layout of settlements and their fortification, or from the absence of walls, from burial customs and surviving artefacts. With the refinement of archaeological techniques, we can establish with increasing certainty important uniformities and diversities and connections. But till we have a written record of the people who built the settlements and used the objects, large areas of their thought and social institutions elude us altogether. Where there is no other evidence, there will always be a temptation to make large deductions from styles of decoration on pottery: but in more articulate epochs we by no means always find a close correlation between pottery decoration and the development of other arts, let alone a correlation with social or political development.

Earlier languages also leave important traces. Greek belongs to the great Indo-European family, but to a branch of it with no close connections that we can now follow. It contains a fairly high proportion of words which we can recognise as foreign, and no doubt many of these were taken over from the languages of previous inhabitants. Place-names in particular are often taken over in this way, like the Celtic names which survive in England, or the numerous Indian names of North America. But philological survivals cannot be set in series and dated in the way that archaeological materials can, nor can one easily estimate how large a body of newcomers is required in any particular situation to impose a new language on a conquered population. Greek itself was split up into a number of dialects, though not to the point where one district could not easily understand another, and the differentiation and distribution of these dialects is an important clue to the earlier history of their speakers—provided we remember that the processes of formation and interaction will have been continuous, and that dialect boundaries will have been fluid. Particularly in dealing with the first arrival of the Greeks in the peninsula, the notion that each dialect represents a separate and compact group of settlers has proved seriously misleading. Recent theory is inclined to doubt whether the Greek language even existed, in any form that we should recognise, till intruders with an Indo-European language had amalgamated with the earlier inhabitants.

Oral tradition presents another kind of problem. The Greeks had a large fund of stories about their heroic ancestors, and there can be no doubt that tradition was in some degree continuous from the Mycenaean age through centuries of illiteracy to the literate age of later Greece. Tenacious accuracy has been claimed for this tradition, especially in the matter of names and pedigrees, but available analogy (and there is plenty of it) suggests that it is usable only where there is confirmation from some other kind of evidence. The stories centre round two main events, the destruction of Thebes and the sack of Troy. The period of these exploits constituted for the Greeks a 'heroic age', like that of Theodoric or Charlemagne for the medieval epics of Western Europe. The poetry which celebrates such an age has no historical conscience, for the poet's business was to delight his hearers; though an oral poet will generally claim to tell a true story, and his audience will accept the claim, neither party can in fact distinguish critically between history and palatable fiction. We cannot hope to tell, merely by looking at the surviving poems, where genuine tradition stops and the poet's fancy begins, though rationalising critics in ancient and modern times have tried their best. Still less can we make such distinctions when we are dealing with later prose reflections of poetry no longer extant. The city which the excavators number as Troy VIIA was violently destroyed by human hands near the end of the Late Bronze Age; and this has encouraged modern critics to believe that we are dealing here with the subject of the Greek legend, that Troy was really sacked by a Greek host led by the king of Mycenae. But there are serious doubts about date and detail, and there are still, as there have long been, scholars who doubt if Troy was destroyed by the Greeks at all. The epic is never by itself a reliable record of events, and its greatest value for history lies in what it can tell us incidentally about thoughts or customs or material objects, either in some past world or in the poet's own time.

*

Where the evidence is subject to these limitations, one must resist the temptation to draw tidy conclusions. Thus, the spread of agriculture from the east was clearly one of the major events of the remote past, helping the Neolithic population to settle in permanent villages, but it is still matter for argument how this new technique arrived in Greece—by peaceful intercourse with Asia Minor, or by the immigration of new people. There was certainly some traffic by sea within the Neolithic period, since many of these settlements used tools made of obsidian from the island of Melos; but that does not decide the question of origins. Again, it should be noted that the skulls surviving from this early time are predominantly of the type called Mediterranean, but with a fair proportion of the Alpine type; so it would not be wise to assume a racially homogeneous population for the Neolithic period, much less for later ages.

Later changes raise similar questions. The transition to the Bronze Age was not a clean-cut affair, complete at one stroke; it would be easy to imagine the piecemeal introduction of metal, along with other innovations of the time, which include the potter's wheel. But in many places there is a break between Neolithic and Early Helladic occupation, or the Early Helladic sites are new, and it seems as if the new mode of living spread from south to north within Greece; indeed, it never fully penetrated Thessaly. The guess is inevitable, that we have here the culture of newcomers who arrived in the first instance by sea. The population grew noticeably thicker than in Neolithic times: there were some elaborate fortified buildings, like that recently excavated at Lerna in the Argolid; Thermi on Lesbos shows a huddled conglomeration of small houses covering a considerable area; further afield, the contemporary citadel of Troy is a narrow but formidable structure fortified by a rich king to protect his treasure. But over most of the Aegean area we find just small unwalled settlements, which rather suggest a long time of comparative peace.

The culture of the whole area, Greece and the islands (including Crete) and western Asia Minor, is fairly uniform, and clearly interconnected. We should probably associate with this a linguistic fact, the wide distribution of a class of place-names which lived on into the Greek period but are not themselves Greek. The most conspicuous items are terminations in -nth-, as in Korinthos (Corinth), or in a sibilant which the Greeks wrote as -ss- or -tt-, as in Parnassus. There are also some vocabulary words with the same terminations, mostly names for birds or plants. Place-names of these types are clustered most thickly in those parts of Greece where there are most Early Helladic settlements. There is obvious attraction in the idea that this was the speech of the Early Helladic population, whose culture was fairly uniform over the area, and that the Greeks took over from this language the names of many places and a certain number of words, especially of fauna and flora not familiar to them in their earlier home.

Whether or not this earlier language was the speech of the Early Helladic people, we must assume at some stage the intrusion of substantial bands of people speaking an Indo-European language, from which Greek itself developed; and the prevailing opinion has for some time been that such an intrusion occurred about 1900, and introduced the Middle Helladic phase of the Greek Bronze Age. It is now clear that Lerna and certain other sites suffered destruction at the transition from the second phase of Early Helladic to the third, and in consequence the invasion of the newcomers is rather to be dated about 2100; or indeed there may have been more than one wave of invasion. Before and after 2000, there is certainly an overall impression of some violence and of a drop in the population, and of considerable regress from the level of civilisation which Early Helladic Greece had attained. The symptoms suggest invasion, but there is no agreement about the direction from which the newcomers arrived. Arguments from styles of pottery seem currently inconclusive, but it may be relevant that other intruders speaking Indo-European languages broke into the Mediterranean and Mesopotamian worlds about this time, Hittites in Anatolia, Mitanni in northern Mesopotamia, Kassites in Babylonia, and these certainly did not come from south or east. After the first violent upheavals, there was a period of quiet recovery and consolidation, a gradual improvement in various techniques, and one innovation of primary importance, the first introduction into Greece of the domesticated horse. The spectacular advance came in the time of the princes who were buried in the shaft-graves of Mycenae (below), who clearly ranged abroad, and whose art was subject to various influences, including that of Minoan Crete.

The people of Early Minoan Crete shared the culture of Early Helladic Greece and contemporary Asia Minor; if the argument from the place-names is valid, they probably shared their language too. In the course of the Middle Minoan period, soon after 2000, they developed an elaborate and refined civilisation which far outstripped anything their predecessors could show, or their contemporaries in mainland Greece. The centres of this great outburst were the cities of central Crete, Cnossus in the north and Phaestus in the south. The palaces of this period, though difficult to disentangle from later building, seem like their successors to have had no very clear plan—just an accumulation of various groups of rooms round a central court. But their mere extent testifies to the power and wealth of those who built them. The frescoes which decorated the walls, and the pottery used in the palaces, reveal most clearly the gay and delicate character of this long lost world. It is disputable how far the new impulse may have begun from contact with the high civilisation of early Egypt; in any case, this is not a mere modification of outside models, but the flowering of a very distinct and individual people.

There are enough representations of ships in their art to show that the sea mattered to them, and the influence of their art abroad was very great, first on the islands and then on the mainland. Greeks of the fifth century were quite sure that the legendary Minos had ruled the sea from Cnossus—and this is the famous Athenian legend too, how Theseus slew the Minotaur and saved Athens from paying her annual tribute of youths and maidens. But, by the time we have decipherable written evidence, the domination of Cnossus over the sea and the mainland (if it ever existed) had been reversed, and we find Greeks apparently in control in Crete. The conflagration at Cnossus about 1400 baked hard, and so preserved for us, a quantity of inscribed clay tablets, administrative documents which have now been deciphered as Greek. This was not the first style of writing current in Crete: there was a pictographic script, and a development of it which we call Linear A, still undeciphered and presumably used for the non-Greek language of Minoan Crete itself. The script called Linear B is a further development, using some of the older signs, somewhat imperfectly adapted to the Greek language, which here makes its earliest known appearance. To discuss what it was doing in Cnossus, we must first turn back to the mainland.

*

Our knowledge of Mycenaean Greece began when Schliemann turned his attention to the strong but relatively inconspicuous citadel of Mycenae in the north-east corner of the plain of Argos. The unrifled 'shaft-graves' of the great circle, just inside the Lion Gate, yielded an astonishing amount of gold, masks for the faces of the dead, dress ornaments, jewellery, cups and the rest, amply justifying the epithet 'rich in gold' which Homer once bestows on Mycenae. Another and earlier grave circle has now been found, outside the walls of the later citadel, and we are now sure that these rich developments, quite unlike anything that had been seen on the mainland before, began before the end of the Middle Bronze Age, at a date close to 1600.

To use the name 'Mycenaean' for this last phase of the Bronze Age, or to call the dominant people 'Mycenaean Greeks', may be misleading or may not, but it is convenient, and by now unavoidable. The unresolved question is whether Greece in the fourteenth and thirteenth centuries was in any degree a unified kingdom ruled from Mycenae itself. There were palaces and rich tombs elsewhere, and nothing in the archaeological record positively implies the dependence of these other centres on Mycenae. The pottery and other artefacts of the thirteenth century show a quite remarkable uniformity of style over the whole area, and for this there must be some reason; but political unity is not a necessary inference from cultural uniformity, nor in itself a sufficient explanation of it. Equally, the deciphered documents concern the administration of the areas centred on Cnossus and Pylos, and in no way suggest that either was dependent on Mycenae: they contain, indeed, no hint at all about the relations between one centre and another.

Belief in the dominance of Mycenae rests on two uncertain props. One is the king of 'Ahhiyawa' who appears spasmodically in Hittite records of the late fourteenth and the thirteenth centuries, as a neighbour somewhere off the western coast of Asia Minor. In spite of some philological objections, it is now widely agreed that this name must be connected with 'Achaioi', the name most frequently used by Homer for the Greeks who followed Agamemnon to Troy. It has been argued, from the Hittite context, that this king was a minor prince whose centre was not far from the Asiatic coast, perhaps in Rhodes. Other scholars maintain that the context requires a more extensive ruler, as the king of a unified Mycenaean empire would be. Secondly, Homer believed that the king of Mycenae was somehow superior to the other kings, though he had difficulty in expressing this relationship, so alien to later Greek ideas. It seems easier to account for this by supposing that the overlordship of Mycenae was a traditional element, imperfectly understood by Homer's time, than by taking it as later invention. However, most of the following discussion is confined by the nature of the evidence to Cnossus and Pylos, and the problem whether there was a unified kingdom is seldom relevant. The term 'Mycenaean' is used hereafter for the whole civilisation, without prejudice.

The palace at Mycenae has partly collapsed into the valley which it overhangs, but we can supplement our picture from the rock of Tiryns, no great distance away, near the shore of the Argolid, and from elsewhere. An elaborate complex has been found at Pylos far in the southwest, in legend the home of king Nestor. There are traces on the Acropolis at Athens, and in Boeotia there were palaces at Orchomenus and elsewhere, besides the rich palace which underlies the modern town of Thebes, and is known to us only from the few corners where circumstances have permitted excavation. Further north, there were palaces in southern Thessaly, a late extension of Mycenaean civilisation. For the most part, these palaces show an agglomeration of groups of rooms not different in principle from the Cretan style. The main distinguishing feature of these mainland examples is what has been called the 'throne-room'. This belongs to a type, common in Middle Helladic Greece, which archaeologists call a *megaron*, a rectangular building with its door in the middle of one of the shorter sides, leading first into a smaller anteroom, from which there is access to the main inner room. The ceremonial variant in the palaces has usually a columned porch, then a vestibule which may be quite narrow, then a large main room whose ceiling was supported by four columns surrounding a central hearth; and against one wall the emplacement for the king's throne.

Besides the palaces, our archaeological material comes from tombs, found by now in most areas of Greece, some of them rich enough to suggest the burial of men who might be called kings. The shaft-graves of Mycenae, referred to above, belong to an early phase. Later we find a more grandiose form of monumental tomb: a square-cut passage leads into the slope of a hill, to the doorway of a circular chamber with a false dome. The first of these to be discovered, the tomb at Mycenae which Schliemann named the Treasury of Atreus, is particularly impressive; and so are the grave-goods which have been recovered from unrifled tombs. It was, however, only at the time of their burial that the dead received this expensive reverence: when the body had decayed, the bones of a Mycenaean Greek were often swept aside to make room for a later burial.

Cretan influence on Mycenaean art was very great. Long observable on the islands, in the sixteenth century it spread to the mainland, and the technique of much that was made or painted there is unmistakably Minoan. In the first excitement of Sir Arthur Evans' discovery of Minoan Crete, it was natural to guess that Crete had conquered the mainland at this stage, but the guess will not do, nor even the notion of a Cretan colonisation. So far as these are artefacts of Cretan workmanship, they are the work of Cretan (or Cretan-trained) artists, working for foreign masters with alien tastes. The vases and the rest, the magnificent inlaid daggers, the sculptures on the headstones of the graves, show an interest in war which is foreign to Minoan art, which indeed was altogether much less concerned with the human figure. On the gold masks from the shaft-graves (pl. 5a), some of which seem to attempt portraiture, the moustache and the curiously cut beard mark the king of Mycenae off clearly from the clean-shaven Cretan.

The Mycenaean Greeks took to the sea on a large scale, with firm contacts far away in the west in South Italy, and trading settlements (if no more) on the Syrian coast. Their pottery was already exported in the fourteenth century, and very widely in the thirteenth, to Troy and Egypt and many other places: often it takes the place of previous imports from Minoan Crete; on a few sites we find a Mycenaean replacing a Minoan settlement. It is no great surprise that they should have taken over Cnossus itself, the richest centre of that strangely unwarlike civilisation, whose cities were unwalled and whose troops wore no body-armour. Recent excavation suggests a date early in the fifteenth century, but the facts are not yet beyond dispute. The Greeks took over the palace, intruding a 'throne-room' into it, though this is not a 'megaron' like those of the mainland. It became an arsenal as well as a store-house, full of chariots and horses and other matters not familiar there before, including body-armour. From the documents, it seems that many other Cretan cities were now controlled from Cnossus.

Then, about 1400, all this was suddenly destroyed in a great fire, while alterations were proceeding in the palace, and to all appearances the Mycenaean Greeks abandoned Crete. It was not that Mycenaean power in general collapsed—indeed, the next two centuries are the period of its widest prosperity—and we know of no outside power likely to have done just this damage and produced this result. Possibly a revolt in Crete convinced the Mycenaeans that they could no longer hold their conquest—it may have strained their manpower to occupy so much as they did. At all events, they went, and Crete, deprived of its old glory, continued in its old Minoan ways through the remainder of the Bronze Age. Some parts of the palace of Cnossus were cleared and inhabited again by Minoan squatters, but it was no longer the centre of anything that much mattered.

*

It is time to look more closely at the contribution made by the newly deciphered documents. The script called Linear B was first identified at Cnossus at the beginning of this century, and the only other large find of inscribed tablets was made at Pylos just after the last war. A few have been found at Mycenae, and recently some more at Thebes; and there are traces elsewhere, principally signs painted on vases at Thebes and other places. With the exception of these last, we owe all our specimens to the burning of the buildings which housed them. Scratched on wet clay and allowed to dry, these were no permanent records, but current memoranda; and they survive only because they were accidentally baked. The character of the script betrays that it was not intended for clay, as were the wedge-shaped impressions which gave the cuneiform script its name. This was a script for pen or brush; if it was used with any intention of permanent record, then, ironically enough, that record was made on perishable material.

It is not easy to guess whether the script was ever used for anything but the meagre administrative documents which we have in their rough clay drafts. Cumbrous and ambiguous as a medium for rendering the Greek language, it might seem unusable except in this special context, where trained scribes knew what sort of things their colleagues would have put down. But scripts as awkward as this were used elsewhere in the ancient Near East for monumental record or diplomatic correspondence. As luck will have it, Mycenaean kings did not try to record their exploits on stone, but they must have sent letters to one another and abroad, written presumably on perishable material. Writing was the monopoly of a small professional class, for the style of the script (and most of the terminology) is identical for the Cnossus documents baked in a fire about 1400, and for the Pylos tablets burnt about 1200. A script used only by specialists for restricted purposes might, like some cuneiform scripts, be as conservative as this, whereas in a fully literate society, which used writing freely for many purposes, the style would be bound to alter largely in the course of two centuries. (The conservatism here postulated is still disquieting, and determined attempts have been made to revise the dates and reduce the gap, especially by dating the catastrophe at Cnossus much later; but the archaeological obstacles seem insuperable.) In any case, in view of the circumstances in which our tablets have been preserved, it is wildly unlikely that we shall ever recover any Mycenaean history or literature in this script.

The scribes worked within a system which was fully familiar to them but is not known to us. They recorded only the detail they needed for each transaction, so that the framework and the general presuppositions to a large extent elude us, as do many of their technical terms. But it is clear that we have here a careful and elaborate palace bureaucracy, which was administratively interested in practically everything anyone might do or fail to do. For all we know, it may have been as inefficient as the centralised machinery of other places and other ages. But the intention of universal interference is certainly there, and that alone makes a very wide gulf between Mycenaean Greece and the way of life that developed after Mycenae's collapse. More immediately, it means that the kings of the Late Bronze Age lived a very different kind of life from that of Homer's Agamemnon.

The king stands at the apex of the political hierarchy, and his title is *wanax*, a word which Homer still applies to his kings; but for him this was a conscious archaism, the word being later reserved for the gods. The *lawagetas*, whose title is at least translatable, as 'leader of the people', has very naturally been taken as the commander of the army, though no text directly says that he was. We have a number of other titles, almost all of them hitherto unknown; among them appears the word which later Greece used for a king, *basileus*, not to all appearance here very high in the scale of importance. We have to grope for the meaning of these persons' titles and the nature of their functions, but the number and variety tell their own tale. Till the time of the classical democracies we shall not meet again this degree of differentiation of function in the public life of any Greek community.

The palace had to know in detail what materials it collected from village, official or individual, and it recorded deficiencies and exemptions. For instance, the authorities at Pylos issued bronze to smiths, noting the amount to each by name, and also the names of those who received no allocation; so we can say today how many such unemployed smiths there were in each of some dozen villages, in the year of Pylos' destruction. Equipment in store was listed, too. Swords, spears, and arrows, body-armour and helmets, chariots and their wheels, are described in detail often unintelligible; even in listing a pair of wheels no longer serviceable, the scribe needed to say what kind of wheels they were. Peaceful furniture was also listed—tables, chairs and foot-stools in words just recognisable, but the technicalities of their decoration are given in terms that were lost when the skills were lost. A fresh vocabulary had to be evolved when Greece again reached a comparable level of technical sophistication.

Archaeology lends some help when we puzzle over lists describing material objects, but the linguistic difficulties deepen when we come to the very interesting series which deals with land tenure at Pylos. Two words for a plot of land occur, one of them wholly obsolete later, the other in use in Hellenistic times in Rhodes, in what appears to be a quite different connection. The latter word is accompanied in the texts by two alternating participles which seem to distinguish two different forms of tenure; with the less intelligible of the two, we meet very often the phrase 'from the people' (see below). This is another case where the vocabulary lapsed with the system, leaving us very much in the dark. To take one most frustrating instance, there is quite frequent reference to dues or services which individuals have not fulfilled, and this opens up interesting possibilities about conditional tenures. But the most complete sets of documents have very possibly a religious context, so that the dues may be sacrifices, not a civil obligation; and the striking fact that many of the holders are described as 'slaves of the god' may be quite untypical of the country as a whole. But the possibility is at least open that property carried a military obligation. We have some military contingents listed (by now, the reader will not be surprised to hear that different categories of soldiers are described in terms hitherto unknown and quite incomprehensible), and some documents about rowers. We must not pretend that we understand the arrangements for the defence of Pylos, but, in a document which is certainly concerned with missing rowers, one dark clause uses the vocabulary of the land-tenure records. It is clearly possible that the occupant of the land had a duty to provide one or more men for the defence of the kingdom.

The labour force was numerous and much differentiated. We have, for instance, a series of short notes about the numbers of women in various categories, and of their children, often with a place-name as a heading, and often with a note of quantities of wheat and figs, which have been interpreted as their monthly rations. The words that describe the occupations of these women are sometimes obscure, but it is striking that these stray groups had to be recorded at all, and that the lords of the palaces required so much specialised service. Male vocations are also highly differentiated, for the service of the king and others: some bear their later Greek names (smith and swineherd were stable vocations, needed just as much after the collapse), others are less certain. Some of those who are listed were relatively free; it was worth the scribes' while to note, of four women in a Pylian village, that their mother was a slave and their father a smith, whereas six others had a slave father—the smith was something other than a slave, whatever good that may have done him or his daughters. There were certainly slaves of individuals as well as the 'slaves of the god' who held land near Pylos, but in some relations slaves seem to be treated in much the same way as free men. Freedom and slavery in this remote society may well have borne shapes which would seem strange to us.

At Pylos, one could apparently hold some sorts of land 'from the people' as well as 'from' individuals, and 'the people' gave wheat and wine and other things to the god Poseidon. This raises questions more interesting than answerable. *Damos* (in Attic speech *demos*, descending to us in the word 'democracy') may signify, as our 'people' does, the whole nation, or the common people as opposed to the nobles; and there were other shades of meaning. Whatever the precise colour here, there is clearly some sort of corporate body distinct from the king, perhaps a village community, perhaps a body serving a particular religious cult. The 'free' men just discussed were available to be organised into such a corporation; but, given the general character of our documents, it is not likely that such a corporation enjoyed a real independence.

What we see of the economic system is the activity of the palace, which exacts produce and no doubt much else from the king's subjects, and doles out rations and materials when something has to be done, with exact notes of what has been received or issued, and what should have been. There is no reference to anything outside the palace system, and it may well be that this covered the whole country. There is no suggestion of money, or of any standard by which values might be compared, items just being counted, weighed, or measured as they stand. Nor is there any direct reference to foreign trade, which must have involved some kind of exchange; and we may reasonably suspect that the palace, which controlled so much, would control this also.

The question insistently presents itself, how the gold and the ivory which must have come from abroad were paid for, and how the whole elaborate hierarchy was supported. These questions are just as insistent for Minoan Crete, too, which had no resources not available to mainland Greece. The land could produce surplus oil and wine, whose export in later times possibly more than balanced the need to import cereals from outside, but it is not easy to see how these kings could grow so strikingly rich on this margin. Later Greeks prospered at sea in the carrying trade, and the Mycenaeans, who established themselves both in the Levant and in the far west, might have made profits as middlemen. It is not so easy to accept the same solution for Minoan Crete, which had dealings with Egypt and elsewhere and also with the Aegean islands, but for a long time none with the Greek mainland, and does not look like a serious intermediary trader. Nor is there any clear indication that Greek craftsmanship in the Mycenaean age had the export value which it undoubtedly possessed later.

The answer possibly lies in the very extensive lists of livestock found in the Cnossus archives, in round numbers and with a high proportion of male animals. There are parallels in estate records from medieval England, and some from the ancient Near East. A recent interpretation deduces an organised industry, with flocks of standard size whose numbers could have been maintained by lambs from the palace's breeding flocks, the object being the production of predictable annual amounts of wool. Another series of records refers to the delivery of both cloth and wool, so some of the wool was woven in outlying villages, and some centrally. This could have served an export trade as well as home use. It may be that the contemporary situation favoured Crete as a wool-producer, as the late medieval situation favoured England. Fewer sheep are recorded at Pylos, and hardly any made-up cloth, but the few tablets from Mycenae include records about wool: textiles may or may not have played the same part in the economy of the mainland.

Not much more than this can be established with any real probability from the documents; though some uncertainties may be resolved by further study, much will continue to elude us. If any continuous literature had survived, we might understand these laconic documents better, and they would be a valuable check on the literature; by themselves they are open to too many alternative interpretations. It is in most cases easier to see that a large and complex operation is being carried out than to determine its precise nature. But the scale and the complexity are in themselves facts of the first importance, and it is of profound significance that these palace officials spent so much time inquiring into matters which no classical Greek state would have thought of asking about.

The collapse of Mycenaean Greece led to a simplification of both system and vocabulary, which was already complete for the epic tradition in which Homer worked. His kings led their own armies and felt no need for all the multiple officials. Their titles vanished from the language when the bureaucratic edifice crumbled, so that *Iliad* and *Odyssey* are no reliable guide to the real lives of Mycenaean kings. It is not that there was a total break in the tradition. For instance, it is noticeable that the names of Homer's heroes are for the most part old formations, many of them actually found in Linear B, not names of the type later generations would invent. These traditional names no doubt belonged in old stories, themselves in their largest lines traditional. Again the epic technique helped to keep the past alive and Homer's listeners expected some archaism, but much was lost even to the tenacious memory of the oral poet. On the whole, so far as the structure of society is concerned, we should treat Homer as evidence of a period well after the Mycenaean collapse, not as evidence for the great days of the thirteenth century.

For Mycenaean Greece, if we are to supplement the fascinating but incomplete evidence of the material remains and the administrative documents, we must look rather to the analogy nearest in kind, the centralised economies of other palaces in Mesopotamia or Syria, whose records are fuller and less restricted in scope. They are not all alike, nor all of a date which would allow them to have been direct models for Cnossus or Pylos. But the attempt to run a whole country, however small, by book-keeping alone was surely not a spontaneous development from the native circumstances of Middle Helladic Greece. We must suppose that the Mycenaeans copied the practice of Minoan Crete, itself no doubt a borrowing made possible by Crete's contacts with the Near East. The pressures generated by the attempt must have been considerable. It is not perhaps our business to speculate on what might have happened to the system if there had been no interference from outside, but it would be fair comment that this was for the Greek nation a false start. In many ways there is a close parallel between the Mycenaean and the later Greeks, in their trade and colonisation, and in their capacity to absorb outside influences and evolve a powerful and individual culture. But the more lasting achievements of later Greece were built on a very different foundation, the co-operation of free men; organisation was not imposed from above by powerful kings.

CHAPTER 3

The dark age and Homer

THE MYCENAEAN AGE ended in a period of destruction and turmoil, in which the palaces were burnt and the administration collapsed, and when the ensuing dark age was over things were very different in Greece and the Aegean. A major new element was the arrival of the Dorian Greeks, who in classical times occupied large parts of the Peloponnese, Crete, Rhodes, and a corner of south-west Asia Minor. Legend represented this movement as the return of the descendants of the hero Heracles to claim what they had inherited from him. They crossed by ship from Naupactus into the Peloponnese, defeating Agamemnon's grandson, and the three brothers who led them founded the three Dorian kingdoms of Argos, Sparta and Messenia. Refugees from Pylos and elsewhere crowded into Attica, which was later attacked by the Heracleidae; an oracle had promised them victory, if they spared the life of Codrus, king of Athens, but he nobly contrived to get himself killed, and Athens was saved. The sons of Codrus led the migration across the Aegean which founded the Ionic cities of Asia Minor, and the Heracleidae also sent out settlers, to Crete and Rhodes and elsewhere. All this bears about the same relation to the truth as the story of Hengist and Horsa does to the Anglo-Saxon penetration of England—it is not so false as to be totally meaningless, but the facts, as revealed by patient archaeological investigation, are a good deal more complicated.

*

The distribution of Greek dialects is almost enough, by itself, to prove that some such movement as this took place. The main division is between what are called West Greek dialects, on the one hand, that is, Doric and the related group labelled North-West Greek, spoken in Elis and elsewhere; and the East Greek dialects, on the other hand,

Ionic and Aeolic and Arcado-Cyprian. Ionic appears in Ionia, in the islands of the central Aegean and Euboea, and in a slightly modified form in Attica. Aeolic was spoken in Lesbos and on the Asiatic mainland opposite, under some Ionic influence; and in Boeotia and Thessaly, with a varying admixture of North-West Greek. The terms, Doric, Ionic and Aeolic, belong to the Greeks' own classification of their dialects: Arcado-Cyprian is a term invented by modern scholars to express the close kinship between the speech of Arcadia and that of distant Cyprus. This kinship is surprising, in view of the fact that, in the historical period, the Arcadians in their mountains were cut off from the sea by the Dorians to the east and south, and by the Eleans to the north-west. Direct and regular contact between Arcadia and Cyprus is unlikely after the prehistoric period, when one might suppose that the common ancestor of their two dialects was spoken more widely in the Peloponnese, on the coast as well as inland.

It was argued above (p. 16) that one ought not to associate the separate dialects of Greek with separate bodies of invaders, but the case of the Dorians is an exception. One of the main characteristics of the West Greek dialects is that, though they are not unintelligibly divergent, they do not show certain changes which all East Greek dialects had undergone, changes for the most part already present in the language of the Mycenaean documents. It can fairly be inferred that the Dorians, and the speakers of related dialects, were not in close contact with the speakers of the East Greek dialects during the prehistoric period when these phonetic changes were taking place, but lived elsewhere at the time, probably outside the area covered by Mycenaean civilisation. The whole situation, including the relation between Arcadia and Cyprus, is adequately accounted for if, as suggested above, some early stage of the Arcadian dialect had been spoken over wide areas of the Peloponnese in Mycenaean times; and if migration had brought the Dorians and the rest into the Peloponnese at a later time, cutting the Arcadians off from the sea. The story of the Dorian migration gives us an explanation which fits the facts.

Most of the peoples who spoke West Greek dialects, or dialects with a North-West Greek component, thought of themselves as relative newcomers. Whereas Athenians and Arcadians claimed to be sprung from the soil they occupied in classical times, and to have lived there always, the Dorians, Eleans, Boeotians and Thessalians believed that they were descended from conquerors who had come in from outside, at a time not long after the Trojan War. It is another conscious archaism in Homer, maintained with almost complete consistency—the most serious exception, which troubled Thucydides, is the presence of Boeotians in the *Iliad*—that he deals with an earlier Greece before the time of these conquests, and that the newer peoples have no part in his story. The opposition of the older and newer races lived on in Greek sentiment, finding expression quite as illogical as any modern racial theory. The conflict between Dorian Sparta and Ionian Athens in the fifth century sharpened the feeling of difference for Thucydides and his contemporaries. In Sparta and Thessaly especially, another by-product of invasion survived into historic times, the subjection of the earlier inhabitants to a form of servitude, the helots of Laconia and the *penestai* of Thessaly.

★

The process by which all this came about becomes slowly clearer as facts accumulate from fresh excavation. Signs of trouble multiply in the Mycenaean world in the latter part of the thirteenth century. Across the Isthmus of Corinth a wall was built, whose siting shows that it was meant to defend the Peloponnese against attack from the north. The fortifications of Mycenae and Tiryns were heavily strengthened, more than once; and so were those of the Acropolis of Athens. The expected blows came somewhere around 1200, when many settlements were violently destroyed and many abandoned, in Phocis and Boeotia, and in Corinthia, Argolid, Laconia, and Messenia. The citadel of Mycenae suffered, the fortress of Tiryns was destroyed, the palace at Pylos was burnt. Athens perhaps lay off the main track of the destroyers, since the Acropolis shows no signs of actual damage.

There was some degree of recovery, but the permanent effects were dire and extensive. The southern Peloponnese, Laconia and Messenia, had evidently been thickly populated in the thirteenth century, but the period after 1200 shows very much fewer signs of habitation. Mycenae itself was reoccupied by survivors, who clung to their old way of life, though at a lower and poorer level, and other sites were still inhabited. In Achaea in the northern Peloponnese, and in the islands off the west coast, occupation is actually denser after 1200, representing probably a refugee movement away from the main scene of destruction. In western Attica, a settlement using Mycenaean pottery clung for a time to the Acropolis; but there was evidently more wealth and security in eastern Attica, behind the slight barrier of Mount Hymettus, where a prosperous Mycenaean community continued in being. The same prosperity is shown among the islands, especially Rhodes and Cos in the Dodecanese; and Miletus on the Asiatic coast belongs to this group. Further afield, Cyprus, which had long imported Mycenaean pottery and bronzework, seems now to have received actual Mycenaean settlers, in more than one wave. What happened in the north of Greece is not as yet very clear, but Mycenaean occupation seems to have continued in Thessaly.

Remembering the Greek legend, historians have naturally thought that the destruction of so many Mycenaean centres should be associated with the arrival of the Dorians and other newcomers. The reoccupation or continued occupation of old Mycenaean sites tells heavily against this suggestion. Indeed, in the Argolid, as the evidence now stands, there is nothing for some 150 years yet that could be taken to indicate the arrival of new settlers. The damage can be explained without invoking the Dorians, for in the years around 1200 the eastern Mediterranean and the adjoining lands were full of destructive migrants. The troubles of Egypt are the most firmly dated: in the fifth year of king Merneptah—his dates are not agreed, but this will be somewhere around 1225—the Libyans attacked Egypt with help from 'the peoples of the sea'; and, about 1190, Rameses III had to face a much more serious advance of these wanderers by land and sea in Palestine. The Hittite empire in Anatolia declined into increasing confusion and vanished by the end of the thirteenth century, and there are similar troubles elsewhere. The disasters which befell Mycenaean Greece are roughly of the same date, whether they were concentrated in a short space of time or spread over a longer period (the archaeological evidence naturally cannot provide exact dates, or even secure synchronisms). If they belong to the same pattern, we should suppose that the migrants who ravaged Greece then passed on elsewhere, most probably to join in the attack on Egypt.

As a result many Mycenaean Greeks moved to the less damaged parts of the land and many, the more active and enterprising, went abroad. At home, the kings with their impressive treasure, the complex hierarchy of officials, the elaborate bureaucracy, were a topheavy and brittle superstructure, unlikely to survive heavy blows. The palace at Pylos was not rebuilt, and it is hardly conceivable that the scribes continued their work somewhere else. Indeed, it looks as if most of the king's subjects had fled. The remnant which reoccupied Mycenae evidently commanded no large resources. But if we ask how these Mycenaean remnants were supported, how the still prosperous Mycenaean enclave was organised in the Aegean and East Attica, what went on in the areas which Mycenaean civilisation abandoned, we are back in the dark with no documents to guide us.

The archaeological record nevertheless assures us that there was some cultural continuity through the twelfth century and into the eleventh. Some buildings remained, dress and burial customs did not alter, new styles of pottery within the Mycenaean tradition were evolved both in the Argolid and in the Dodecanese, and there was interaction between these areas, and between them and the last phase of Minoan Crete. That shows that people, with at least some of the social habits of the old ruling class, maintained themselves in the Argolid and Achaea and elsewhere; and to do that, they must have controlled at least some of the land. The community on the Acropolis of Athens must have been supported from the plain below. The sea was still, in some degree, open for these people, and still more for the Mycenaean Greeks of the Aegean, who continued to import luxuries from abroad; and at this stage a little iron is found in this area. But it is no use trying to guess how these Aegean Greeks were governed in the twelfth century; we do not, indeed, know how they were organised in the days before the mainland disasters. As for the areas in which Mycenaean continuity is not attested, we could suppose them still tilled by a peasantry, whose overlords were dead or gone, and whose quiet lives left no archaeological trace; or it may be that some districts remained merely waste and empty till they were occupied by newcomers.

The Dorians and the other newcomers are distinguishable from the other Greeks mainly in terms of their dialects. The Dorians also had certain religious festivals in common, and some institutions, notably their tribal system, which is discussed in Chapter 5. But in archaeological terms there is hardly any specific feature that can plausibly be associated with them, except perhaps a simpler form of dress, a modified blanket fastened with large pins at the shoulder. Otherwise, we must presume that, when they came, they largely took over and adapted what they could use of the relics of the civilisation that went before them. Their situation through most of the second millennium B.C. is not altogether easy to envisage. In some respects, mainly in their language, they must be regarded as an integral part of Middle Helladic

Greece; but they had no part in the rich civilisation which arose in the south around 1600, though they were so far in contact with it that they were not total strangers when they migrated southwards. At present, it seems most likely that they had been living in the archaeologically almost unexplored north-west—roughly speaking, in Epirus.

Their arrival in the south is not marked by any datable trail of destruction, and the most plausible if not the only solution is to place it at the point when most of the old apparatus of Mycenaean life finally disappears. Recent evidence from the Argolid suggests a definite cultural break in the middle of the eleventh century. In some places, the habitation centres shifted a little, and in at least one case new graves were made in the ruins of old houses. The dead were buried singly in stone-lined graves of the kind archaeologists call 'cists', not by successive interment in family chamber-tombs in the Mycenaean manner. Other Mycenaean features disappear, and the signs of change are varied enough to justify us in taking this as the time when the Dorians gained possession of the land they were to occupy through the classical period. At about the same time the Mycenaean communities in the Aegean and East Attica also came to an end.

The settlements in the Argolid, which have here been ascribed to the incoming Dorians, used pottery which is closely related to that of contemporary Athens. This was in the earliest style of Iron-Age Greece, called Protogeometric because it looks forward to the later Geometric style. In West Attica, we can watch the birth of this style. There, a generation or so before the earliest Protogeometric tombs of the Argolid, a new cemetery was started in the Ceramicus (at the gates of later Athens) in which the dead were buried singly in cists. The pottery in the earliest of these graves is in a decayed style to which the name 'sub-Mycenaean' has been given, and out of this there developed without any sudden break the Protogeometric style, which spread to other areas including the Argolid. This raises further questions about the relation between Mycenaean and post-Mycenaean settlement. Single burial in cists was not new in Greece—indeed, it was the regular style of the Middle Helladic period, and had appeared sporadically since—but the Ceramicus cemetery shows a change, in that it has only cists and no chamber-tombs. It is tempting to suggest that we have here a resurgence of older burial habits, the subject population coming to the surface when the Mycenaean upper class could no longer maintain itself. Alternatively, and to my mind more plausibly, it has been argued that, if the cist-burials of the Argolid belong to newcomers, then the cist-burials of the Ceramicus also belong to newcomers of some sort, who had infiltrated into lands long underpopulated, and eventually amalgamated with the Mycenaean remnant. The continuous development of the pottery could fit either hypothesis, for neither requires a convulsion of a kind that need interrupt the pottery industry.

One way or another, essential changes took place, and Greek civilisation was set on a new course. At the time, in the late eleventh century, the diversity of this civilisation must have been more apparent than the factors making for eventual convergence. We cannot hope to unravel more than a little about the ways in which Greece settled down, but it may be useful to distinguish three patterns of settlement, which will to some extent reappear in later chapters. (1) In some areas the conquerors entirely prevailed, and succeeded in assimilating the earlier population. Thus, the Argolid shows some signs of the survival of pre-Dorians of various social classes (p. 95), but in the classical period it was wholly Dorian in speech and institutions and there is no trace of internal racial feeling. The Boeotians, though their speech was a mixture, seem also in later times to have felt themselves to be a homogeneous race. (2) In other places the conquerors remained a self-conscious minority ruling subjects of a different race. This is conspicuously the case with Sparta, where rulers and ruled alike spoke Doric, and in Thessaly, where the dialect of the conquered contributed more than that of the conquerors to their common speech of later times. (3) Other areas remained unconquered, like the interior of Arcadia; or the speech of the earlier population might prevail over that of the newcomers—as happened at Athens, if Athens was in fact penetrated by newcomers at this time.

Differences of this kind combined with the geographical structure of the land to produce a fragmentation probably more thorough than that of earlier or later ages: for instance, it seems to have taken time before the whole territory of Attica was united under Athens. We cannot hope to discover much about the feelings of the Greeks of this dark age, towards one another or towards the outer world, though it should be noted that the name of Hellenes was adopted for the first time during this dark age as a general national name. When communications became more free in the eighth century, the society which emerged was conscious of a certain unity as against the outside world, for all were Hellenes, worshipping the same gods in much the same manner. The crucial period, though it has left us no documents beyond its pottery, must be the time immediately after the Dorian immigration, when these various kinds of Greek-speakers settled down together to become a new people, distinct in various ways from their predecessors, the Mycenaean Greeks. This radical change of direction affected the unconquered areas fully as much as the conquered. Whether Athens in the eleventh century absorbed or repelled her invaders, one might be tempted to think that memories of the Mycenaean age would be more lively there than in places where the older population was fully absorbed or subjugated. It has, very naturally, been guessed that Athens was the main channel by which traditions of the Mycenaean age were transmitted to later times in the form of legend. Whatever the truth of that—and it is a fact that the legends were somehow transmitted—neither Mycenaean memories nor the continuous development of her pottery allow any inference that in other respects society continued to run on Mycenaean lines. There were material changes, in dress and burial customs, but it is more important that Athens felt herself to be fully a part of the new post-Mycenaean Greece—indeed, to judge from the evidence of her pottery, she took a leading part in its formation.

A secondary movement settled or resettled the islands and the Asiatic coast. Much remains dark here. We do not know what became of the Mycenaean Greeks of eastern Attica, for we have only their tombs, which simply come to an end: discovery of the settlement to which they belonged might clarify the picture. On one or two of the islands, the settlement using Protogeometric pottery cuts across the lines of Mycenaean habitation and burial, as the new settlements in the Argolid do, which may again imply some change of population. At Miletus, the Mycenaean settlement was violently destroyed, and the first pottery of the succeeding settlement closely resembles what was made at Athens at the transition from sub-Mycenaean to Protogeometric. The tradition that most or all of the cities of Ionia were founded by leaders from Athens is firmly supported by community of speech, tribal organisation and festivals. The finds at Miletus suggest that the movement called the Ionic migration took place at much the same time as the Dorian occupation of the Argolid, in the eleventh century. The migrants were not all of them Athenians. It is not easy to suppose that Attica at this time had so large a surplus population, that it could spread out over the whole of this area; nor are there archaeological signs of such overcrowding. Herodotus thought that the population of Ionia was very mixed, including settlers from many areas of Greece, and there is some detailed evidence to support him. We should probably suppose that the immigration of the Dorians and others did displace a mixed body of refugees, for whom Athens supplied the leaders.

Further north up the coast of Asia Minor, the Aeolic occupation of Lesbos and the mainland opposite is still wrapped in an archaeological darkness which prevents us from tracing its connections and development. The supposed descent of the founders from a son of Orestes is not very helpful; but the connection of their dialect with the speech of Thessaly and Boeotia is unmistakeable, and this bond of kinship was still strongly felt in the fifth century, when it played a small part in the course of the Peloponnesian War. To the south of the Aegean, the Dorians spread out over Crete, over Rhodes and the Dodecanese, and over the adjacent corner of Asia Minor, in sufficient numbers to give this area Dorian speech and Dorian tribes. Archaeology gives no clear clue to the date when the Dorians reached it: confused legends put these foundations a few generations after the arrival of the Dorians in the Peloponnese: we know so little of the situation at that time that we can make no good guess about the pressures which stimulated this movement.

*

By now, it will be apparent how history has been simplified and romanticised in the legend outlined at the beginning of this chapter. The Dorian legend, how they were led by the descendants of Heracles, recovering their rightful heritage in the Peloponnese, was always suspect, as an attempt to legitimise Dorian usurpation of lands which in Homer belonged to Agamemnon and the other Achaean kings. No great faith need be placed in the earlier stages of the genealogy by which the later kings of Sparta were linked to Heracles. The romantic story of Codrus' self-sacrifice may be a stylised version of a genuine repulse of migrants from the borders of Attica, or it may merely cover up the fact that some of these migrants did enter Attica. But the legend may give a fair reflection, at least in outline, of Athenian leadership in the Ionic migration, and of the synchronism between this movement and the arrival of the Dorians in the Peloponnese.

I have so far left out of account the most famous legend of all, the ten-year siege of Troy by a combined Greek army under Agamemnon, the background of Homer's *Iliad*. This is because of the deep-seated difficulty of coming to a firm conclusion about its historicity. It is partly a chronological question, whether the destruction of the relevant stage of the city of Troy can be dated to a time when such a combined expedition would be plausible; and partly a matter of the correct interpretation of the lists of the Greek forces and the Trojan alliance in the second book of the *Iliad*. It is doubtful if either problem can be convincingly settled, on the evidence now available. If there was such an expedition, Homer is no certain guide to its character, as is clear from the single fact that he represents it as the siege of a great city, sheltering armies of Trojans and allies, whereas it can be seen today that the whole circuit of the citadel was no more than 550 yards. If the war of Troy is only legend, the poem is none the worse for that; and Homer's value for this enquiry, as our sole articulate witness to the state of a society which had vanished before Greece again became literate, does not depend on the historical fact about the destruction of Troy.

*

However, there was clearly some continuity of tradition from the Mycenaean period to Homer. Suspicious as we may be of detail, no one supposes that the heroic age of the poets was all free invention. More than the bare bones of a story can be preserved by the techniques of oral poetry in an illiterate society. The epic 'formulae' are the basic mechanism, not just the stock passages describing a sacrifice or food or fighting, which strike every reader of the *Iliad*, but a complex web of less obvious uniformities. The oral poet has to keep his head, and the attention of his audience, while he unrolls in verse a story of considerable length. In Greek epic, the stories were very long, and the metre rigid and exacting. The general course of the poem and its episodes must be planned before the singer starts, for he cannot stop in the middle to consider how to treat an episode, or to weigh the merits of one phrase against another. The details must be left to the technique he has learnt; and here the important element is his stock of formulae, whole lines and smaller phrases, a large part of which are just combinations of noun and adjective. In Greek, the requirements vary with the case of the noun and the position of the phrase in the hexameter line, and for any particular position the noun has usually one invariable adjective.

This was a formidable technique to master, but one that had tremendous possibilities, once the poet knew how to use it. Passed on from one generation to another, it tended to conserve detail as well as story. When the detail became obsolete, it might still be acceptable to an audience which expected its heroes to be different from themselves, and might be uneasy at innovation. Nevertheless, the technique could hardly remain static over a long period: a great singer could not fail to leave his mark upon the art, and the background would change in some respects as the heroic age faded further into the past. Further, no poet sings the same tale twice in exactly the same manner, so that the text of an oral poem is exceedingly fluid, at any rate in the practice of its original creator; and the art dies out when poets begin to write, so that it is a considerable problem how the Greek epic came to be written down at all. Some have guessed that the poet lived in a transitional age, when writing was beginning again in Greece, and that he himself dictated his songs; others, that disciples learnt by heart these long texts, which had made an unusually deep impression; or other solutions might perhaps be imagined.

Happily, most critics would now allow that the *Iliad* and *Odyssey* each bear the mark of a great creative mind. The notion that these rightly cherished masterpieces are a collection of lays, strung together haphazard, is a dated curiosity of scholarship; but it is still disputed whether the different tone of the *Odyssey* means a different author, or a change in the same poet who composed the *Iliad*. When the poems were composed, how long an interval passed before the text was fixed in writing, how much it was altered during such interval (or indeed before the text we have was accepted as authoritative), are also matters of lively controversy. More critics would now assign the *Iliad* to the eighth century than to any other, and most would allow that outlying portions of both texts are later additions, but the argument shows no sign of ending.

We may expect that the background of the story will reflect an earlier stage of society than the poet's own, but we need not expect that all features of it will derive from the same time. The conventions of Greek epic are no doubt partly artificial, as its language certainly is, and we need not try to think that any particular generation of Greeks lived in all respects the kind of life which the poems presuppose.

Mycenaean reminiscences are mostly matters of concrete detail. Some baffling words were retained, and formulaic combinations lived on, many of them of the kind that serve to distinguish one individual hero. The great shield 'like a tower' which protected Ajax is a relic earlier than any conceivable Trojan War, for in the thirteenth century the Mycenaeans had abandoned the large body-shield and relied on a smaller, round shield with a central hand-grip. Another remarkable antique is the helmet lent to Odysseus in the tenth book of the *Iliad*, a cap with rows of boars' tusks sewn to the outside, described in some five lines of detail though equally obsolete in the thirteenth century. Phrases to describe these objects must have been worked into the poets' repertoire remarkably early. More general are certain exclusions —the fact that there is very little iron in the story, and that the political geography of the post-Mycenaean world has been kept out.

On the other hand, the organisation of the palaces has been completely forgotten. The patient scribes known to us from Cnossus and Pylos might never have written. Not that one would expect the bureaucracy to play a substantive part in either poem, but there is not even incidental allusion; and Homer's kings positively behave as if they had not got such machinery at their disposal. The titles of the Mycenaean officials have vanished, leaving only *anax* and *basileus*, both now words for 'king'; the vocabulary of land-tenure has vanished too. This is very much what we might expect from the mechanics of transmission, which would tend to conserve hard matters of technical fact: concrete details imperfectly understood have a romantic charm, denied to concepts of government and administration, which lose interest when they can no longer intervene in one's life. But the social system which the poems presuppose is nevertheless older than the poet's own time. In general, it may be assigned to the time when Greece had settled down after the migrations, though it must be repeated that the background is not necessarily all of one piece.

The political structure is frustratingly vague. The king is right in the centre of Homer's picture, and he is an autocrat, at least in the sense that no one has any clearly defined rights against him. But he was not an autocrat in the style of those rulers of highly organised states, who work through an elaborate hierarchy of ministers and servants. In these, the monarch's will is effective only to the extent that he can trust his servants, at every level; and almost all the subjects' business is done with such servants, who, however loyal, inevitably have interests other than the mere execution of the king's will. The Mycenaean documents presuppose just such a hierarchy, and we can only guess at the extent to which the king himself was really in control. In Homer, there is no such machinery at all.

Agamemnon may summon the other princes to a council. A king may have an attendant warrior of his own class, whose vague title *therapon* is sometimes translated 'squire', though the same word is freely used for servants of any degree; and there are heralds and other attendants. But there is no one whose specific concern is administration. Subjects may honour the king with gifts; and when Alcinous, king of Phaeacia, has made expensive presents to Odysseus, he proposes to recompense himself and the other donors by collecting gifts from the people. But there is no sign of regular taxes, or of tax-collectors. It is noticeable that the kings do a great many things for themselves. It is natural enough that Odysseus should be able in an emergency to build his own raft, but a little unexpected that, peacefully at home in Ithaca, he should have made with his own hands the royal bed on which he and Penelope slept. Homer mostly speaks as if his heroes did their own cooking. Except that these kings are credited with great possessions and imposing treasures—tradition demanded that much—they lead relatively simple lives on a relatively small scale.

But if there is no organisation in the Mycenaean style, there is not much resemblance, either, to the later Greek system, though the elements of that system seem to be present in rudimentary form, as they perhaps were not at Cnossus or Pylos. Agamemnon was expected to call a council at need, and did so, though there was no clear convention about its membership and no means of compelling him to take its advice. Indeed, the opening scene of the *Iliad* shows him acting flat contrary to its unanimous opinion. He may also summon the whole army in assembly, but it has no formal rights, either. This is not simply because an army abroad is a special case. At home and at peace, the people of Ithaca are still more comprehensively inert in the curious situation that has arisen, in the twenty years of Odysseus' absence, between his son, Telemachus, and the suitors who besiege Odysseus' wife Penelope and feast off his stores. It is hinted, more than once, that the people might be dangerous and that their anger might totally defeat the suitors or Telemachus. But in fact nothing happens, not even when Telemachus calls an assembly, the first for twenty years.

There is no sign of an Ithacan council, but there was no acknowledged king present to call one.

The important point about these curiously indeterminate institutions is that they should have been there at all, and that the poet should devote space to them. When they worked harmoniously, the king's hand was strengthened by consulting his council before a decision, and by announcing it to the people afterwards. If there was opposition, the king might think again, or (in real life, if not in the *Iliad*) that might be the end of his kingdom. The possibilities of development are obvious. If the council now can only tender advice, it may one day, under weaker kings, gain the right to enforce its will. If the people now can only applaud, or remain silent, or perhaps in extremity rebel, they may one day use their meetings to criticise or reject or amend the proposals announced to them. Meanwhile the king's right to command is limited only by the possibility that he may lose the confidence of his followers. It seems that the overriding need of this society was for clear leadership in an acceptable direction.

For cohesion, the system depended entirely on the direct relation of the inferior to his king: in war, on that loyalty of *hetairoi* (the standard translation 'companion' renders this rather palely) to their leader which pervades the *Iliad*; in peace, on the effective functioning of the king's extensive but relatively simple household, more fully exemplified in the *Odyssey*. The basic assumptions are the same for both poems, but a story whose background is a large army fighting abroad naturally emphasises a special aspect.

In the *Iliad* the great heroes are *hetairoi* to one another, companions in a common enterprise who must for honour's sake come to the rescue when one of their number is in danger. This aspect of the fighting is much more prominent than any direction of the battle by Agamemnon as commander-in-chief. Equally, the followers of an individual hero are his *hetairoi*. There is a hint that the nucleus of this following might be his own kindred, but a rather faint hint, and it is clear that the army of the *Iliad* was not built up on the basis of regular kinship units, like those discussed in Chapter 5 below. The contingents were, however, not merely the personal following of their leaders, but ethnic groups, large or small, with their distinctive names. Within the contingent, some were socially on a level with the king, and specially his *hetairoi*, like Meriones, the constant attendant of the Cretan, Idomeneus. But the rank and file, present in great numbers, though playing a shadowy role, are *hetairoi* too, when the story allows us to see them. For instance, the crew of Odysseus' ship is always so described. Intermittently in the *Iliad*, other forms of organisation are mentioned or planned, but the poet soon forgets them, whereas the relation of *hetairoi* to their leader is dominant throughout.

The purpose of this large, loose organisation was to sack Troy. The leaders' claim to loyalty depended, apart from their birth, on their effectiveness in furthering that purpose. That meant, primarily, their prowess in those weird and often inconclusive duels of which Homeric fighting consists (many of them have to be inconclusive, because the major heroes cannot lightly be killed off before they have played out their own story; but the slaughter is fierce enough among the minor characters who appear only in order to meet their carefully variegated deaths). The poet likes to say that his great men were good in council as in fighting, but there is hardly anything that could be called rational military planning. Perhaps the fixed form of the tale of Troy left too little latitude, whereas minor raids, like those which Nestor describes from the Pylos of his youth, gave more opportunity for cunning and stratagem. For the *Iliad*, Nestor's long experience means chiefly that he has a larger store of heroic examples to use in exhortation; and he was clear and eloquent, foreshadowing the part which rhetoric was to play in later Greek life.

Splendour was almost as much a duty as prowess. The high birth is, of course, part of this. Heroes traced their descent from gods, at no great remove, and the gulf was fixed and wide between them and ordinary men. A king's immediate ancestors should preferably have held the kingdom before him, and a king must have treasure and land at his free disposal. Most of all, he must show his heroic temper in resenting slights to his inflamed and dangerous honour; and, with so many kings gathered together, the competition in prestige was specially explosive at Troy, whence the wrath of Achilles and the whole plot of the *Iliad*. Agamemnon himself had some reserve of authority in that he was 'the most kingly', an indefinite concept—the poet does not clarify it by adding that he ruled over the most people, for, clearly, the kings were not in general graded according to the number of their subjects. But this extra authority was no help to him when Achilles withdrew to his tent.

Much of all this arises directly from the way in which poet and audience imagine a hero, larger than life not only in his strength and wealth but also in his code of honour. But just as the sense of honour is no more than an exaggeration of the normal attitude of upper-class Greeks in a later age, so probably the other attributes have some roots in reality. We ought to try to find a place in history for these kings, who were neither the apex of a Mycenaean hierarchy, nor subject to the constitutional limitations imposed on later Greek kings. The loose structure, the need for clear command, perhaps even the rampant individualism of the heroes at Troy, are all suitable to a people on the move; it may be that the epic tradition had, at some stage, used as a model for the army before Troy an idealised version of some of those bands of colonists who settled the coast of Asia Minor in post-Mycenaean times.

Apart from the large section of the poem devoted to the hero's magic wanderings, the *Odyssey* stays at home in Greece. Its background is a heroic household at peace, for all the tension of the suitors' doomed siege of Penelope. The picture is anything but complete, for Homer has eyes only for the palace, and sees the lesser figures only in their relation to the princes. His language is so much geared to this high level that, when the scene shifts to the hut of the swineherd, Eumaeus, some of the palatial magnificence rubs off on that, and Eumaeus himself is a 'leader of men'.

Odysseus has ample flocks and herds on Ithaca and on the mainland. His house in town is conspicuous by its size and magnificence, well stocked with clothing, oil, wine and everything the household needed. There is treasure, too, in plenty. The involved architecture, some of it inextricably woven into the story, recalls the complexity of such palaces as Tiryns. There is some Mycenaean reminiscence here; but it is also true that much of the story could be played out in a much smaller house, that much of the magnificence is mere multiplication of simple things, and that the hero and his wife are not wrapped in the care of specialised attendants in the Mycenaean style but do much of the work themselves. When the hero was not hunting or feasting, showing his athletic prowess or listening to song, his time would be amply filled in looking after his estates, by personal inspection. So, for instance, Telemachus felt the need to excuse the infrequency of his visits to Eumaeus by his preoccupation with the doings of the suitors in town. Women are prized for their skill in weaving and the like, Penelope no less than her servants, and they look after the storerooms themselves like later Greek wives.

Almost everything the household needed could be produced from its own resources, and imports from outside are mainly slaves and metal. Slaves are mostly women, and the straightforward source of supply is the sack of cities, with the slaughter of their men. But Eumaeus, kidnapped by Phoenicians, was acquired by barter by Odysseus' father, Laertes; and Laertes had given the worth of twenty oxen for Eurycleia, who in her old age manages the house under Penelope. The only traders are Phoenicians, and the poet is not seriously concerned to describe their operations—their function in the story is to kidnap a hero, or otherwise transport him from one place to another—but he represents them, for the most part, as offering precious objects, and in at least one case they seem to take natural produce in exchange. Other seafarers are apt to be pirates, an occupation open to heroes and no more discreditable than war.

The metal most in evidence is gold, some of it in use on the table, but mostly locked away to be brought out when a present is needed for a visiting hero. Gifts play an enormous part in heroic life, sometimes to appease offence, but mostly in courtesy to visitors; a journey abroad might collect treasure in imposing quantity. The heroes delight in its value, and the giver frankly expects adequate return when he goes visiting. Nevertheless, the gifts are mainly tokens, circulating only in this high-flown way, the value enhancing the status of giver and recipient. The unavoidable need for useful metal brings a hint of more prosaic transactions, as when the goddess Athena, in disguise, tells Telemachus she is on her way to Temesa for bronze, carrying iron in her own ship. This is one of the rare places where iron is allowed to intrude into the heroes' world of bronze. Another instance is the great lump of iron, given as a prize during Achilles' funeral games for Patroclus, which 'would keep the winner's household for five years, and neither shepherd nor ploughman would go wanting'. This, for once, is a gift to be expended in use, but there is no hint of trade here, for the iron is booty, won by Achilles.

Trade was not for heroes. It was a dangerous insult when a young Phaeacian told Odysseus he did not look like an athlete, but like a man who sailed for gain in trade. The word 'merchant' is not employed here (or in reference to Phoenicians), but a circumlocution. The whole thing might be an intrusion from the poet's own time, when Greek merchants certainly sailed the Mediterranean for profit: but it may reasonably be doubted if the Greeks ever gave up trade entirely, even in the dark post-Mycenaean age. But the merchant had no place in the heroic household, and thus almost escaped attention, an uncomfortable outsider.

In general, safety lay in belonging to a hero's household. The worst kind of life that Achilles can conceive, in a famous passage of the *Odyssey*, is that of a hired labourer working for a poor master. Here is another hint of what might go on in the interstices of this world of princely houses, where the poet is not, in general, looking. Otherwise, work on the land or in the house is done by slaves or servants. The minor heroes who have their separate houses in the town are in some degree the king's retainers, and in normal circumstances—unlike the injurious feasting of Penelope's suitors—might eat at his table. The king is naturally their leader in war, an ever-present danger. So, when Telemachus called the Ithacan assembly together, the first question was whether he had news of a hostile host, or of some other public emergency. The king is their shepherd in peace as well: the community will prosper under a good king, who rules with a father's kindness—though the only concrete evidence a heroic poem can offer is the kindness of Odysseus and Penelope to individuals. This is a settled world, but not, except for stray details, the Mycenaean world; and that is the main basis for the view that the society here reflected is, substantially, that of the time when Greece had settled down after the migrations. It was settled, that is, in comparison with the disastrous time when the Mycenaean palaces were wrecked, but still insecure enough, imperfectly protected against local war and individual violence; a time when king or noble might, with luck, provide an element of stability, otherwise lacking, when the dependence of the weaker might safeguard them against everything but their protectors.

*

Apart from what we can read out of Homer's stories, our evidence for the dark age is entirely archaeological. Even when the dark age, in the strict sense, ends in the latter part of the eighth century with the revival of Greek literacy, our information from written sources is for a long time so scrappy that we must continually press the archaeological evidence for historical conclusions. That means a heavy reliance on the evidence of pottery, with those dangers of over-interpretation to which I have already called attention; but the fair deductions that can be made from pottery are very far from worthless.

We can see, for instance, that Athens took the lead in developing Protogeometric pottery out of sub-Mycenaean, though Athens had no monopoly, and distinguishable styles were developed elsewhere. The full Geometric style which followed varies more from place to place, but the Attic product is still the most impressive, exercising the most influence on other centres. Graves of this time show that Attica was less poor and less isolated than other areas. The Geometric style takes its name (the names of these styles are of course modern: no ancient literature classified, these long-lost objects) from the characteristic geometric elements in the decoration. These range from simple zigzags and triangles to great maeanders and other elaborate patterns, which covered the whole surface of even the largest vessels in a tight careful network, using the bolder bands of pattern to emphasise the contours of these admirably made vases (pl. 6). In the eighth century, Geometric artists began to draw pictures, in which the figures are schematic silhouettes, patterns energetic in action (pl. 8). On the vast funerary vessels which held the ashes of the dead Atherian or stood on his grave, we have funeral scenes and the attendant games, but there are also battles, and ships, sometimes in action against an enemy on shore. Apart from pottery, we have mainly small bronzes, animal and human figurines which are almost equally schematic. There is no stone sculpture, but wooden cult-images, reputedly very ancient, were venerated in some later temples; and some of these may have dated from this time. Architecture was reduced to cottage terms, as may be seen in the clay model of a temple, from an archaic shrine near Corinth, with thatched gable and two columns to represent a porch.

Still more important, archaeology can document for us very amply the change which brought the dark age to an end, the resumption on a large scale of communication and trade with the East. Sporadic imports are found in Greek graves of the dark age, but they become frequent only in the eighth century, the main flood in the second half of it. The effects are first obvious in Greek metalwork, then near the end of the century in pottery, introducing what is distinguished as the orientalising style. Floral ornaments curve in an un-Geometric way, and the lotus-bud and palmette take their place among Greek patterns. The human form is no longer a diagram but begins to take its own shape, looking distantly forward to the free naturalism of later Greek art. Sphinxes and griffins and wilder mixed winged shapes appear.

The first source of all this was Syria and Phoenicia. These were unsettled times in the Levant, when first the small states of north Syria, which continued many features of Hittite civilisation, then the Hebrews and Phoenicians, began to feel the revived power of Assyria. The development of Greek metalwork, especially an important series of Cretan bronzes, has suggested that Phoenician craftsmen actually emigrated to Greece. But the main channel was simply the growth of trade, with the Greeks taking the initiative. Cyprus played a large part in this, and a link with Mesopotamia was provided through the Greek site at Al Mina, at the mouth of the river Orontes in Syria. The installations excavated here are strictly commercial, warehouses rather than habitation: the river has carried away the earliest levels, so that we cannot be sure whether there was a Mycenaean settlement on this, as on some other Syrian sites; but Greeks from the islands, especially from Euboea, were active here from near the start of the eighth century. The valley of the Orontes gives access to the interior, and thence, across inhabited land, to the great bend of the Euphrates and Mesopotamia.

Greek explorers were no less active in the eighth century to the west, in the direction of Italy and Sicily. Here they met, for the most part, tribes at a lower level of civilisation than themselves. The outcome was not trade in luxury products or the learning of techniques long lost to Greece, but the occupation of agricultural land on which the surplus population of the homeland could settle. But in the Etruscans they found an established civilisation, which the Greeks were to influence very strongly, and a source of the metals that Greece so signally lacked. The earliest Greek colony in the west, before the middle of the eighth century, was at Cumae in the Bay of Naples, and the location suggests that traders had sought contact with the Etruscans for the sake of metal. The main wave of agricultural colonisation begins later, in the 730's.

*

Even at the first stage of renewed contact with the East, when the Greeks, and especially their artists, were pupils rather than masters, it would be right to stress the diverse originality which they showed, not only in things they invented for themselves but in their treatment of what they picked up from others. They may have borrowed their griffin from abroad, but they transmuted the dumpy original into a creature of slender, fierce curves which make it purely Greek. The limestone statuettes, which they now began to carve, show in the sharp features of their faces a style far removed from the more fleshy oriental model. For large-scale sculpture and architecture, we have to wait till the middle of the seventh century, when the Greeks were more familiar with Egypt. Then there is the same transformation. The naked male statues called *kouroi*, often more than life-size (pl. 7), are rigid enough in pose. But in the earliest of them there is already some hint of movement, an indication that they are the first stage in a long process of experiment, not a fixed model for conventional copying. And if the Greek temple owed anything to Egyptian colonnades, it was given a combination of strength and delicacy quite unknown to the original.

The originality of the Greek adaptation of the Phoenician alphabet is fully as striking. The script which Greece had once possessed, and then lost, was a syllabary, a system found in many parts of the world. This requires a large number of signs, almost all them standing for combinations of consonant and following vowel; in Linear B there are also signs for vowels standing alone. This is simpler than some forms of writing used in the ancient world, but it is inconvenient, not only for the number of signs required, but because it cannot represent a consonant without a following vowel. Greek, like most Indo-European languages, has frequently a consonant at the end of a word. To deal with this, a syllabary must use a sign which brings in a following vowel which is not there in speech, and which the reader must disregard—unless, like Linear B, it just omits all final consonants. The same difficulty arises where there are two adjacent consonants within a word.

The Phoenician script worked on a different principle. It had far fewer signs, but these were virtually all consonants, the reader being left to fill in the vowels for himself. This was up to a point manageable for a Semitic language, but Greek has far too many words with the same series of consonants, which need the intervening vowels to differentiate them. The Greeks, however, grasped the fact that a syllable can be broken up into its components, and that you can have a separate sign for each consonant and vowel. On this genuinely alphabetic principle, so familiar to us that we take it for granted, any combination can be written down without either inserting vowels that are not spoken or omitting vowels that are.

This alphabet was not learnt in the way of professional scribal training, as the Mycenaean script must have been, but informally acquired in use—presumably, in the first instance, for business purposes. It was quickly used for verse as well; the earliest surviving writing in the new alphabet is a strictly frivolous hexameter, scratched on an Attic jug made about 725 (pl. 14). This is not in the regular Atherian script. It retains one or two Phoenician features which were not eventually adopted in Greece, which suggests that this was an early experiment, from the time when writing was in the process of being introduced. It marks the end of the dark age, four centuries or more when nothing at all had been written in Greece. The new invention spread very rapidly, and from an early date a high proportion of the Greek people was fully literate.

CHAPTER 4

Outlines of political history

WHILE WE ARE reasonably well informed about the late fifth century and the fourth, the earlier history of Greece can be reconstructed only partially and with difficulty. Greek interest in the past was for long turned towards the legends of the heroic age, which various writers tried to reduce to a system, and historical interest in the more immediate past was delayed till much of it was irrecoverable. It was not till the end of the sixth century that anyone sat down to write anything like a historical record of events, and the first whose work survives in full collected his information in the middle of the fifth century.

This was Herodotus, born at Halicarnassus in south-west Asia Minor about 490. A wide traveller of splendidly comprehensive curiosity, he ranged over the history and ethnography of the accessible parts of Asia and Egypt, South Russia and Libya, in the first half of his work, tracing the growth of the Persian Empire and providing in incidental digressions what comes near to a continuous history of Greece from the middle of the sixth century; in the second part he described the Greek wars with Persia from the Ionian Revolt of 499 to the defeat of Xerxes' invasion of Greece in 479, matters of living memory to many whom he questioned.

Thucydides, an upper-class Athenian intellectual, born soon after 460, in exile from 424 to 404, turned wholly to contemporary history and described, after careful sifting of reports from many sides, the first twenty years (431–411) of the Peloponnesian War between Sparta and Athens. His history is austerely bare as a military record, but memorable for his passionate concern with the causes and working-out of political events, expressed mainly in the elaborately composed speeches of the actors. By this time, the record can be filled out from the surviving comedies of Aristophanes and from the beginnings of a long series of law-court speeches; with the decrees and public accounts which the Athenian state inscribed on stone (e.g. pl. 15) and a sprinkling of inscriptions from other cities. In the fourth century the speeches and inscriptions continue and multiply; so did the writing of contemporary history, though little of this survives except for the work of another Athenian exile, Xenophon, whose somewhat partial and selective history took up the Peloponnesian War where Thucydides left off and continued the story till 362.

The writing of history in these discursive or analytic styles was something new in a world which had hitherto yielded only the personal record of a king's achievements, or (another startling exception) the Jewish chronicles with their strong religious orientation. Greek historiography rose in a century from nothing at all to the remarkable heights of Herodotus and Thucydides, but thereafter it lost its creative curiosity. The standard work on archaic history was the earlier part of the universal history of Ephorus of Cyme, written soon after the middle of the fourth century and known to us from explicit quotations and from the influence it exerted on later compilations. It seems to have been itself a conscientious compilation of what was then available, with little depth of imagination or power of judgment, and heavily influenced both by the style and by the moralistic outlook of the rhetorician Isocrates. Almost all Greek historians, from now on, proclaim their intention of setting examples of virtue and vice before the young. Useful work was, nevertheless, done in other directions. In the course of the fourth century, historians began to realise the value of documents, such as there were, for the study of earlier history. Aristotle and his school made extensive collections of laws and constitutions; but little remains of these, except the greater part of Aristotle's *Constitution of Athens,* and that only because it was luckily recovered from an Egyptian papyrus, published as lately as 1891. Aristotle's nephew, the historian Callisthenes, also systematically exploited the early poets, whose poems were then available in their entirety, whereas we have only stray quotations; and some reflections of Callisthenes' work have come down to us. But Greek attention to the past, in whatever period, was not all in the way of disinterested critical enquiry, and we have to be on our guard against writers whose view of the past was coloured by contemporary prejudice.[1]

For the time before the generation of Thucydides and Aristophanes

1. For further discussion of the historians see pp. 260–3

we are not nearly so well served. From the middle of the sixth century, some fifty years or more before his own birth, Herodotus can give us continuous narrative with enough credible detail for us to see, not merely what happened, but in some measure how it happened. There is no hard and fast line, and the degree of detail available varies as the person or event concerned is intrinsically more or less memorable; but, roughly speaking, the further we go back before about 550, the more we can expect legend and folk-tale to intrude and distort. The quality of Herodotus' information about Periander, the tyrant of Corinth, at the end of the seventh century and the beginning of the sixth, is markedly different from the quality of what he has to tell about king Cleomenes I of Sparta, who died in 490, around the time of the historian's own birth. For the remoter past, when we can be reasonably sure of an event at all, we can seldom grasp more than the bare fact, without the detail which would make it intelligible.

To supplement the historians, we have for the early period the two poems of Hesiod; and quite numerous scraps of seventh-century verse, to tell us what individual men hoped and feared. The first laws to be inscribed on stone belong to the late seventh century, scrappy enactments of Cretan cities which for some reason rated this form of permanent record. Inscribed tombstones and dedications to the gods become increasingly common. We still depend heavily on the evidence of pottery and other artefacts, which at least have the advantage that what they have to tell us has not been distorted by the prejudices of later antiquity. The distribution of pottery, found away from the centre of its manufacture, tells us something of the movements of the Greeks who used it or sold it; and when, towards the end of the sixth century, the production of other local centres largely ceased and left the market in fine pottery to Athens, we are rewarded with a magnificent series of pictures of daily life, which not only delight the eye but illuminate the record of formal history.

*

The society depicted in Homer was held together by its kings. By the time the historical record opens these have almost vanished. Sparta kept its hereditary kings till the end of the third century, and many of them played a leading part in her history, but effectively their formal powers had been reduced to the command of armies outside the borders of the state. Probably till the end of the seventh century, there was a king at Argos who was something more than a formal figurehead; and the colony sent off to Cyrene from the Dorian island of Thera about 630 was led by a king, who transmitted his title to seven generations of his descendants, down to the middle of the fifth century. In almost every other state of which we have any knowledge at all, political control had very early been stripped from the king and distributed among an aristocracy of birth.

Stories are related of the decline or overthrow of kings, but it is a remarkably thin and dubious tradition. The most we can safely say is that, while a few kings are said to have been violently removed, the transition in most places seems to have been gradual and peaceful. When Aristotle says of Athens that weak kings first lost the command in war, that looks like someone's commonsense guess; and maybe it sometimes happened that way. The king's religious duties might seem to pose a more obstinate problem, but evidently the sense of hereditary right was not, even in this sphere, too strong for the transfer of such priesthood to magistrates,[1] elected or even, in the end, appointed by lot for a year. The title 'king', arousing none of the deep repugnance which the word *rex* caused the Roman republic, survived in Athens as the title of an annual magistrate, who conducted the ancestral rites that went with the title, but otherwise was no more than one magistrate among the rest. In other cities, we later find one or more magistrates with this title.

But political control had passed to the nobles, a definable and exclusive caste. Herodotus remarks of the Bacchiadae, who controlled Corinth in the early seventh century, that they married only among themselves. These were reputedly all descended from a king of Corinth, named Bacchis; but in the wider area of Attica, where there were other local centres besides the city of Athens, the caste was made up from a number of families, claiming various lines of descent but all classed together as Eupatridae, the 'families with noble fathers'. This, too, is seen from later vestigial remnants of privilege to have been a closed caste. Other names occur elsewhere, either indicating the descent of the aristocratic group or describing them in some other way, as the Hippeis or 'Horsemen' of Eretria in Euboea.

By the time Greek history is observable in any detail, the nobles

1. 'Magistrate' in this book does not refer as in English to the judges of small local courts, but is used in the original Roman sense, there being no other word available, to mean the higher officers of state.

were beginning to lose their political monopoly, and not much is known of the organisation of the cities when their power was at its height. Many noble families lasted on into the classical age, their inherited prestige a political as well as a social asset under later systems of oligarchy or democracy, their feelings expressed vividly enough for us to be able to imagine something of the spirit in which their ancestors had exercised their power. But for the practical detail we can only resort to guessing on the basis of later survivals—for instance, in what we know of the kinship organisation of Athens and elsewhere (Chapter 5), or in the field of cult and sacred law. But we can say certainly that it was under these aristocratic regimes that Greek contact with the outer world revived, as described at the end of Chapter 3, and that the first great wave of colonies spread out over the Mediterranean. These were no mean achievements.

The Greeks of the homeland could work out their social and economic changes without fear of external interference, but the East Greeks on the coastal fringe of Asia Minor could never disregard the powers of the interior. That meant, in the first instance, the kingdom of Phrygia, with its centre relatively far to the east at Gordion, near the modern Ankara. This was destroyed around 700 by invaders who came from South Russia by way of the Caucasus, the Cimmerians, whose destructive raids went on through the earlier part of the seventh century and sometimes reached the Greek coast. By the time the Cimmerians were defeated and dispersed, mainly by the Assyrians, the new kingdom of Lydia was established, with its capital at Sardis in the valley of the Hermus, barely three days' journey on foot from the coast at Ephesus or Smyrna. It was not to be expected that the Lydians would leave the coast alone; and the East Greeks had to wage intermittent war, till by the middle of the sixth century all the cities of the Asiatic mainland were paying tribute to the last Lydian king, the famous and wealthy Croesus. But the Greeks were also friends with the Lydians, who absorbed Greek culture to the point that Croesus, for all the different scale of his wealth and power, was felt to be almost one of themselves. Fighting did not hinder the rapid growth of East Greek prosperity, and it was in the seventh century that Miletus, in particular, colonised the Black Sea and its approaches, and took the lead in opening up relations with Egypt.

The seventh century speaks to us mainly through its poets. Hesiod in his *Works and Days* had spoken of his own troubles, the dispute with his brother over their inheritance and the corruptness of noble judges. Personal feelings and vicissitudes were much more freely ventilated among succeeding poets, who broke away from the epic style in various metres. Many are mere names to us, and none of their works survive complete, but enough remains to show that there was no sudden break in social habit or feeling when the kings gave way to the aristocrats or when the latter lost their political monopoly; rather, there was a continuous development, corresponding to the continuous increase of Greek prosperity and contact with the world outside. The downfall of the aristocrats was a strictly political phenomenon, however much social and economic discontent may have contributed towards it.

The change came mostly in the form of revolution under the leadership of a tyrant. The foreign word, *tyrannos*, introduced during the seventh century, was in origin no more than a synonym for 'king'. In certain contexts it continued to be used so, but it was early taken over in ordinary speech for a special type of monarch, the man with no hereditary claim who seized power by his own effort. Then, in the course of the political struggle, as the tide turned against this kind of government, it acquired the overtone of condemnation that it had for classical Greece and has had ever since. But the first tyrants were welcomed as leaders of revolt against aristocratic government, a clear example being Cypselus, who overthrew the Bacchiadae of Corinth a little before 650, killing or expelling the nobles and confiscating their property.

The grounds for discontent were various. We have clear evidence of agrarian distress and debt in Attica around 600, and may reasonably suspect it elsewhere. No doubt in other ways too, economic growth spread its benefits very unequally, widening the gulf between powerful and weak, rich and poor. Solon in the 590's rebuked the greed of the governing class at Athens. About the same time Alcaeus of Mytilene, and a little later Theognis of Megara, complained with great bitterness about the power of mere wealth and the disregard of the claims of birth. Evidently, one source of disturbance was the existence of numbers of wealthy men who were not nobles, and who had been excluded from power under the aristocratic regime. In Mytilene, and a little later in Athens, we can see how the nobles added to the turmoil by quarrelling for power among themselves; and we may guess that, in the later stages, their government was often incompetent as well as oppressive. But if, in the earlier and more clear-cut cases, the tyrant answered a real need, the continuance of one-man rule met increasing opposition from those who were thus excluded from power. Few tyrannies lasted beyond the second generation. The revolutionary example was in itself dangerous, encouraging some very dubious aspirants for power.

By the middle of the seventh century, the character of Greek warfare had begun to be radically altered, when the heavy infantry, called 'hoplites', were organised in close formation, the formidable hoplite phalanx. The adoption of this new style of fighting, which proved its effectiveness abroad as well as at home over some three centuries, must be linked with economic growth, because it depended on the ability of a sufficient number of landholders to provide themselves with fairly expensive armour. It has been suggested, by myself among others, that the emergence of a new and more widely based defence force provided support for revolutions like those of Cypselus, but on the archaeological evidence at present available it looks as if this view puts the matter back to front, as if it was rather the tyrants' strong government that was needed to create the new army.

The first 'age of tyrants', roughly from 650 to 510, also saw the first law-codes committed to writing—a step of vital importance for the administration of justice—and the adoption from neighbouring Lydia of true coinage. A war in the 590's for control of the sanctuary at Delphi, the first of several 'Sacred Wars', draws attention to the rise of the oracle there, from small beginnings in the eighth century, to become a focal point for all Greece. It marks, also, one of the few successful interventions of Thessaly, whose great resources were more often neutralised by political disunion. The great festival at Olympia, whose games were of only local importance when the regular numbered series began in 776, had already grown to national importance by the middle of the seventh century. Next in rank after Olympia was the Pythian festival, instituted at Delphi after the Sacred War; and the other two great athletic events, named Isthmia and Nemea, were also regularly organised at the beginning of the sixth century. The internal bonds of Greece grew tighter at the same time that her external contacts widened.

One state conducted a very different kind of reform, or revolution, in the course of the seventh century, and never underwent tyranny. At a time when other states were unloading their surplus population to colonies abroad, in the latter part of the eighth century, the Spartans conquered Messenia, seized the land, and reduced the inhabitants to the same status as the helots of Laconia, a large step along the path which was to make Sparta different from other Greek states.[1] There was a long and dangerous Messenian revolt in the seventh century, and this put a heavy strain on a system already distorted by the original conquest. It is not certain how these tensions are related to the reforms which tradition associated with the name of Lycurgus, but Sparta emerged with a social system and an interior discipline which other Greeks found surprising, and with a political system which gave great latitude to kings and council and the magistrates called ephors, but mainly reserved decision to a large assembly. The 8,000–9,000 full citizens were theoretically equal: the other free inhabitants, called *perioikoi*, to some extent self-governing in the towns and villages they lived in, had no say in the conduct of state affairs; the helots and Messenians were slaves.

The Spartan aristocracy owned an abnormally large territory, and the number of full citizens was abnormally large by the standards of later Greek oligarchy, though small enough if we compare it with Athens. The helot system, though a great and permanent internal danger, relieved the Spartans of continuous close attention to their own farms and set them free to train as soldiers, producing an army whose professional competence far outran that of the ordinary city's militia. Inevitably, this army was used. The end of the seventh century seems to have been a time of quiet and prosperity, but before long Sparta set out on further conquest in Arcadia. The first intention was, apparently, to reduce the Arcadians to the same servitude as the Messenians, but then, after a heavy defeat, Spartan policy was radically changed. A series of alliances, first with her main Arcadian opponent, Tegea, and then with other states, reinforced by military successes which cancelled the effect of the earlier defeat, brought all the Peloponnese except Argos under her leadership and formed the powerful organisation which we call the Peloponnesian League. This growth of Spartan power was the most important political event of the sixth century inside Greece, and by the end of the century the League was an established institution with something like a constitution of its own.

Externally, other events were overshadowed by the rise of the Persian Empire. The great Cyrus based his new kingdom on the foun-

1. For the helots see further pp. 93, 139–40

dations laid by the Medes, once his overlords, but he ranged further than they had. In one short campaign, about 545, he overthrew Croesus of Lydia, and then went on to conquer the Greek coast. Though Cyrus himself came no further west, the Persian Empire under his successors was still bent on expansion, on a scale beyond preceding empires, and when Darius I (521–486) conquered Thrace and frightened Macedon into submission the threat had come very close to the Greek homeland. Frequent appeals to Sparta for help against the Persians drew attention to the danger. Sparta sent no help; and Greece, for the most part, went on with its own quarrels, making no visible effort to organise resistance. But a nucleus for resistance already existed in the Peloponnesian League.

The life of the conquered was not desperate, for Persia was, on the whole, tolerant of local custom and religion; but still the East Greeks had exchanged their familiar neighbour, Croesus, for a remote and enormously more powerful master, who demanded tribute, general obedience, and on occasion military service. The worst grievance was political, that the Persians found it convenient to rule the Greek cities through tyrants, nominated by themselves. The Greeks felt that they had outgrown tyranny; and the Ionian Revolt against Persia (499–494) began with a general deposition of tyrants. Sparta again gave no help, but Athens and Eretria sent aid in the first year of the Revolt, and the sea-borne force, sent across the Aegean by Darius in 490, was directed specially against them. It was Athens' special glory that her troops faced this army at Marathon, and defeated it before the Spartans arrived. The much larger army, brought by land round the north of the Aegean in 480 by Darius' son, Xerxes (486–465), was directed to the general conquest of Greece. Forced to organise in a hurry, the Greeks naturally rallied round Sparta, whose League commanded the greatest resources for land fighting. At sea, the navy newly created for Athens by Themistocles was disproportionately larger than any other contingent, but there was no question of the allies submitting to Athenian leadership, even at sea. Of the great battles of 480, even the decisive naval action at Salamis was fought under nominal Spartan command, and the crowning victory by land at Plataea in 479 was very much the victory of Sparta, and of her general, the regent Pausanias. Sparta's concentration on military technique has that claim to our gratitude, that the tide of Persian conquest was turned; and so, that Greek civilisation rose to its great heights unhampered by foreign domination.

Meanwhile, Athens was set on a new political course, though the factors making for democracy cannot have been altogether apparent to contemporaries in the sixth century. Attica was, again, a large territory by Greek standards, and her internal resources were much greater than those of the average city. On the evidence of tombs and pottery, Athens in the dark age was more prosperous than most, perhaps also more powerful. The latter part of the seventh century was, however, a time of strain, including the unsuccessful attempt of one Cylon to make himself tyrant. In the first years of the sixth century, Athens was on the brink of revolution, mainly owing to an agrarian system which was reducing the poor to a state which could be described as slavery. The crisis produced a reformer of singular humanity, Solon, who is known to us as a person through the surviving quotations from his verse. He was appointed to the chief magistracy in 594, with the mission of reconciling the contending classes.

The details are matter for argument, but Solon certainly rescued the poor from their worst troubles, and abolished debt-bondage for the future. On the political side, his largest change was to set up a system of four classes graduated by income. The various offices of the state were reserved for the higher classes; the lowest class was restricted to a vote in the assembly, which also acted as a court of appeal from the decisions of magistrates. To make wealth, rather than birth, explicitly the basis for political privilege was a change in line with the times, but Solon's reforms did not prevent the establishment of tyranny at Athens, though they may have delayed it. It still did not come easily; it was only at the third attempt that Peisistratus established his power, soon after 550, a power which he exercised mildly, and handed on in 527 to his son Hippias. The basis of the tyranny was the need to restrain the internal conflicts of the governing class. When Hippias was expelled with Spartan help in 510, these conflicts broke out again, till in 507 one of the contenders, Cleisthenes, the second great Athenian political reformer, in Herodotus' phrase 'took the people into partnership'.

From the effects, we see that this was a real and momentous change, but the mechanics of it are not quite obvious. To Greek eyes, the basic reform was the change from four tribes, based on kinship, to ten new tribes, based initially on territorial division (see Chapter 5). But, though one can appreciate the effect of this on army organisation and on civil administration, it is not so easy to see how it helped to transfer real political power to the people. The answer probably lies in the part assigned to the smallest of Cleisthenes' subdivisions, the 'demes' of Attica. Most of these were based on existing villages (*demoi*), though the demes of the city must have been artificial creations. They had their own local administration, and also put forward candidates for membership of the council and for other offices; and political activity in his own small local nucleus encouraged the ordinary man to take a more effective part in the politics of the state.

This was in effect a change in the spirit in which Athenian institutions were worked. Later on, the belief grew that Solon was the conscious creator of Athenian democracy, which is certainly a distortion, in that nothing resembling the developed democracy could have entered the mind of an early sixth-century reformer. But it is true that Solon provided a constitutional framework in which democracy could grow, a framework which the tyrants left undamaged; and that the limited rights which Solon gave to the lower classes were capable of further development, particularly (as Aristotle stresses) their right to sit on juries in a court of appeal. The tyranny, repressing the quarrels of the noble and wealthy, rested on popular support, or at least on the negative presumption that the people would not support any kind of counter-revolution—a presumption which held till the very end of Hippias' reign. By the time the upper-class squabble was resumed in 510, a generation had grown up which was no longer content to watch such faction, or to be mobilised on one side or another. The popular appeal of Cleisthenes' reforms lay in the fact that his scheme allotted a real function to the ordinary demesman, a function in which he did not need to enrol himself in an aristocratic faction or rely on a tyrant as his champion. In other ways also, Cleisthenes undermined the local influence of the nobles, and circumstances helped him by identifying his opponent Isagoras with outside intervention by Sparta. Much yet remained to be done before Athenian democracy took the developed form which Aristophanes caricatured and Plato held in contempt, but Cleisthenes' reform of 507 marks a decisive step. Herodotus was justified in calling him the man who set up democracy at Athens.

A new element had thus been introduced into Greek politics at large. The sixth-century question was still mainly about tyranny; and in the latter part of the century Sparta built up for herself a reputation as the great opponent of tyrants, so much so that Herodotus and Thucydides take her crusade against tyranny as an established fact—though, apart from the conspicuous expulsion of Hippias from Athens, we cannot point to many tyrants actually overthrown. There were elements in her own system which were clearly not for export, but, with her large complement of theoretically equal citizens, Sparta could make some show of being the champion of constitutional government, as against the monarchs who allowed no equals inside their own city. There can be little doubt that this line of propaganda helped Sparta to expand her alliances and her influence. But, in the fifth century, tyranny ceased for a while to be a continuous threat among the states of southern Greece. With the emergence of conscious democracy, the centre of conflict shifted to an area where Sparta could only be seen as conservative or reactionary, the contrast between oligarchy and democracy.

It is unlikely that any class of Athenian had ever been formally excluded from the city's assembly, but Solon still assumed, as a matter of course, that there would be 'leaders of the people' to guide them in their choices. In many places, mere tradition and convention will have kept government longer and more effectively in the hands of a restricted class. We know of specific cases, other than Sparta, where the qualification for full citizenship was hereditary in the classical period. It is known, in general, that many later oligarchies had a franchise which depended on the possession of a fixed amount of property, though the earliest specific example is the constitution imposed by the Boeotian League on its member cities in 446. Possibly, in many classical oligarchies the restriction of full citizenship only became explicit and formal in answer to the democratic claim that all free adult males had the right to a vote. Not indeed that in Athens more than a small proportion habitually attended—at a time when there may have been as many as 45,000 qualified voters, it was rare for as many as 5,000–6,000 to exercise their right—but it is clear that men of all classes did attend. The principle that no one should be denied that right was the essential principle of democratic freedom and equality.

The principle worked with all the more explosive force because of the sudden and dramatic rise of Athens to power. In addition to her other resources, there were silver mines in the south-east corner of Attica at Laurium, and a new rich vein was opened there at the beginning of the fifth century. Themistocles secured that the windfall should be used to build a fleet of two hundred ships, a quite unprecedented number. The same Themistocles was the principal architect of the naval victory at Salamis in 480, and—strenuous as the effort of expansion must have been—Athens emerged from the war immensely stronger and more confident than ever before. At the same time, Sparta, whose organisation and traditions made her an awkward leader for a war now mainly transferred to Asia Minor and the eastern Mediterranean, withdrew from the further prosecution of the struggle against Persia. The personal disgrace of Pausanias, the victor of Plataea, damaged her prestige still more: so the unexpected sequel of her successful leadership in 480 was that she withdrew wholly inside the Peloponnese, and had to face serious disaffection there. Athens meanwhile stepped forward as the organiser and leader of a new maritime league, the Confederacy of Delos, based on a programme of liberating the East Greeks and continuing the war against Persia.

Not only did this league cover a wider area than any seen before, but the conditions of naval war imposed a different kind of control. The allies of Sparta were geared to land warfare in the established style, short campaigns by the cities' militia of hoplites, who brought their own rations with them and needed no more than that. Naval war meant that ships must be built, and rowers paid and fed; the Delian Confederacy from the start demanded substantial money contributions from its members. As time went on, most of the allies found it burdensome to contribute their own ships and men to League expeditions, and the nominally allied force turned increasingly into an Athenian navy, financed with allied money. So the disproportion in power increased, and Athens' allies were in effect disarmed; whereas on the Peloponnesian side Sparta continued to need allies with efficient armies, and her opportunities for intervening in the internal affairs of allied cities were that much reduced.

Athens used her disproportionate power, and by the middle of the fifth century the Confederacy had turned into an empire, subject to what decrees the Athenian assembly chose to pass. Athenian magistrates were installed in a majority of the cities, legal cases involving the more serious penalties were referred to Athenian courts, land was confiscated (usually after a revolt) and allotted to Athenian colonists, and much more. These developments, and the use of allied money for building Athenian temples, were moral issues for some contemporaries: they exercised the powerful and uneasy mind of Thucydides, and were much discussed in the 350's when Athens' second Confederacy (see below) was drifting apart. It is, perhaps, a result of the Greeks' own preoccupation with the topic, that Athenian imperialism still continues to excite moral condemnation beyond what is usually dealt out to strong powers who have used the opportunities open to them. The Athenians were certainly not always perfectly just or wise, whatever colourable excuse could be found for particular actions. For instance, it was reasonable at the very beginning to prevent the secession of the island of Naxos, for if every member were free to renounce its sworn obligations the Confederacy would soon have ceased to be any protection against Persia. But it was complained that the settlement imposed on Naxos, when her attempt was defeated, was unjustifiably severe, amounting to 'slavery'. So with many other oppressive acts, which the Athenian assembly might justify to itself, but not to all the world.

This needs to be seen in perspective, more particularly in relation to the Greek situation, and to the ideological conflict between democrats and oligarchs. It became a commonplace that Athens everywhere encouraged democracies, and Sparta oligarchies; and though there were exceptions, the rule cannot be denied. Imposition of democracy was an act of tyranny to those who feared and distrusted the people, generally the propertied classes, the men who actually paid the tribute-money which went to Athens; but to the inarticulate lower classes Athenian rule might at least offer protection against their native oligarchs. No doubt, if it had been feasible, the inhabitants of the smaller cities, democrats and oligarchs alike, would have preferred to settle their own affairs in that complete independence which all Greeks so passionately desired; but the ideal could not be realised in a world dominated by the conflict between Athens and Sparta, each of them only too ready to liberate the small city from a regime favourable to the other side.

For some time after the Persian War, the two great cities lived in comparative concord. Athens' attention was set on the prosecution of the further war against the Persians in Asia, in which some notable successes were won; Sparta was preoccupied by her own troubles within the Peloponnese. But, as Athenian power grew, its weight was increasingly felt inside the Greek world—the war against Persia eventually died down, and was closed by a formal treaty in 449— while, as Sparta's strength revived, her help was bound to be invoked by any victim of Athenian aggression. A war which broke out soon after 460, between Athens and her nearest neighbours, eventually involved Sparta also. The peace which concluded this war in 446 lasted for only half of the thirty years for which it was made.

This interval of comparative calm (446–432), before the outbreak of the great Peloponnesian War, was a period of high hope for Athens, the time when Pericles dominated Athenian politics. On the Acropolis, the Parthenon and Propylaea were built, and many other buildings elsewhere, under Pericles' supervision, with the sculptor Pheidias as one of his principal agents. Sophocles was perhaps at the height of his long career, and Euripides at the beginning of his long series of controversial plays. Protagoras of Abdera and others of the group called 'sophists' frequented Athens as their natural centre, and the city had become, in the phrase which Thucydides gives to Pericles, 'the school of Greece'. Pericles also acted a principal part in converting the Athenian alliance into a close-knit empire, and was the man most obviously responsible for appropriating to Athens' use the accumulated savings of the allies' contributions in money. In spite of the expense of the great buildings, the bulk of this sum was intact in 431, and Athens entered the ensuing war with large financial reserves, a case unique in Greek history.

It was not easy for the two diverse and powerful cities to coexist in Greece, and the war which broke out in 431 between Athens and the Peloponnesian League, the subject of Thucydides' history, was primarily a struggle for power, for the domination of Greece. As Thucydides put it, 'the growth of Athenian power alarmed the Spartans and compelled them to war'. The ideological component, the conflict of the two ideals of democracy and oligarchy, must not, however, be ignored. It had a very practical effect on the course of the war, finding supporters for Sparta among the men of property in cities subject to Athens, and sympathy for Athens among the lower classes in opponent cities; but the latter, in general, were less effective because these were not the men who bore arms. The length of the war, twenty-seven years only minimally interrupted by the compromise Peace of Nicias in 421, was due partly to the strength of feeling aroused by Athens' bid for empire, but mainly to the difficulty the combatants had in getting to grips with one another; the land power of the Peloponnesian League could not interrupt Athens' sea-borne supplies, the navy of Athens could not strike at the inland resources of her enemies. Athens tried to break the deadlock with her large, ambitious expedition in 415 to Sicily, whose cereals were mainly exported to the Peloponnese. The annihilation of this force in 413 was a turning-point of the war, the end of Athens' total domination of the sea. Even so, Athens rebuilt her fleet and held on with astonishing tenacity; and the decision in 404 was reached only through Persian help to the Peloponnesian fleet, which got control of the Hellespont and cut Athens' supplies from South Russia.

The material damage was very great. Peloponnesian armies had devastated the countryside of Attica, first by brief invasions, after 413 from a fortified post north of Athens. Megara suffered as heavily from Athenian invasions in the early part of the war; and Corinth, a naval power vulnerable to Athenian attack, never recovered her earlier strength. The psychological damage was no less important, especially at Athens where the long tension of the war showed itself in an outbreak of hysteria about certain acts of sacrilege in 415, in the brief oligarchic revolution of the Four Hundred in 411, and in the irregular trial and execution of six victorious generals in 406. After the surrender in 404, a second oligarchy, that of the Thirty, was imposed by Sparta. Civil war followed, and in the autumn of 403 Sparta acquiesced in the restoration of democracy. The strain of these upheavals must be taken into account before we too much blame Athens for the trial and death of Socrates in 399.

Victorious Sparta had its own internal troubles. Lysander, who had established a working relationship with the Persians and organised the Spartan victory, was a singularly ruthless politician. He organised tight oligarchies in the cities which came under his control, and planned to replace the Athenian empire by a still more extensive and more rigorously controlled Spartan empire, by land and sea. But at Sparta, as at Athens, there were those who had scruples about ruthless imperialism, and a steep and continuing decline in Spartan manpower made extensive commitments more difficult and more dangerous. Lysander's solution for Athens, the oligarchy of the Thirty, was soon repudiated, and he himself for a time lost his influence. Even so, Spartan rule was felt to be unconscionably harsh—their own domestic discipline tended to make them unimaginatively authoritarian in their dealings with other cities, not accustomed to such discipline—and in less than ten years Sparta found herself at war (395–387) with a coalition which included the reviving power of Athens. Sparta had also supported, in 401, the younger Cyrus' attempt to wrest the Persian throne from his brother Artaxerxes II, and had been engaged ever since in desultory

war with Persian governors in Asia Minor: but the earlier pattern re-
asserted itself, Sparta and Persia each having less to fear from the other
than from Athens, and in 387 Sparta once more with Persian help got
control of Athens' lifeline through the Hellespont. The ensuing peace
was formally based on a formula sent down from Susa by the king of
Persia.

The 'King's Peace' of 387 became the framework of Greek inter-
city politics for a generation. Southern Greece was weary of war. The
Peloponnesian War had involved unprecedented effort and destruction over an appallingly long period, and the defeat of Athens had
proved to be no solution. Already, in some abortive negotiations in
the winter of 392-1, the concept of a 'common peace' had emerged, a
peace which should embrace not only the present combatants but all
the cities of Greece. The King's Peace was to be on this model, guaran-
teeing the autonomy of all cities alike, except the Asiatic cities which
were assigned to the Persian king. This abandonment of the East
Greeks to Persia was a feature of all Spartan treaties with Persia from
411 on—a point eagerly stressed by the Athenians who, if often harsh
themselves, had kept the Persians out of these cities for some seventy
years in the fifth century. For the cities declared free, the problem
inevitably arose of sanctions against an aggressor who threatened some
city's autonomy; but the Greeks were no more successful than modern
nations in establishing machinery for the enforcement of peace. Southern
Greece was, in any case, long familiar with the concept of the hege-
mony of one disproportionately strong city over the other members
of its alliance. In the fourth century, the city which was currently
dominant felt entitled to interpret 'autonomy' in a sense favourable to
itself. The Spartans in 387 insisted that the Boeotian League be dissolved, in the name of freedom for its constituent cities; the Thebans
later maintained their League, but insisted on the independence of
Messenia from Sparta. There was never a General Assembly of the
Greek cities, nor a Security Council for the leading powers to quarrel
in: so far as common peace was ever achieved, it was imposed by
conquerors from outside, Macedonians or Romans.

The westward expansion of the Persian Empire had ceased with
the defeat of Xerxes' attempt to conquer Greece in 480. There was no
doubt of the superiority of Greek heavy infantry over any oriental
force that could be brought to bear against them, and increasing use
was made of Greek mercenaries in the orientals' own warfare. The

most impressive example was the famous body of the Ten Thousand, who followed Cyrus against his brother in 401, and after Cyrus' death made their way under improvised leadership out of Mesopotamia through inhospitable mountains to the Greek cities on the Black Sea coast, the adventure story so graphically told by Xenophon in his *Anabasis*. The mere survival of the Ten Thousand suggested that the empire was vulnerable. There were other signs of weakness, such as the increasing tendency of Persian provincial governors to follow policies of their own making; and notably the revolt in 404 of Egypt, whose independence, under native kings, was preserved against numerous counter-attacks for sixty years till its brief reconquest by Artaxerxes III in 343. The conquest of Persia, under one leader or another, was long preached by the Athenian pamphleteer, Isocrates, as a remedy for the troubles of Greece; but the obstinate fact remained that Persia had recovered control of the East Greek cities, and still exercised a far from negligible influence in Greek affairs. This was partly due to respect for its immense resources in manpower, however slow to mobilise and unwieldy to handle; but much more to the empire's wealth, and the Greek states' need of subsidy, either to maintain a fleet of any size or to pay the mercenaries who played an increasing part in Greece's internal wars. The Persian Empire had obvious weaknesses and might seem in decay, but it still held together an immense territory, more than Alexander's successors could maintain as a unity.

In the early fourth century, the power wielded by Dionysius of Syracuse was also a factor in Greek politics. Since the foundation of the first western colonies in the latter part of the eighth century, the Greeks had spread round the coasts of Italy and Sicily till, in the early sixth century, they reached what proved to be their permanent limits: to the north, they stopped short at the confines of Etruscan territory; in Sicily, they never penetrated the western third of the island. In the interior of Sicily, the native Sicels and Sicans were partly subjugated and effectively penetrated by Greek culture: the larger hinterland of the South Italian states could not be digested in this way, and the native tribes, like those of the interior of Thrace, sometimes brought disaster to the cities of the coast. The cities themselves developed, in some ways with a slower rhythm than the older-established cities of the homeland, but essentially along the same lines, and with their more favourable soil and climate they grew exceedingly prosperous.

Syracuse was originally governed by landowners, the descendants of the original settlers; and conditions were probably much the same else-where, sometimes provoking tyranny in the style familiar in the home-land. In the early fifth century, military monarchy in a different style was set up, first by Hippocrates of Gela (498–491), then by his suc-cessor, Gelon (490–478). Gelon conquered Syracuse in 485 and made it his capital, transferring to it half the population of Gela and the upper-class inhabitants of certain other cities which he wholly destroyed. Though Gelon's power was not, in the first instance, founded on sup-port from any kind of lower class, he won great personal popularity by his victory over Carthage in 480 (below), and handed on his monarchy to his brother Hieron (478–467); but a revulsion after Hieron's death led to the establishment of democracy, which lasted some sixty years till Dionysius gained power in 405. It is something of a question how these military regimes, with their mercenary armies, conquest of neighbouring cities, and transplantation of citizens, were able to achieve the success they did in the west. There was no lack of opposition, and the fiercely anti-monarchical bias of surviving Greek accounts makes it hard to form a balanced judgment. The odes which Pindar composed for Hieron and others do not do much to restore the balance. Indeed, they make it clear that the tyrants' wealth and magni-ficence were so much out of the normal Greek scale that they seemed dangerous in themselves.

The struggle of Greeks and Carthaginians in the fourth century made it easy for later historians to regard Carthage as an immemorial enemy. But it does not seem, in fact, that Carthage took very much notice of Sicily before 500, though the Carthaginians were concerned to keep others out of the areas where they mainly traded; they cut off the promising contact which the Phocaeans of Ionia had made with south-west Spain, and combined with the Etruscans against a Phocaean colony in Corsica in the late sixth century. The quarrel in Sicily which came to a head in 480 was a strictly Greek quarrel, in which Gelon's opponents appealed to Carthage for help. The only factor which might suggest that Carthage had ulterior designs is the size of the army which was sent over under Hamilcar. This army was decisively defeated at Himera by Gelon, who then exacted a large indemnity from Carthage; but he did not proceed against the three small Phoenician colonies at the western end of Sicily, which Carthage had by now taken under her protection. In 474, Hieron won his share of glory by a naval victory at Cumae (near Naples) over the Etruscans, who by this time had passed the maximum of their territorial expansion in Italy and were never again a threat to the West Greeks.

In the seventy years after 480, Carthage consolidated her power in Africa; and when, in 409, another large army intervened in a Sicilian dispute, the intention of wider conquest was quickly made clear. The commander, Hannibal (the names familiar from Roman history constantly recur), was the grandson of the Hamilcar who perished at Himera, and his personal desire for revenge may well have been a serious factor in Carthaginian policy. Over some years, the Greek cities of the southern coast were successively reduced by elaborate siege. This eventually precipitated a political crisis in Syracuse, which ended in the establishment of Dionysius, first as sole general, then as tyrant. This formidable figure remains an enigma to us, since we know him only from accounts which are uniformly hostile, and the history written by his adherent Philistus is lost except for a few unhelpful quotations. An effective demagogue who denounced upper-class mismanagement of the war, Dionysius had also rich backers, and we cannot fully analyse his rise to power. Almost at once he was forced, in 405, to accept a peace which assigned the greater part of Sicily to Carthage; when he started another war, he had to endure in 396 a nearly disastrous siege of Syracuse: but for most of his reign the Carthaginians were confined to the western end of the island. The Greek area and its hinterland were effectively in Dionysius' hands, and Athenian decrees in his honour describe him as 'the ruler of Sicily'. He also controlled the toe of Italy, with alliances and dependencies reaching far up the Adriatic. This was military monarchy on a grander scale than had yet been seen in the Greek world; and it evidently depended for its existence on the exceptional talents of Dionysius, whose performance over a long reign of nearly forty years shows that he cannot have been merely the monster that Greek writers depict.

Athens more than once angled for Dionysius' friendship, but the democracy was hardly a natural ally for him; his support was regularly given to Sparta, who had befriended him while he was establishing his power. A naval squadron from Syracuse helped Sparta to gain control of the Hellespont in 387, and thus to force Athens to accept the King's Peace; later, when Sparta and Athens combined against Thebes, Dionysius more than once sent bodies of mercenaries to help them. After his death in 367, Syracuse was of less account under his son, the younger Dionysius. In 357 the latter was driven out by a small force

brought over from Greece by his kinsman, Dion, a friend of Plato and
at that time in exile. For all Dion's parade of liberating Syracuse, this
was hardly more than a fight for power within the dynasty; and the
struggle continued in a series of debilitating upheavals, in which Dion
and others were murdered and Dionysius II eventually returned to
power. In the end, he withdrew in face of another small expedition
from Greece, brought by one Timoleon from Corinth in 344 at the
invitation of a Syracusan party. Timoleon gained a great reputation as
a virtuous liberator, but so far as he brought any real respite it was of
short duration, and the round of tyrannies and Carthaginian wars was
renewed. The tradition of self-government, never so firmly rooted in
the west as in the Greek homeland, had effectively died out.

There would be no advantage in chronicling here the inconclusive
wars of the homeland, between the King's Peace of 387 and the victory
of Philip of Macedon at Chaeroneia in 338. Sparta exploited ruthlessly
the strong position which the King's Peace gave her, and provoked a
reaction which it was beyond her power to repress. Athens in 378
formed a second naval confederacy, whose constitution endeavoured
to eliminate the remembered faults of the fifth-century empire; but
the new league prospered only so long as its members shared a common
fear of Spartan aggression. In 371, Thebes defeated the Spartan army
at Leuctra. The Greek world was shaken by the overthrow of Sparta's
long-established military superiority, but Sparta was still a danger to
her Peloponnesian neighbours. The Theban attempt at domination
provoked new problems, without solving those which had plagued
Greece for so long. In 356, the Phocian leader, Philomelus, seized the
sanctuary of Delphi; and the temple treasures financed a mercenary
army through the ten years' Sacred War which followed, weakening
Thebes and multiplying confusion. Through all these years, one conference after another tried unsuccessfully to organise universal peace—
and through the same years Plato wrote his masterpieces at Athens.

A hint of coming change was shown in the career of the Thessalian
tyrant, Jason of Pherae, who organised the great resources of his land
and, till his murder late in 370, prevented the Thebans from exploiting
their victory at Leuctra; but his successors could not hold Thessaly
together. No contemporary observer could have guessed that a king of
Macedon would succeed where Jason had failed, for the potential resources of this tough mountain people had so far been neutralised, by
their own backwardness, by the pressure of Greeks from the south and

wilder mountain tribes to north and west, and by the interminable civil wars of its royal house. When the great Philip succeeded his brother, killed in battle against the Illyrians in 359, he quickly showed by his mastery of external and internal dangers that he was to be one of the strong kings of Macedon. But there had been others before him; and the Greek world did not quickly realise the use he could make of his reorganised kingdom, further strengthened by his capture of the Thracian gold and silver mines. Access to southern Greece was secured to him when he gained possession of the Thermopylae pass in the final phase of the Sacred War, which he forcibly settled in 346. The apprehensions of Demosthenes at Athens were justified: as Philip showed, he needed the co-operation of Athens and her navy rather than her subjection, but the establishment on any terms of Macedonian power must eventually have ended the political career of the city. Resistance was not easy to organise. While Philip lived and held his existing power, he was not easy to fight; many Greek cities rather hoped for his help against their neighbours than feared his domination; Athens itself was long divided. In the end, it was an alliance of only Thebes and Athens that was defeated at Chaeroneia in 338. Philip then organised a reluctant Greece in the League of Corinth, under his leadership.

The idea of a general war against Persia had long been familiar in Greece, and Jason was believed to be planning one when he died. It is not clear, exactly when Philip began to see it as a practical possibility, but his preparations were well advanced, and a bridgehead in Asia Minor had been established, when he was murdered in 336. According to all precedent, this should have been the signal for the collapse of Macedon in new civil wars. But Alexander, Philip's greater son, and probably the instigator of his murder, was of age and fully capable of mastering the situation. Rapid campaigns to north and west secured his outer frontiers, and Greece was stunned by the destruction of Thebes. In 334, he was able to resume his father's plan, and crossed the Hellespont, launched on a career of conquest which undid the Persian Empire and led Alexander as far into India as his troops could bear to follow.

The acquisition of these vast new territories set the Greek cities in a new perspective. Alexander himself had no further need of their troops, and not much of their approval. In the strife of his successors, the great Hellenistic monarchies, the cities' political weight was not great, though their old prestige still counted for something; and

Greece was still the source of civilisation. The cities themselves were by no means reconciled to their place in this new world. Athens could still fight bitterly in the Chremonidean War of 267 against Antigonus Gonatas of Macedon. Sparta's revolutionary kings, Agis IV and Cleomenes III, sought to revive the old austere way of life; but Cleomenes' ruthless skill, after momentary triumphs, united too many and too powerful enemies against him. The growth of the Aetolian and Achaean Leagues in the third century showed that Greece was still capable of creating new political forms. Only the final Roman conquest flattened her into quiet provincialism.

*

An eager and combative particularism stands out as the main characteristic of the political life of the Greek cities. The political institutions which they developed in their meagre territories were more open, and called for more comprehensive participation by the individual citizen, than anything the world had yet seen; and this participation was possible only in small units. Representative government, by delegates elected to a central institution, was not wholly unknown in the larger units; but it never replaced direct government by the primary assembly of all qualified citizens, which was still of the utmost concern, even to oligarchic states where the qualified citizens were few in number. Even in larger states, there was an intimacy of political and social life, which would have been lost if the effective decisions had been taken in a distant capital: even in the smallest, for whom genuine independence was in the classical period an unattainable ideal, much remained for local decision, not lightly or readily surrendered to a greater power. Conscious though they were of their nationality as Greeks, the individual city had captured their emotions, and the larger nation could not claim an overriding loyalty. So all attempts at wider union failed. The most hopeful was the fifth-century empire of Athens, for all its much publicised oppressions, but even this never reached the stage which Rome successfully passed, where pride of local independence was swallowed up by the glamour of the central power.

Just enough of Greece united to resist the Persian invasion of 480, but the performance was never repeated. This was due, not only to the direct influence of city particularism but, almost more, to the disruptive secondary effect of this particularism on the stability of the individual city. Oligarch or democrat, the Greek cared passionately about the form of the institutions of his native city. If they were not to his liking, he could be sure of finding support or shelter in some nearby state which shared his ideological feeling. The major constitutional issues could not be settled at a national level, but were continually fought out anew at a level which we might think of as municipal. The familiar political disease of the Greek city found its own peculiar name, *stasis*, which must have meant originally the stance or position one took with regard to public questions; but it was widened to mean either a party of persons with a common political aim, or the mere state of strife between such parties. The same spirit of faction necessarily permeated all other discussion of serious political issues, war and peace and alliance, the use of public money, and all the rest

These were the basic factors: the passion for city autonomy; the practice of direct, not representative, government; the endless strain of faction. They certainly contributed to the deepening confusion of the fourth century and to the eventual loss of Greek independence, but the political history as a whole is anything but merely melancholy. On the central question of internal dissension, it would be well to remember that it was only the comparative openness of Greek politics that allowed it to be manifested at all, whereas the subjects of the Persian king had, formally speaking, only the choices of obedience to central authority and revolt against it. The principle that the community should vote, and should as a whole accept the majority decision, was first exemplified in Greek history. Indeed, it may have been in Greece that it was first employed at all; and with it came a whole new range of political activity, not available at all under autocratic monarchy. The principle is not always allowed to operate today, and we must not too much complain if these early pioneers were sometimes impatient of it.

CHAPTER 5

Tribes and kinship groups

REFERENCE HAS BEEN made in previous chapters to tribal organisation in various parts of the Greek world, and an analysis of Greek
society should perhaps begin with the frameworks within which its
members were variously grouped. The issue is almost entirely about
the internal organisation of the individual city, the ways in which the
units of its army were built up, and the ways in which the population
was divided for purposes of civil administration. Some confusion arises
here from the presence of two quite distinct principles of organisation,
locality and kinship.

Organisation by locality will cause no difficulty: this is what we
are all accustomed to, in the shape of parishes and counties, states,
parliamentary constituencies or electoral precincts, and the like. It may
be harder to visualise the entirely different system which groups its
members according to kinship. The units of such a system are based, at
least theoretically, on common descent, so that a man may find himself
enrolled for civil and military purposes with his remote cousins living
in quite another part of the country, not with his familiar neighbours
from the same street or village. Kinship organisation is, however,
exceedingly widespread, and traces of it can be found in the background
of the history of most nations. The Celtic peoples of the British Isles
had a highly elaborate system, persisting conspicuously in the clans of
Scotland: the North American Indians are the classic example, the
study of which gave a basis for this sector of modern anthropology;
and many kinship systems, of various types, still survive to show us
how such things work in practice.

Among the city-states of Greece, the kinship principle seems to have
been most effective at an early stage of their history, towards the end
of the dark age and in the earlier part of the fully historical period.
The primary division of the citizen body was into tribes (*phylai*): below

them come phratries (or 'brotherhoods'), the most widespread term, though others are found, such as *hetaireiai* (groups of 'companions') at Gortyn in Crete: the smallest units are variously named, *genē* at Athens and elsewhere, *patrai* in some places, and I shall use the term 'clan' for units at this level. Almost all of these are terms which imply literal kinship. At very varying dates, most states went over to a territorial principle; but when they did so they were apt to retain for their new kind of division terms, especially 'tribe', which originally belonged to the kinship system. At Athens certainly, and very possibly elsewhere, phratries and other kinship groups survived as social and religious units, after the change-over to organisation by locality. The Athenian citizen of the classical period was thus simultaneously involved in two different types of group, which overlapped in the untidy way which historical development so often imposes on social organisation.

*

The basic unit for archaic and classical Greece is the individual city, but the larger groupings are in some degree relevant. The names, Hellene and Hellas, in Homer's usage almost entirely restricted to a particular corner of southern Thessaly, spread by some process which we cannot now follow to become, by the time Greece was once more literate, the standard names for the whole race and the area it inhabited. Herodotus and Thucydides both thought that the name Hellene covered some diversity of racial origin, but the unity which it expressed had a firm basis in community of language, religion and social customs, and above all in the feeling of community among those who used the name. In a way that is characteristic of their thought, the Greeks expressed this feeling by saying that the hero, Hellen, was the son or brother of Deucalion (the Greek Noah, who survived a universal flood to become the ancestor of subsequent mankind) and the father of Dorus and others, from whom came the Dorians and other divisions of the race. Greek literature is littered with such 'eponymous' heroes, artificial constructions to account for the origin of a current name, seldom more than cardboard figures whose thin stories never come to life. They may serve here to bring out the point that alleged kinship is sometimes no more than a genealogical fiction to express the unity of a body which has been formed on a quite different principle, a point which is of some importance as regards the origin of phratries and clans.

Within the whole body of Hellenes, certain major groups stand out, notably the Dorians and Ionians, whose combative racial feelings have been mentioned earlier. The links between the Dorian cities are particularly clear. Besides the general character of their dialect, they tended to concentrate on particular religious cults and to celebrate festivals, like the Carneia, which were common to them all. In all Dorian communities about whose internal arrangements we know anything at all, we find the same three names for tribes—Hylleis, Pamphyloi, Dymanes—which strongly suggests that this triple division already existed among the Dorians as a whole before they entered southern Greece in the eleventh century and founded the states we find in classical times. In many Dorian states, an additional tribe or tribes can be found, which are usually interpreted as a means of incorporating some part of the pre-Dorian population in the system. Where this occurred, a genealogical link of some kind would be provided, as at Argos, where the fourth tribe, Hyrnathioi, was traced to a daughter of the Dorian founder of the city. Among the Ionian cities, community of dialect, cult and festival is equally noticeable, but tribal names are less uniform. Athens had her four old Attic tribes, the basis of the archaic state down to the reform of Cleisthenes in 507 (below), and these survived vestigially, for religious purposes, down at least to the beginning of the fourth century. These four names, together with two others not found at Athens, crop up among the cities of East Greece often enough to show that there was some common Ionian tradition in this matter. But the regularity is much less marked than among the Dorian cities, reflecting perhaps the mixed origins of the East Greek states. For other sections of the Greek race, there is no comparable evidence.

These tribes were, however, very much units of the individual city. They may be symptoms of a common origin, but in later times there was no organisation to comprise, for instance, all cities of Dorian speech and institutions; and no suggestion that there could be a feeling of solidarity between the Hylleis of one Dorian city and the Hylleis of another. Where the situation allowed or encouraged it, feeling between two races could be used, as on the occasion when Brasidas, in Thucydides' history, encourages his men by reminding them that they are Dorians, and accustomed to defeat Ionians. But the Dorians never hesitated to fight among themselves, indeed the traditional hostility between Argos and Sparta was a factor of continuing importance in the history of the Peloponnese.

Some more compact racial groups did, however, achieve a measure of unitary organisation. The cities of Boeotia, with mountain barriers to divide them from their Athenian and Phocian neighbours, were always separate cities but also conscious of a racial unity. This they expressed, for instance, by putting an abbreviation of the Boeotian name on their coins (pl. 13, No. 11); for much of their history, they formed a Boeotian League, with federal officers and council whose decisions were, apart from occasional dissension, binding on the whole league. The Arcadians were equally conscious of their racial character, but their very broken territory was unevenly developed. There were some old-established cities, jealous for their independence, and some more loosely organised areas, ready to unite and found the new city of Megalopolis in the fourth century; their efforts to form a unitary league were less successful. Further afield, where Greek culture tailed off towards the north and west of the peninsula, the Aetolians and others had virtually no city organisation at all in the classical period. The powerful Aetolian League developed on a somewhat different basis in the latter part of the fourth century, to become an organisation with considerable weight in the Hellenistic world.

*

The Greek *phrater* is the common Indo-European word for a brother, illustrated in the Latin *frater* and indeed in our own word. Since all Greek dialects use a quite different word for a literal brother, and since *phrater* was restricted to members of phratries, it can be argued that the loss of the original meaning of *phrater* goes back to a time before the Greek language split up into dialects, and that phratries in the full later sense already existed among the Middle Helladic people before they first entered Greece. There is no means of verifying that. The Mycenaean documents, though they sometimes record the status of parents and children, had no such occasion to speak of brothers, and we do not know what word the Mycenaean Greeks used. The most that can be said is that the lists which deal with soldiers and rowers do not, on the face of it, look as if they were based on kinship divisions.

Homer is possibly more informative. Near the beginning of the *Iliad* (ii. 362) Nestor advised Agamemnon to organise his army by tribes and phratries, so that tribe might help tribe and phratry help phratry; and he would know exactly who was fighting well and who was holding back, since they would be fighting in these separate units.

This principle of organisation makes no appearance at all in the rest of the poem, where the essentially formless Homeric army marches and fights and flees simply as an indeterminate background for the exploits of the great heroes; and Nestor's own contingent shows no sign of organisation by phratry, when Agamemnon visits it later. Similarly, the only other reference to phratries in the *Iliad* presupposes a comprehensive social system of phratries, which simply is not there in the rest of the poem; and there are no phratries at all in the *Odyssey*. The natural inference from all this is that the epic conventions which formed the poet's starting-point made no allowance for phratries. But the poet himself was familiar with them, and thought they were the natural units to employ in the organisation of an army, and he said so once, in passing; but to reform the whole diction of his long poem to conform with this principle would have been a large effort for no very valuable result. So he dropped them again, and the inconsequence of his casual mention of phratries was not a kind to worry the hearers of an oral poem.

That would imply that phratries were at least no conspicuous part of the society in which these epic conventions had been developed, but that they had beome part of the regular framework of Greek life by the poet's own time, roughly the eighth century. In political terms, that would mean that they became important at a time when the rule of kings was dying out and the cities came increasingly under the control of exclusive aristocracies. We might then risk the guess that phratries, of the kind known to us from survivals in the classical period, were formed at the close of the dark age as a way of organising the followers of particular groups of nobles.[1] Once such an association was formed, it would in the Greek way quickly acquire a common ancestor and take on all the colour of a genuine kinship group: at the start, indeed, it would inevitably include large family groups, and membership thereafter would be hereditary, in the strict male line.

Some features of Athenian phratries and clans fit this guess well. There has been some controversy, whether originally the whole body of Athenians had been organised in such clans (*genê*), or only the nobility; but, for the classical period and later, it is certain that the clans

---

1. The reader should be warned that most historians take the phratry as a solid inheritance from a much more remote antiquity. The passages from Homer seem to me a serious obstacle to that. For the view taken above, see my articles cited in the Bibliography.

were exclusively aristocratic groups, and it is likely that they always had been. Their main function in later times was to provide priests for certain cults, some of them state cults of great importance. There is some doubt whether they were all genuinely kinship groups in origin. Most of them have names of 'patronymic' form, the name of their supposed ancestor with the termination -*idai* added, but there is reason to think that in early times this termination could be used to designate groups with some basis other than common descent; and a few of the names look as if they were taken, rather, from the clan's religious function. Whatever the truth of that, bodies with names of this form would certainly be assumed in the classical period to be groups descended from a common ancestor.

In Athens, in the late fifth and fourth centuries, a particular clan is found in several instances exercising the remains of authority within a particular phratry, in a way that suggests that its authority had once been very much greater. It suggests, in fact, that the clan had once controlled entry into the phratry and formulated its rules; whereas in later times, such matters were decided by a phratry meeting at which all members voted, a small-scale version of the general assembly of all citizens, in the democratic manner. Further, some phratries, and rather more clans, had strong roots in particular parts of Attica, and this is very possibly true of the rest. This may suggest that the phratry had once been the local following of the local great family. If this is on the right lines, clans with their attendant phratries were principal elements in the political struggle within the city at the end of the dark age. But that is a period of which we have no detailed history.

In sixth-century Athens, which we know slightly better, we hear mainly of the actions of individuals; so far as we encounter continuing units they are not the clans but the individual great families, which Greek like English is apt to call 'houses'. Such a house was that of the Alcmeonidae, which we meet first in the person of Megacles, who was chief magistrate of Athens at the time of Cylon's attempt to make himself tyrant in the late seventh century, and was held responsible for the execution of Cylon's supporters after their surrender. There may have been a clan, called Alcmeonidae, to which this house belonged: the question is disputed, but it is not in dispute that the persons whom our sources classify as Alcmeonidae were all direct descendants of Alcmeon, the son of the Megacles just mentioned. It was this family, rather than the clan as such (if there was one), that played the public role. Again, there are signs that Athenian politics in the sixth century were heavily affected by the regional loyalties of particular districts of Attica, most noticeably in the period of strife which preceded Peisistratus' tyranny. It is possible that locally based phratries played their part in this regional faction, but there is no direct evidence. The general impression remains that clans and phratries had already ceased to play much part, as such, in Athenian politics, well before the reform of Cleisthenes in 507.

*

One main reason for changing over from kinship to local organisation must always have been the need to provide a more efficient basis for the army. Greek armies almost always consisted of regiments based on tribes, *phylai*, whether these were kinship groups or territorial units called by the same name. The advice of Nestor in the *Iliad* (above), though it stands quite isolated, is still adequate evidence that phratries were used as subdivisions of the military tribe. As warfare grew more complicated and needed stricter training, the loose organisation of the kindred became less and less suitable for the army. The difficulties would increase where, as seems to have happened in Attica (below), landowners became more mobile and the members of kinship groups to a lesser extent lived round the original local nucleus. Accordingly, it is not surprising to find many states changing, at one time or another, from kinship tribes to 'tribes' based on locality. For Sparta, a line of Tyrtaeus guarantees that the army was once ordered, as one would expect, in the three traditional Dorian tribes: the context leaves a little uncertainty whether this army of the kindred had lasted into the poet's own time, the seventh century, but the chances are that it had not long been reformed when he wrote. It was probably in his time that Sparta formed, instead, five army units based on locality, on the four 'villages' of Sparta itself, with the small town of Amyclae as a fifth, a few miles to the south. Argos, on the other hand, shows an army still, in the fifth century, based on four traditional tribes, the Dorian three with one added (p. 78); and these same four were still the basis of her civil organisation in the Hellenistic period.

Between these extremes comes the instance best known to us, the reform of Cleisthenes at Athens in 507. In place of the four old Attic tribes he created ten new ones, still called by the old name *phylai*, and also, as the old tribes had been, divided into thirds called *trittyes*. The new system had its local roots in the smallest units which we call 'demes'. One of the many uses of the word, *demos*, was for the villages which had always existed in the Attic countryside, and the bulk of Cleisthenes' demes were based on such villages; but the demes he created in the city were wholly artificial, and in some rural areas his demes were not simply natural units. From these demes, thirty *trittyes* were built up in a somewhat intricate manner, mostly but not all blocks of contiguous territory, ten in the city and its surrounding area, ten round the rest of the coast, ten inland. Each new tribe had assigned to it by lot one *trittys* from each of these three categories. The new tribes were put under the protection of ten heroes, chosen from a longer list by the Delphic oracle, and the worship of these heroes gave the tribes their cult centres. The demes mostly had their own cults already, and even the more artificial *trittyes* have left some record of their communal sacrifices.

Though a need to reorganise the army may here, as elsewhere, have given a start to reform, the change of system meant change in the whole framework of civil life as well. In addition, Cleisthenes used his reform to prevent certain old associations in the country from exercising as separate units a local political influence. This was part of his general tendency to neutralise, but not to abolish, traditional institutions with religious overtones. Thus, his new demes replaced the phratries as the smallest units in the build-up of the tribe, but the phratries continued in existence side by side with the demes, and the noble clans continued to provide officiants for traditional cults. The ten new tribes provided the regiments of the army, the subdivision into *trittyes* here playing a practical part, and the ten generals[1] were elected, one from each tribe. The Council of Five Hundred, which Cleisthenes instituted to replace the older Four Hundred of Solon, was made up of fifty members from each tribe, chosen by lot from the candidates put forward by their demes, which were represented according to their size. For all kinds of public business, boards or committees of ten were appointed, again one from each tribe; and for many public offices the candidates were for long put up in the first instance by the demes.

At their different levels, tribe and deme were essential elements in the political and administrative machinery of the state, and each attracted strong loyalties. The tribe had its own assembly and the cult of its tribal hero, and it competed against other tribes in various festivals.

1. For the generals see pp. 158–9

The deme under its demarch managed its own local affairs and kept a register of its members. These registers were the primary means of determining who was or was not a citizen of Athens, there being no central list. Speeches in court constantly stress that a man's deme best knows what sort of man he is, and his standing with his fellow-demesmen is the best witness to character that he can produce.

But, though the basis of the system was territorial when it was instituted in 507, and though its local roots continued to be important, membership of a deme was thereafter hereditary; a man did not change his deme if he went to live elsewhere. This a curious testimony to the continuing strength of the principle that a man's descent should determine his place in the framework of the state. It had a further incidental result, which slightly assists the historian of Athenian society. Since a Greek, unlike a Roman or an Englishman, had in principle only a single name, and the stock of names was not unlimited, some further determinant was necessary to identify a particular person. By the end of the fifth century at Athens, it was normal to identify him by his father's name as well as his own and by his deme membership, e.g. Pericles son of Xanthippus of the deme Cholargus; even so there were often duplicates, especially within a single family. But to add the deme-name tells us, not where the man himself lived, but where his direct male ancestor had lived in 507; and so, where we have the full official names for several members of a family or a kinship group, we can see how widely they were scattered at the time of Cleisthenes' reform. The scattering seems already to have been extensive by 507, a fact we could not otherwise have known, and that would certainly have made difficulties in training and mobilisation for an army still based on kinship groups. This could be the reason why a change in the organisation of the citizen body was needed at Athens in the late sixth century.

*

When Cleisthenes changed the basis of citizen organisation from kinship to locality, he did not abolish clans and phratries but only took them out of the political system. The kinship groups remained as social units, in which the individual family could feel that it had a place and a context. It may have been technically possible for a fourth-century Athenian to be a citizen without belonging to a phratry, but it is clear that such a man would be in an uncomfortable and questionable position. In some rare cases, the phratry had still a public function.

The archaic law of Dracon which dealt with unintentional homicide, passed over a century before Cleisthenes, but reaffirmed in 409 as the law of the state, appoints that if the dead man has no close relatives ten members of his phratry shall settle with the killer. At a more normal level, phratries also owned property and engaged in lawsuits, and no doubt did much else that we do not hear of.

A few decrees of phratry meetings or lists of members are preserved on stone, but we encounter the classical phratry mainly in courts of law, where its evidence might help to establish a man's status. His father might have celebrated his marriage by giving a feast to his *phrateres*, though it does not seem there was any compulsion to do this, or even any strong social pressure. He would certainly offer a sacrifice on behalf of an infant son, at the age of three or four, and another shortly before the son's formal introduction and admission to the phratry at the age of eighteen. This took place at the annual festival of the phratries, the Apatouria, held in the late autumn, very much a family festival. On the latter occasion, the father swore an oath that the son was the legitimate issue of a valid marriage. The phratry, like the deme, kept a register of its members, but what was required in an Athenian court was not the document itself or an attested copy, but the oral witness of members who had been present at the litigant's enrolment. They could attest that he had been accepted as a legitimate son of his family, and that his father had performed all the proper rituals. Witness of this kind was even more important in the case of an adopted son than with a natural son, the fact of adoption being easier to contest in court.[1]

Though these family matters were the special concern of the phratry, the marriage itself did not consist in any ceremony performed before the phratry. It seems, rather, that in an Athenian marriage the essential act was just the handing-over of the bride to the bridegroom by her father or guardian, attested in the Greek manner by oral witnesses rather than by a written contract. All that the phratry could do was to attest that it had accepted the father's oath on the validity of his marriage and the legitimacy of his son. In 451, a law proposed by Pericles confined Athenian citizenship to those whose parents on both sides were Athenians, whereas before 451 the son of an Athenian father and a foreign-born mother had qualified as an Athenian citizen. After Pericles' law, the oath which the father swore before his phratry included also the statement that his wife was Athenian-born. On all these

1. These are adoptions of adults, not infants; see pp. 112–13

matters, the evidence of the *phrateres* could be important, because they were matters of concern to the phratry as such, which should have been satisfied about them before it admitted a new member. Similarly, an adopted son had to be introduced into the adopter's phratry, and the *phrateres* could bear witness to the fact of the adoption and the status of the adoptee.

The phratry, surviving as a social unit alongside the territorial demes, was a useful witness precisely because it was a kinship group and therefore interested in these family matters. The deme, of course, was interested in the same range of facts and required to be satisfied about them before it enrolled the natural or adopted son of a member, so that, in cases about inheritance and the like, a litigant would want to call the evidence of his demesmen, not only of his *phrateres*. Indeed, enrolment in a deme was a more basic requirement to establish one's citizenship. When in 346 the Athenian state ordered a general check of the whole body of its citizens, having no central list of voters, it could only proceed by ordering the demes to go over their lists and scrutinise the claims of each member named in them. The demes, even after the loss of Athenian independence, had still a function to perform and survived. The phratries, on the other hand, for whatever reason, faded away during the Hellenistic period and became a matter for antiquarian research among the scholars of a later age who wrote commentaries on the Attic orators. After Alexander's death and the Macedonian conquest, Athenian citizenship was a matter of less concern, at any rate to the lower social classes. It may simply be that, in this time, they found more comfort and satisfaction in other forms of social and religious association and no longer bothered with the phratry.

The clans, on the other hand, persisted into Roman times, protected by their social prestige and exclusiveness. They had long lost what corporate political influence they had had in early days. The possession of a noble name was always an asset in Athenian politics. The Greeks easily believed in an élite, and like others they were ready to suppose that all sorts of characteristics are transmitted mainly in the male line, along with the name and the property. But, as was said above, it was the individual great 'house', not the clan, that counted in the classical period. We seldom know to what clan a prominent Athenian belonged, or whether he belonged to one at all: when we do, it is usually as a kind of nickname to distinguish him from other persons of the same name. Thus a certain Demostratus, who is mentioned in connection with the preparations for the Athenian expedition to Sicily in 415, is distinguished as 'Demostratus of the Bouzygai'. Again, while the phratry continued in the fourth century to be a matter of concern to the ordinary man, the clan lost its authority within the phratry, and the phratry assembly made its own rules. But, in the same fourth century, the clan had still a social value for the upper classes, who had leisure for purely decorative activities, and the important priesthoods which attached to some clans helped to keep them in being. Among the most conspicuous were the offices which played their part in the Eleusinian mysteries; and though the two great clans which provided the main officiants, Eumolpidae and Ceryces, had some curious vicissitudes in the post-classical period, the offices continued in being. The decline in the value of citizenship enhanced the social value of clan membership, not diminished it.

*

This discussion has centred mainly on Athens because almost all our material comes from there. At Athens we can, to some extent, see how citizenship, while Greece remained free, progressively lost its original dependence on the framework of kinship institutions—it makes no difference to the argument whether the kinship was in origin genuine or fictional—and became a more purely political concept. Elsewhere the general movement was certainly in the same direction, though at different speeds and with different stopping-places, but from these other states we have no such comprehensive evidence as we have from Athens.

Citizen birth was naturally everywhere the normal criterion for citizenship, but not all states insisted on a citizen mother, as Athens did after 451. Clans of one kind and another are mentioned sporadically, mostly in aristocratic contexts. It may be worth noting the case of Samos, where a democratic revolution resulted in the creation of a whole new set of clans, in which not only the nobles but every citizen was enrolled; and these artificial units had the name, *genê*, like the Athenian clans—a word which linguistically ought, more than other terms, to convey literal kinship. Phratries are more often attested. For instance, the Labyadai of Delphi inscribed their rules on stone, a record as elaborate as anything we have from Athens. We may note that, at Gortyn in Crete, there was a distinct class of persons who belonged to no *hetaireia*, the institution corresponding there to the phratry, and their status before the law was very markedly inferior. It was still thought necessary for Alexander's most famous foundation, Alexandria in Egypt, to have a set of phratries; but, having no traditional names available, the Alexandrians gave their phratries numbers. Parallels and variants to the Athenian institutions could be further multiplied.

CHAPTER 6

Landowners, peasants and colonists

IN GREEK SOCIETY, as in other pre-industrial societies, land was very much the most important form of property. In a world without large liquid resources and without the large credit structure which supports our civilisation, other forms of investment familiar to us either did not exist at all or were exceedingly risky in comparison with land. Land, or a house, cannot be surreptitiously removed, and these were the solid and obvious forms of security. The right to own land within the territory of a state was everywhere reserved to the citizens of that state. At Athens the resident aliens, called 'metics' (pp. 130–2 below), in whose hands lay most of the commerce and industry and most of what liquid capital there was, were excluded from purchasing land.

There was not too much land available. As was stressed in the first chapter, Greece is mostly bare mountain, and though the soil of the alluvial plains is generally rich, it could not by itself support a large population. Pressure on the land was certainly a main factor in the foundation of so many colonies abroad, in the late eighth and seventh centuries, and at least contributed to the agrarian distress which troubled Attica around 600, and to the revolutions which established tyrannies elsewhere from c. 650 onwards. Whatever the position had been in the seventh century, the eventual result for classical Attica was a countryside mainly occupied in independent small holdings, which were at the free disposal of their occupants. That was not an inevitable result. In the main plains of Attica, concentrated estates of a fair size are technically possible and have been seen in more recent times. In ancient Thessaly, the nobles held much larger estates in their wide plains; but even there, there was no development comparable to the vast Roman *latifundia* worked by gangs of slaves. The Attic model seems to have been the general one in Greece, apart from a few special cases, and it is an important though not entirely answerable question how this came to be so.

Greek tradition in these matters might well be varied. It is no use even speculating about the systems that may have been imported by prehistoric invaders like the Middle Helladic people, for more than fifteen centuries separate their arrival in peninsular Greece from the Athens of Thucydides and Aristophanes. That is roughly the span which separates the collapse of Roman rule in Britain from current British systems of land tenure, time enough for extensive changes, peaceful or violent. The installation of the Mycenaean kingdoms would have been enough, in itself, to blot out the primitive arrangements of the earliest Greeks. Nor is it much use speculating about survivals from the system imperfectly revealed by the Mycenaean documents, for the disappearance of this section of the Mycenaean vocabulary and the very different situation seen in Homer shows that the old fabric was effectually torn up when the palaces were destroyed and the bureaucracy vanished. We have no direct means of discovering what happened to the land in areas where the invaders dominated, as the Dorians did in Sparta and Argos, and the Thessalians in Thessaly; or what kind of changes came over the areas which were not thus invaded.

Here, Homer's preoccupation with the princes obscures our vision. Clearly, the great prince, with his palace and his numerous flocks and the rest, disposes of the land as he pleases, settling his servants as he likes, even giving large tracts away as Agamemnon proposed to do to appease Achilles. Some of this will be not so much reflection of any historical situation, as the way the epic poets, looking back from their own world, thought that the great kings of legend ought to act. Agamemnon's project of giving seven cities with their inhabitants to Achilles, is, on the face of it, a political act, quite unlike that of a land-owner, however great, disposing of part of his land. We are nearer domestic life in the *Odyssey*, where the circumstances are indeed con-fused during the absence of the king, but it seems that the great property will remain with Odysseus' son, Telemachus, even if he is not in the end accepted as king. Here, there are clearly landowners other than the king, though their presence is indicated only by implication, or incidentally, as when one of Penelope's suitors offers to settle a beggar (who is Odysseus in disguise) as a labourer on his land. The system also contained still smaller landholders, hardly noticed by

Homer, like the poor and needy man imagined by the ghost of Achilles (p. 47 above).

Two models of settlement mainly offer themselves. One is the situation in historical Thessaly, where in the classical period there were very large estates, quite different in scale from those of southern Greece. This system looks like a survival from archaic times, and by the fourth century it was beginning to be seriously eroded. Great estates in this style are clearly one possible outcome of migration and conquest. The other is the colonial model, with a 'lot' of land assigned to each individual colonist—maybe literally assigned by lot, but this word (*kleros*) came at an early stage to mean any parcel of land, as 'lot' does now in America. Allotment in this style is heard of from the very beginning of the eighth-century colonial movement, in the story of an improvident Corinthian who, during the voyage out, gave away the lot which he was to receive at Syracuse in exchange for a honey-cake. Such allotment might equally be the pattern of the original Dorian settlement in the Peloponnese, and of other conquerors elsewhere. These two systems, though they both employ the word 'lot', suggest a difference in social organisation. The Thessalian distribution of land would be appropriate for conquerors, led by a strong nobility able to carve out large domains for themselves, in the style of the Norman conquest of England: the colonial pattern implies rather a community, conscious of the need to maintain the individual as a soldier, parcelling out the land in adequate and perhaps (with suitable exceptions) equal lots. The evidence we have from later periods suggests that the pattern of original settlement was, in fact, rather more diverse; the diversity probably depends in part on the proportions between conquerors and conquered in different areas.

Aristotle ascribed to the shadowy early figure of Aleuas 'the Red' both the standard division of Thessaly as a whole into four regions, and a division of the land into lots, each of which was to provide forty horsemen and eighty heavy infantry for the federal army. The diagram of precise equality is no doubt bogus—Aristotle had a similarly precise and implausible diagram for the social organisation of early Athens—but it leaps to the eye that the 'lot' here is on a quite different scale from the more modest estates of southern Greece. Contingents of troops are here to be raised on a territorial basis, not out of the city's tribes and their subdivisions, as was done in the south in historical times. We know so little about the development of the system that we cannot be sure whether the scheme ascribed to Aleuas was really a reorganisation carried out a long time after the migration, or reflects the situation created by the original conquest.

The general development of Thessaly in the classical period was away from mere domination by the landed nobility and towards the city-state system of the south. The earliest Thessalians who are more than just names to us are those nobles who, at the beginning of the fifth century, attracted poets like Simonides and Pindar to their great houses, and whose birth and wealth were celebrated in almost Homeric terms. At this time, such nobles could act as independent powers, as is illustrated in the story of Meno of Pharsalus (an ancestor of the Meno who gave his name to one of Plato's dialogues). He raised 300 cavalry from his *penestai* (below) and came to the help of the Athenians in one of the early campaigns of their Confederacy, against Eion, at the mouth of the river Strymon in Thrace, in 476. No Athenian or Corinthian aristocrat could act on a scale like this, nor any individual Spartan. The development of cities was already beginning in Meno's time; by the end of the fifth century, we find a tyrant in the city of Pherae, whose port Pagasae (the modern Volos) is the only effective entrance into Thessaly by sea. His successor was the briefly powerful Jason, who succeeded during the 370's in uniting Thessaly under his rule. It is to be noted that the federal army which Jason organised drew its contingents from the cities, not from quasi-independent estates: the land of Thessaly must by then have been firmly divided up into city territories.

We do not know to what extent there were smaller free landholders in between the great estates, but it is likely enough that there were such, attracting no more attention than their counterparts in the world of Homer. Below them were men of servile status, the *penestai*, whom ancient writers put in the same category as the helots of Sparta, and who are usually taken to be the conquered remnants of the pre-conquest population. We hear less in detail about them than we hear about the helots. They are known to have been numerous, and their revolts a standing danger to the ruling class; but, as in the anecdote about Meno of Pharsalus, they might be loyal enough to be usable as an armed force. The dialect mixture of Thessaly, with the Aeolic of the conquered a rather stronger element than the North-West Greek of the conquerors, again suggests that the conquerors were originally a minority, but one cannot guess at the proportions implied.

South of Thessaly, the Boeotian plain was rich land, though not on the scale of Thessaly, and the Athenians affected to despise the agricultural sluggishness of their neighbours, the 'Boeotian pigs'. Here, for once, we have some quite early testimony, the poem which Hesiod wrote for the instruction of his fellow-farmers, probably late in the eighth century or early in the seventh. Hesiod deals entirely with the problems of a farm of moderate size, run by a single master and his slaves. He complains freely about his own troubles, mainly the division of the family property with his brother Perses, and alleges that Perses sought the favour of the 'bribe-devouring princes' to gain more than his share. But he seems to be entirely free himself, not dependent on these corrupt nobles except to the extent that they may pervert the course of justice. This can hardly be the whole picture. We cannot suppose that the nobles themselves were all restricted to single-family farms of the sort that Hesiod describes. But he gives no hint, how the nobles ran their estates, or what sort of labour cultivated them. Remembering the different situation not far away in Thessaly, we have to be careful about taking Hesiod's picture as typical for land-distribution in Greece generally; but he certainly attests the existence of a whole class of free and independent farmers, operating on a small scale in Boeotia around 700.

The Dorian Peloponnese again shows some diversity. The situation of Sparta was in many ways abnormal. The ruling aristocracy, the full citizens called Spartiates, had their extensive lands tilled for them by their helots, slaves who actually lived on the land and had to render some of the produce to their masters. This is represented as a heavy burden, and their conditions were in other ways hard. But they belonged to the state, and were not chattels disposable by their masters. They kept what produce remained and, at any rate in the post-classical period, many of them were able to accumulate respectable amounts. The Spartiates, by Herodotus' estimate, numbered 8,000 men in 480, but by the end of the fifth century they had sunk to less than half this number, and by 371 they were hardly more than a thousand. Even when they were at their most numerous, the average size of their estates must have been large by Athenian standards. Side by side with them lived the free men called *perioikoi* in the minor towns and villages, managing their local affairs and apparently leading quiet lives in the ordinary Greek style, except that they were under Spartan supervision and had to serve in the Spartan army. We have no figures to show the proportions of the available land occupied by these two disparate communities, but there is no doubt that the *perioikoi* were the more numerous, or that the Spartiates kept large tracts of the best land for themselves. The *perioikoi* seem to have been content with their situation, and few of them ever revolted: no doubt they felt the advantages of being protected in their quiet prosperity by the formidable army to which they contributed.

The *perioikoi* spoke Doric (but so did the helots) and are not distinguishable racially from the Spartiates by any criterion that we can apply; and the term 'the Lacedaemonians', the formal name of what we call the Spartan state,[1] included *perioikoi* as well as the full Spartiate citizens. Since we know so little of the condition of Laconia when the Dorians arrived, or of the number of the Dorians when they entered Laconia, we can only guess at the way in which this exceptional situation came into being. Ancient writers, ignorant of the gap we call the dark age, and assuming that the Dorians took over flourishing kingdoms from the grandsons of Agamemnon and Menelaus, mostly treat the conquest as an act achieved in one swift movement, after which the Dorian kingdom was established over the whole land. Some, however, maintained that the conquest had been spread over many generations, and that Sparta only gradually emerged as the controlling centre. Neither tradition can have been based on much knowledge of the facts, but the anomalies are perhaps more easily explained if we suppose that a relatively small body of Dorians settled in Sparta in the first instance, then expanded their control from there, absorbing what then became the perioikic communities and no doubt confiscating part of their land for Spartiate use. In that case, however, there could be no question of an original division of the whole territory into single lots at a particular moment.

The position is further complicated by the belief that the remote Spartan lawgiver, Lycurgus, had divided the available land up into equal lots for the full citizens. The idea of an exactly equal distribution of land always had an attraction for the Greeks, and it appears in Plato's *Laws* and in other utopian contexts; and in the same spirit it might be projected into an ideal past. In this case, there may be some limited justification. A tradition which seems to be based on Aristotle

1. Greek did not use geographical terms, as we do, for the names of states. Where we say that 'Athens' did something, an ancient author says that 'the Athenians' did it.

said that there were two categories of land at Sparta: the 'ancient share', which the holder was forbidden by law to sell or otherwise alienate; and the rest of the land, whose sale was frowned on by convention but legally permissible. The phraseology suggests a deliberate allocation at some time in the archaic period. We know that citizenship at Sparta depended on a man's ability to pay his dues in kind to one of those all-male messes which were a special feature of Spartan life. The inalienable 'ancient share' may then have been instituted at a particular moment, in an attempt to ensure the economic existence of a sufficient number of citizens, and thus of soldiers in the all-important army, while leaving over another category of land, disposable by its owner without the same restriction. If this took place, it was probably in connection with the seventh-century revolt of Messenia. We cannot hope to reach further back and determine the nature of the earlier allocation of land at the beginning of the history of Dorian Sparta.

Whatever the racial composition of the *perioikoi*, it would be reasonable to guess that the Laconian helots were predominantly of pre-Dorian origin. Their enslavement by the relatively small body of Spartiates created a problem which haunted all Spartan history, the problem of security against helot revolt. In the north-east Peloponnese there was no such built-in tension. In Argos and Sicyon we hear, barely, of the existence of a class regarded by ancient lexicographers as comparable with the helots. It is natural to think again of the enslavement of part of the pre-Dorian population; but this did not create a problem to dominate the whole history of these states, and we must presume that here the numbers were not so dangerously disproportionate. Moreover, the fourth tribe which in Sicyon existed beside the three traditional Dorian tribes was certainly the tribe of the non-Dorians, and we may presume the same of the similar fourth tribe at Argos. It would seem that here the upper class of the pre-Dorian inhabitants was incorporated into the civic organisation, at the start or later, a measure which was never taken at Sparta.

Once more it is not easy to distinguish what belongs to the original pattern of settlement and what is due to subsequent developments, but on the evidence it seems more likely that in these cases the newcomers outnumbered the remnants of the older population, and that the two groups combined peaceably. At Sicyon, and in some degree at Corinth, racial feeling was an ingredient in the situation which led to the installation of tyranny in the middle of the seventh century, but there is no such record of division at Argos; and, by the classical period, all three cities seem to be regarded as homogeneously Dorian. There is no tradition here of equal distribution of the land. Aristotle, indeed, refers briefly to a very ancient lawgiver at Corinth who thought that the existing distribution of property, even if unequal, should be stabilised as it stood, which suggests that some plan for redistribution into equal lots had been put forward unsuccessfully in the early archaic period. So far as we can tell, the eventual pattern here, as in Attica, was of a large number of relatively small units at the free disposal of their holders.

Without going into further instances, which would not seriously alter the picture, this review suggests that the colonial model of a controlled and purposive distribution of land is hardly at all applicable to the migration period, and that attempts to produce an equal distribution were the product of later crises. The situation in Thessaly may be due to the fact that the invaders were led by an aristocracy strong enough to seize most of the land for themseves, but further south the social structure of the invaders was such as to result in a less unequal distribution. The exceptional situation at Sparta was achieved by the pertinacious aggression of the Spartiate aristocracy, very probably after the migration rather than during it. That may have been aided by the isolation of Laconia behind its mountain barriers, whereas Argos, Corinth and Sicyon were more open to the outer world and less of a geographical unity in themselves. The primacy of Argos was recognised, especially in the religious sphere, but she never united the north-east Peloponnese politically.

The situation in early Attica is as hard as any to determine. Whereas in the states just considered we can legitimately speculate on the various possible effects of migration and invasion, in other places we know only that, roughly at the time of the arrival of the Dorians in the Argolid, their society went through an important transformation, dropping the last relics of the Mycenaean way of life and looking forward rather to the future developments of archaic Greece. The nature and mechanism of this transformation remains obscure, and we cannot begin to estimate its effects on the tenure of land—we do not even know what the previous position was. It is only for Athens that we have any early evidence at all; and there, our knowledge does not begin until the agrarian crisis which confronted Solon in 594, and is based on the remains of his own poems and on whatever we may judge to be valuable in later descriptions of his reforms. The nature of that crisis must be discussed later in this chapter in a different context. Here we need note only the statement of Aristotle, that before Solon's time the land was in the hands of the few—a statement which accords so ill with the later condition of Attica that it has been generally disbelieved —and the fact, which is not contested, that at that time much of the land was cultivated by a class of poor men called *hektemoroi*. These were obliged to pay over one-sixth of the produce of their land to members of the rich upper class, and were in the process of lapsing into outright slavery.

*

   Before proceeding further, we should consider another question which has much distracted the discussion of Greek land tenure, the question whether, in the early stages, land was the collective property of a family unit, or of a kinship group of the kind discussed in the last chapter, the current occupier having no right to dispose of it; or whether, on the contrary, it was the individual property of an owner who could sell it or give it away or mortage it to another. Systems are well known in which land is the inalienable property of a kinship group; and though this was certainly not the situation of classical Greece there is no reason why the early Greeks should not have gone through a stage of this kind. The possibility has been much discussed, especially in relation to Solon's agrarian problem. Indeed, a recent theory holds that one main category of land in Attica remained inalienable, right down to the great upheaval of the Peloponnesian War at the end of the fifth century; and this theory has found some believers.
   There is no doubt at all that the Greeks had a well-developed feeling that property ought to remain in the family. This comes up in many forms in the speeches that survive from property cases in the Athenian courts in the fourth century. The natural desire to leave land to one's own posterity was reinforced by the religious need to maintain a family shrine and to cherish the tombs of ancestors. For an instance of Athenian feeling on this point, candidates for the archonship, the principal magistracy, were asked at their preliminary examination about their family shrines and tombs and whether they took care of their parents; and they might have to produce witnesses to these and other matters. The law of inheritance at Athens again shows a strong

bias in favour of keeping land in the family. Nevertheless, a strong sentiment is not the same thing as a legal prohibition. In many civil-isations, a wide distinction is made between what an owner may do in his lifetime and what happens to his property after his death; and in fourth-century Athens, for all its restrictions about inheritance, there was no prohibition against selling land in one's lifetime.

Where we hear of positive prohibition, it usually affects only the sale of particular categories of land. The distinction at Sparta has been discussed above, and probably represents the need to safeguard an artificial allotment of part of the land. The same need might arise with a colony, as we see clearly in a late case where the rules were inscribed on stone and survive, the settlement of Black Corcyra (Korčula off the coast of Yugoslavia) about 385, where, among other things, it is laid down that a proportion of the colonist's 'original lot' may not be sold. When Aristotle says that in early times there were laws in many cities forbidding sale of 'the first lots', he was very possibly thinking of colonies like his own birthplace, Stagira, in the north. This was founded as early as the middle of the seventh century, but that would be late enough to allow for laws in writing, capable of surviving till Aristotle's own time.

Where the law thus forbids the sale of one category of land, the implication is clear that other categories might be sold. Where there is a total prohibition, the implication still remains that land might have been sold but for the prohibition, as with the Locrian law, praised by Aristotle, by which a man had to prove his necessity before he could sell land. We should need traces of quite another kind to identify a system in which individual sale was impossible because the land did not belong to any individual, in which sale was something which could not even be contemplated; and it may fairly be said that there are no such traces from the articulate period of Greek history. On the contrary, Hesiod around 700 adjures the farmer to respect the gods, 'so that you may buy another's lot, not another buy yours'. This makes it clear that the sale of land, however unwelcome the necessity might be, was a possibility to be reckoned with in Boeotia in his time. The notion that land was collective property, not alienable by the current holder, is not plausible for Solon's time, around 600, let alone for the late fifth century.

*

Greece as a whole was underpopulated when the Dorians arrived in the peninsula and the Ionian migration occupied the coast of Asia Minor, but in the dark centuries which followed there was ample time for growth. The possibilities of internal colonisation, a process which we may understand better as the archaeological coverage of this period improves, were limited by the small proportion of the land that is cultivable at all. We need have no hesitation in believing that land hunger was the main stimulus to the colonising movement which began in the latter part of the eighth century, under very different conditions from those of the older migrations. The first wave of western colonisation was clearly directed at the grain-growing areas of Sicily and South Italy. Colonies at Leontini and Catana, founded by Chalcis in Euboea, occupied the extremely fertile plain under Mount Etna; and Achaeans, from the narrow strip of cultivable land along the Peloponnesian coast of the Gulf of Corinth, were mainly responsible for settling the rich lands of south Italy.

For an instance, Herodotus tells us in two versions the story of the foundation of Cyrene on the north African coast about 630. The colonists came from the Dorian island of Thera, the southernmost of the Cyclades, the strange and striking remnant of the rim of a flooded volcano, good soil for vines but not extensive. The story begins with the Delphic oracle's order to colonise Libya (the term covers all Africa west of the Egyptian border). The Theraeans neglected this order to their cost, and in one version their punishment is specified as seven rainless years. After this, they sent the colonists, 'choosing brother from brother by lot'—Herodotus does not seem to contemplate families with only one son—the whole body perhaps 200 in number. It is common to both versions that two fifty-oared ships carried them all. When the colonists were discouraged and tried to return home, they were driven away again by force. A later inscription from Cyrene, partly consistent with Herodotus, gives more detail: if any of those conscripted refused to sail, the penalty was death, and the colonists might return home only if five years' fair trial proved the venture a failure.

Some of these details may well be drawn from a genuine seventh-century decree of Thera, though not from a verbatim copy; others, more than I have given, will have been through nearly 200 years of oral transmission before Herodotus recorded them. The result is naturally mixed, but some outlines appear, more than we get for any other single

early colony. The appearance of Delphi is not unique—not all groups
of Greek cities were equally devoted to the oracle, especially in early
times, but it was often consulted, and some of the responses on record
look to be genuine, even some of the earliest—but its role on this
occasion has, no doubt, been dramatised a bit. The seven years'
drought may perhaps be allowed to stand as a symbol of the difficulty
of feeding the whole population from the city's own land. The taking
of one brother from each family brings up another point, the general
tradition in Greece that the family property should be equally divided
among brothers. This system does not produce the injustices associated
with systems of primogeniture, but it meant that instead of securing a
livelihood for the eldest son and letting the younger members fend
for themselves the Greek family was in danger of going under as a
whole, as its land was further and further divided. So we find Hesiod
already remarking that the way to prosperity for a house was to have
but one son. To take one colonist from each family would, for the
moment, hold up this process. We cannot usually guess at the numbers
of the original colonists, but it is likely enough that the first pioneer
venture was often on the small scale attested for Cyrene. In this case,
it was a decision of the state to send the colony, a point which other
records pass over. Nor do we hear elsewhere of conscription, though
there is another tale of colonists being refused return home; these were
Eretrians, who were driven out of Corcyra by the Corinthians, and
were then repulsed with slings from their home town, after which
they went north to found Methone. Cyrene is like some other colonies,
in that it prospered and grew much greater than its founder, Thera.

Given the basically agrarian character of this early Greek colonisation, the questions most at issue are whether colonies were at all
regularly sent out by state action, and how far their founders may also
have been influenced by thoughts of future trade. On the first point, it is
essential to grasp that these were not colonial possessions in the modern
sense, exploited for a longer or shorter period under the direct control
of the home government. A Greek colony was a new city from the
start, in principle as independent as any other, with its own government and its own foreign policy, and its inhabitants were citizens of
the colony and no longer of the mother state. Religious and sentimental
ties of course subsisted in the vast majority of cases, and in politics
mother city and colony might expect support from one another where
this was relevant and practicable; but the opposite was always possible,

as in the notoriously bad relations between Corinth and Corcyra. There were certain limited exceptions. The Corinthian tyrants planted a series of colonies along the north shores of the Gulf of Patras and up the coast to the north-west, many of them ruled by sons of Cypselus or Periander, and, though the personal tie was broken when the Corinthian tyranny was put down, the political link between these colonies and Corinth remained specially close. A similar link between Athens and Sigeum near Troy, forged in the time of Peisistratus, had less lasting effect. Even these were still separate states, not mere dependencies, and no Greek city operated a 'colonial policy' in the manner of our nineteenth century.

The looseness of the tie is not, of course, decisive against foundation by state action, for the founding state might feel an urgent public necessity to unburden itself of mouths it could no longer feed. State action fits the language of ancient accounts, for though they often ascribe a colony to its individual founder by name they rather more often say that 'the Corinthians' or 'the Milesians' were the founders. There is also the specific case of Thera and Cyrene, already discussed, and a limited number of later cases where the state decree providing for the foundation is preserved. But by the classical period, one may suspect that another consideration makes the consent of the state necessary, the question whether it can afford to lose a substantial number of fighting men.

The distribution of colonies raises another question. Certain colonial areas were almost monopolised by particular founding cities, north-east Sicily by the Chalcidians of Euboea, the Black Sea and its approaches by Miletus, and so forth. It cannot be that these states suffered overcrowding markedly worse than others who sent out no colonies; indeed, they can hardly have supplied so many colonists in so short a time from their own citizens alone. This is particularly clear in the case of Achaea, and it seems inevitable, though we have no detailed account of the procedure, that particular colonising cities acted as agents to organise the emigration of a wider area. For instance, the Achaean cities might have acted for the landlocked Arcadians to the south of them, always populous and land-hungry. The experience of Chalcis or Miletus, both of them great trading centres, would specially fit them for this role. The question remains, what were the advantages, apart from simple civic pride, in having a large number of colonies labelled as Chalcidian or Milesian, and whether there was any political or commercial gain, immediate or prospective, in organising colonies.

To anticipate what must be further discussed in the next chapter, it is conspicuous that in the classical period no Greek state took action to acquire or safeguard export markets for goods produced in the city. This is a modern conception, foreign to the ideas of ancient Greece. Their cities were often concerned about essential imports, especially food. By the classical period, the colonies were very important for the provisioning of Greece; and they did, in fact, provide a market for Greek exports. But there is nothing in the tradition to suggest that colonies were founded with these ends consciously in view, nor do we know much about their early performance, or about the time it took for a colony to take firm root, or how soon the export of grain began. On mere balance of probabilities, one would think that good agricultural land was the first consideration, attracting settlers who could no longer make a living at home, or were positively expelled by their native city like the colonists of Cyrene; and, if the venture succeeded, it could take off further emigrants from the overcrowded motherland. The export of the colonial surplus will have been a secondary development.

That is not to say that traders were of no importance at all. There is no doubt that Greek trade abroad began before the start of the colonial movement. The Greek site at the mouth of the Orontes in Syria was there as a trading station at least from the beginning of the eighth century. Somewhat later, about the middle of the eighth century or a little before, the two great cities of Euboea, Chalcis and Eretria, jointly founded a settlement which is by some twenty years or more the earliest colony in the west, originally on the island of Ischia in the Bay of Naples, then at Cumae on the mainland opposite. It is striking that this first colony should have been planted at such a distance, and that its founders should have passed by so much fertile land which was later to carry colonies of the ordinary agricultural type. When we remember Greece's perennial shortage of metal, we may suspect that the first Euboeans to come here were looking for the iron of Etruria rather than for land to farm. That suggests that, when the next group of colonies was founded in Sicily, the sites were already familiar to traders, and the farmers did not have to feel their own way west. Sometimes, again, the siting of a later colony suggests interests not purely agricultural. So, when Chalcis settled both Rhegium (Reggio Calabria) and, on the

Sicilian side of the strait, Zancle (later Messana, now Messina) on relatively barren land, it may fairly be supposed that the state of Chalcis was interested in protecting the route north to Cumae; no doubt, because Etruria was a source of necessary metal, and not to assist the export trade of Chalcidian citizens.

By the middle of the sixth century, the west gave no further room for the foundation of colonies. Some two-thirds of the coast of Sicily was occupied, and there was continuous occupation along the south coast of Italy. Sybaris reached across to found ports on the north coast of the toe of Italy, and there were a few more colonies north of this, up to Cumae. Further afield, Phocaean Marseilles was firmly enough rooted to survive, with a group of smaller cities along the Riviera coast, and a further group down the coast of Spain, less often mentioned in the literary tradition; but Etruscan and Carthaginian opposition prevented wider expansion in these directions. On the east coast of Italy, archaeological excavation has now revealed the unrecorded prosperity of Greek Spina at the mouth of the Po, but not much else took root here, nor was the other coast of the Adriatic occupied north of Epidamnus.

No similar resistance constricted Greek expansion to the north and north-east. Here, the coast shows a continuous string of Greek colonies, with only a small opening left to the Macedonians between Thessaly and Thrace, but the wild tribes of the interior prevented penetration inland, in spite of the attraction of the mining area round the lower Strymon and opposite Thasos. The Gallipoli peninsula and the shores of the straits were still more thickly settled, though the north side was in constant danger from the Thracians. On the shores of the Black Sea, there were prosperous cities on the north coast of Asia Minor which had reduced the natives to helot-like servitude. Others stretched up the coasts of present-day Bulgaria and Rumania, leading on to the south Russian colonies which achieved a satisfactory symbiosis with the Scythian princedoms in this area, especially with those of the Crimea which were so important for Athens' food supply in the classical period.

Along the south side of Asia Minor the fully Greek cities thin out: Cyprus, more than half Greek from Mycenaean times, was a world apart, mostly subject to mainland powers. On the Syrian coast the Greeks had one or two footholds, but in general there was no place for them in this crowded area of old civilisation. Egypt, still more xenophobic, tolerated only the single trading post of Naucratis, managed by a whole consortium of Greek cities. To the west, there was more room in Libya, where the rainfall in ancient times allowed a wider belt of cultivation. Cyrene planted several further colonies in her own fertile neighbourhood, but when the Spartan, Dorieus, at the end of the sixth century tried to settle further west he was driven out by Carthage.

Before the middle of the sixth century, the Greeks had reached the limit of available territory in a congenial climate. This does not mean that all emigration ended, for we can assume that most colonies were small to begin with, and that their natural increase was supplemented by fresh migration. But we hear of this only when it is interesting for some extraneous reason, as when a body of Samians took refuge in the west in 493 after the collapse of the Ionian Revolt, or on occasions when the fresh colonists quarrelled with the older settlers. There was still just room in Thrace for Athens to found one or two new cities in the fifth century, and there were some fresh attempts to settle the Adriatic, mostly inconclusive. By the fifth century the extra mouths had to be fed by other means, that is, by imports from abroad which had to be paid for.

*

Even at the height of the colonial movement it is not likely that it carried off anything approaching the whole surplus of the population at home. There are always those who prefer to endure the hardship of their present situation, rather than face the risks of a new start elsewhere. The pressure on the insufficient land might be expected to continue, and it is no surprise to find traces of agrarian discontent in the seventh century. The crisis at Athens, which came to a head in 594 and caused the appointment of Solon as mediator between rich and poor, comes to life for us because the reformer was also a poet whose verses were still available for study in antiquity—propaganda put out before his reforms, and self-justification after them, with other pieces of general reflection and some that were frivolously cheerful. Some of the surviving excerpts are long enough to give us an idea of the issues and of Solon's attitude to them, but they are not informative in detail. The poet and his audience alike were familiar with the circumstances and had no need of the kind of explanation which we require. His law-code also survived for study and would be the natural source to go to for points of detail, but ancient writers do not quote from it extensively. These laws, again, took much for granted which cannot now be reconstructed. Quite apart from that, their archaic language was already an obstacle to understanding in the late fifth century, and this must have hampered ancient inquiry.

Tradition was almost unanimous that the centre of the problem was 'debt', that Solon cancelled all private and public debts, and that this was the *seisachtheia*, the 'shaking off of burdens', which was his main immediate remedy. It is certain that he abolished debt-bondage at Athens for the future, a humane measure which was not followed in all other states. The word translated as 'debt' (*chreos*), is, however, a wide term, which embraces other kinds of obligation than those that arise from borrowing; it would include rent or taxes or other kinds of dues. The main reference here must be to the class called *hektemoroi*, into which Aristotle somewhat sweepingly puts the whole mass of the poor, men who paid to someone else a sixth part (*hektemorion*) of the produce of the land they worked.[1] If they failed to pay, they and their wives and children could be haled into slavery. The word, *hektemoroi*, was obsolete in Aristotle's day, but was no doubt to be found in Solon's poems or laws in a context which made its meaning more or less plain. Another archaic and later obsolete word is quoted from the laws as meaning the 'portion' which the farmer handed over to another. This was evidently some system of share-cropping or *métayage*, an institution familiar from other civilisations, but in such varied forms that no argument from analogy will determine the precise form it took in seventh-century Attica.

Aristotle quotes at some length from a poem in which Solon claimed that he had fulfilled all the purposes for which he had originally called the people together. His best witness, invoked in solemn language, is the earth itself, formerly enslaved but now free, from which he had plucked up the many *horoi* (below) fixed in it: then, he had brought back to Athens many who had been sold abroad, some illegally, some legally, and many who had fled from dire necessity, wanderers who had lost their Attic speech; and he had set free those who were in slavery at home and trembled before their masters. After some fifteen lines of this, he takes only two to refer to his code of law as fair to all classes; and then boasts more generally that another in his place would

1. The alternative interpretation, that they kept the sixth part and handed over five-sixths, is less well supported by the sources and improbable in itself.

not have been able to control the people, that if he had joined one side or the other the city would have lost many men.

The city knew what he meant, and he did not need to explain in what sense the land had been enslaved or what sort of *horoi* he removed. The commonest meaning of this word is 'boundary-stone', which gives no good sense here; but it often also means a stone or other notice put up to give publicity to some form of encumbrance on house or land. The main point made by the poem, the liberation of the land, must have something to do with the class mainly in trouble, the *hektemoroi*, and the easiest answer is that the *horoi* of the poem acted as markers for the obligation to pay one-sixth and that their removal meant the cancelling of the obligation. But, if that were right, it still would not tell us how the obligation had arisen or what new system Solon devised in place of the old one.

For Aristotle in the fourth century B.C., and Plutarch in the second A.D., it was natural to think in terms of mortgage or the like, and of borrowing in money, as was normal in their day. In Solon's time, the coining of money had just begun in Greece, but not in Athens, and not in the small denominations that would be needed for the transactions of the poor. If there was borrowing, it was in agricultural terms, in seed or the use of oxen or equipment, such as we find in Hesiod earlier (but there there is no mention of penalties, nothing like the exploitation of the poor that troubled Solon's Athens); and we must understand the obligation to pay one-sixth or fall into slavery as the standard terms of credit in a harsh age. But there is no word of debt in the poems of Solon which are cited to illustrate his reform, and the terms in which Aristotle defines the *hektemoroi* do not belong to the vocabulary of borrowing. The alternative remains open, that these were simply the terms on which the rich got their land cultivated, a kind of rent from a kind of tenant. That would fit rather better with Aristotle's statement that the land was in the hands of the few and that the *hektemoroi* were working the fields of the rich. This has been taken as a mistake, mainly on the ground that large estates were not the rule in later times, and that there is no reason to attribute to Solon or to any later reformer an extensive redistribution of land. But in this case Aristotle is clearly not just projecting the assumptions of his own day into the remote past, and it may be that his statement deserves more consideration.

Whatever the precise nature of the system, it was found unendurable at the opening of the sixth century. Payment of one-sixth does not seem mountainously oppressive, and it is not difficult to conceive that dues on this scale might have been paid for generations without hardship. But the lighter exaction of a tithe has sometimes been bitterly resented, and any standard exaction may in adverse conditions become oppressive—or be made so by powerful men in charge of the operation. Solon said squarely that the troubles of Athens in his time were due to the rapacity of the rich, and the poem paraphrased above shows that they sometimes went beyond their legal rights. The ground for rapacity is probably just that by this time there was so much more that a rich man could do with his wealth. Hesiod in his time had thought of wealth in purely agricultural terms, having more grain in your barn than another: Solon speaks of the accumulation of silver and gold (it makes no difference that it was not yet coined), and complains that there is no end to the piling up of this kind of wealth. Silver was usable abroad, and a substantial part of Greece's increasing trade with the outer world was in the luxuries that appealed to the rich. There was that much more motive for exacting from the poor whatever could be turned into silver, or for selling the poor themselves as slaves. It has happened in other periods of expansion that at any rate the first effect is to benefit the economically strong and depress the weak.

Uncertainty about the nature of Solon's problem means equal uncertainty about the nature of his solution. If it was a question of free smallholders who had got into trouble through borrowing, the cancellation of the debt restored them to free possession of their land, and the prevalence of small holdings in later Attica means that they somehow kept out of trouble thereafter. If we are dealing with an old-established system for tilling what might be called the lands of the rich, the question is a little more complicated. Again, the later pattern of land tenure in Attica would compel us to suppose that Solon left the former *hektemoroi* in full possession of the land they had been working. In that case, he did make a serious change in the pattern of land ownership, in effect creating a considerable class of free smallholders. There is no good reason for thinking that this did not happen.

However we resolve these far from easy problems, we must not suppose that the very rich and the *hektemoroi* were the only classes concerned with farming in Attica. Aristotle's simple dichotomy is too neat, and the existence of a class of free farmers on Hesiod's scale is guaranteed by the terms of Solon's political reform which graduated the citizens of Athens in four classes according to the annual produce

of their land. Really poor men like the ex-*hektemoroi* will have belonged
to the lowest of these classes, the *thetes* with less than 200 bushels a
year: the class above them, the *zeugitai* with 200–300 bushels, roughly
the class which provided the hoplite army, must have been in active
existence before Solon legislated. But the troubles of the very poor
were his first problem. He makes it clear that their condition, near
slavery in itself and liable to lead to outright slavery, had created the
revolutionary situation with which he was called to deal. The poor of
Athens were on the way to being reduced to something like helots,
but they resisted, and found a humane and able champion who was
able to get his solution accepted.

Elsewhere, reformers did not justify themselves in verse, and it does
not seem that information about the condition of the poor peasant in
the seventh century was extracted from the laws of other great cities.
No doubt there were parallel phenomena, and the pressure on the
land was dangerous elsewhere. When Cypselus of Corinth overthrew
the aristocracy of the Bacchiadae, in the middle of the seventh century,
he killed and exiled and confiscated thoroughly enough; but Herodotus
was not concerned with the question of what he did with confiscated
land, how his revolution affected the really poor, what their condition
had been. There are other indications that agitation against the landowning rich played its part in promoting tyranny; but we still lack
detail, as for instance in Aristotle's passing reference to the Megarian
tyrant, Theagenes, 'taking the flocks of the rich as they pastured beside the river and slaughtering them'. It would be interesting, and
might be instructive, to know the full story of that. No doubt tyranny
benefited, in the main, the immediate supporters of the tyrants, and
they were probably to be found in the layer immediately below the
dispossessed aristocrats. Where the upper class had a grip on the land
comparable to that exercised by the Athenian rich, the tyranny is
likely to be the stage at which it was broken. The final result seems to
be, in general, much the same that we find in Attica, predominantly
free smallholders, though there were no doubt many variations in
detail, with a larger or a smaller proportion of the land in the hands of
the great families. The exceptional conditions in Sparta and Thessaly
have been enough discussed above.

For Attica, and for states with a similar pattern, the further question
arises how the rich got their land cultivated when the upheavals of the
age of tyranny were over. Under the old order in Attica, the *hekte-*

moroi were, one way or another, a large part of the answer. Whether or not their trouble arose from borrowing, there is no doubt that literal debt was one of the factors that caused unrest in Solon's Athens; and, as Aristotle saw it, the debtor was liable to fall into slavery if he defaulted. We have to consider this from the creditor's point of view as well as the poor debtor's—what the creditor hoped to gain by lending seed or anything else in small quantities, how either party saw the future prospect at the time the loan was made. Comparative material from Mesopotamia and elsewhere suggests that the creditor's object might be, not repayment of the loan with interest, but the debtor's labour. In these other civilisations, a borrower often, in effect, sold his or his family's labour for an indefinite time rather than borrowed to tide over a temporary difficulty. It may be that this was the way 'debt' worked in seventh-century Attica. If so, the borrower became in effect a slave when he took the 'loan'. But we encounter debt-bondage at Athens only at the moment of its abolition, and elsewhere we have only a few random glimpses of what it meant; so we can only speculate about its role for early Greek agriculture, noting the possibility that it acted as a source of labour for the rich. The abolition of such bondage in Athens and the rescue of the *hektemoroi* may have created something of a labour problem for the men who owned land beyond the needs of their own subsistence.

Beyond reasonable doubt, the main solution was a large increase in the number of chattel slaves, obtained primarily by purchase from abroad. Hesiod already worked his one-family farm with the help of slaves, and in classical Athens it is clear that all but the poorest normally owned slaves, employed not only in household tasks but in tilling the land. The rich had more slaves, no doubt more specialised for particular tasks, and slave overseers to manage such land as they did not let to tenants. Free labour existed, but is not so conspicuous. The commonest form was for men to hire themselves out as casual workmen at the harvest or other busy times, no doubt working side by side with the owner's slaves, just as free men worked side by side with slaves on the great buildings at Athens. A more permanent relationship is illustrated in the opening of Plato's *Euthyphron*, the case of a man whom Euthyphron describes as 'a dependant of mine', certainly not a slave, but having some unexplained personal relationship to Euthyphron and working on the family farm. From the way this is described, it is clear that a permanent relationship of this kind was nothing unusual, but it

seems not to have been common either. It certainly did not develop
into a large-scale regular system like clientship at Rome. Much land
will have been let out to tenants. The nature of our evidence is such
that we hear of leases more often in connection with land belonging to
a god or a hero, which could not be sold, but was leased by the state or
by a cult association; and the terms of the lease were sometimes recorded
on stone. Rich private owners also let parts of their land: but private
leases were naturally not inscribed on stone like leases granted by a
corporation. It should be noted, in this connection, that the Athenian
rich owned for the most part numerous small farms, scattered round
the countryside, rather than larger holdings, concentrated in one place,
a factor which would tend to make tenancy the easiest way to get a
good return from the land.

*

The centuries which followed Solon's reform saw no major change
in the pattern of Attic landholding, though there were, of course,
vicissitudes. Athens did not at once settle down to the new order;
before Solon was dead, Peisistratus had made his first attempt on the
tyranny. He may perhaps have confiscated some of his opponents'
land, and distributed such land in small holdings, but no ancient account
says that he did this. In general, his policy was rather to conciliate the
great families. Once in power, he encouraged small farmers with
loans, and his activities will have helped to consolidate the pattern of
small holdings.

Pressure on the land did not cease in the sixth century, and its
closing years saw the beginning of a new type of settlement abroad,
the Athenian cleruchy. When Athens defeated Chalcis in Euboea in 506,
the land of the Chalcidian aristocracy was confiscated and divided
among 4,000 *klerouchoi*, literally 'holders of lots'. In the fifth-century
empire, this practice was extended and developed, beginning with the
seizure of land in Naxos after its revolt in 470. The distinguishing
feature of the cleruchy was that the settlers did not, like ordinary
colonists, cease to be citizens of the mother-city, but remained organised in their Athenian tribes and could exercise their rights at Athens
whenever they came home. In a late instance, the cleruchy established
on Lesbos in 427 after the revolt of Mytilene, the settlers did not even
reside on their newly acquired land, but rented it to local inhabitants
and stayed in Athens as absentee landlords. This confiscation of land

was one of the most bitterly resented oppressions of Athens, and was explicitly renounced when her second confederacy was founded in 378.

The Peloponnesian War of the late fifth century had a dangerously dislocating effect. For five out of the first seven years of war (431–425), the countryside, which in accordance with Pericles' policy the Athenians had evacuated, was devastated by Peloponnesian armies which far outnumbered the Athenian force. From 413 to 404, the enemy occupied a permanent post at Deceleia, north-east of Athens. In the ordinary way of Greek warfare, devastation over a much shorter period would have ended the war, but the population of Attica could retire behind the walls of the city and the Peiraeus and the five-mile corridor between them, relying on food imported by sea. The damage to the countryside was, nevertheless, important. Vines and olives are not quickly replaced. In addition, Attica was specially vulnerable to the plunderer because, as Thucydides stresses, a large part of the population lived in the country rather than in the city. In states with narrower territories, the farmer lived in the town and made his way back there in the evening. Attica was too big for that, and had many larger or smaller inhabited centres—Eleusis, Marathon, Brauron and others— not all of which could provide adequate protection against an army. When the countrymen were evacuated into Athens, they left behind possessions which an enemy could destroy or remove. Greek plunderers could be very thorough about that, even to stripping roof-tiles and removing woodwork.

Many farms will have been derelict when the twenty-seven years of war at last ended. It has further been guessed, though there is hardly any explicit evidence, that many of those who crowded into the city during the war stayed there afterwards and made no effort to recover their country livelihood; and it has been supposed that the post-war period saw a considerable concentration of property in the hands of those who could afford to buy up abandoned farms. (The central character of Xenophon's *Oeconomicus*, a treatise on the farming life which is moral rather than technical, tells Socrates how his father had made a lucrative business of buying up neglected farms and selling them at a profit when he had set them in order. He refers to neglect and incompetence rather than to war damage, and the treatise is very probably to be set in a later period; but there will have been large opportunities for this kind of rehabilitation in the years after 404.) In the process of Athens' economic recovery, which in general was remarkably rapid, the rich and resourceful may have made some quick profits, but it cannot be demonstrated that there was a significant change in the pattern of landholding. The picture presented by fourth-century lawsuits is still of a country divided into small parcels of land, changing hands at a fairly brisk rate.

Among the hardships of the evacuation of the countryside at the outbreak of war, Thucydides reckons the abandonment of ancestral shrines. The need to care for family tombs and shrines formed an element of stability in all this movement. A distinction is sometimes made between ancestral property and property acquired by purchase, and there was certainly a strong sentiment in favour of keeping family property together. But it is very doubtful if the law made any distinction between these two categories of land in respect of the owner's right to dispose of them. In court, this was rather an emotive plea, the orator inviting the jury's sympathy if no one is left to perform the proper rites for the deceased owner and his forbears.

*

Our information about Athenian land in the fourth century comes almost entirely from the speeches which were composed by professional writers for litigants in property cases and were then published as models of oratory; and from miscellaneous records on stone, some private and some public. The topics about which we hear are mainly the Athenian law of inheritance, and the use of land and houses as security.

An Athenian had hardly any freedom as regards the disposal of his property by will. If he had legitimate sons, the main property went to them without question. If he had none, the usual remedy was adoption, and that meant, not the adoption of an infant in the style which is familiar to us, but the adoption of an adult who could take immediate charge of the property and continue the adopter's line. The man adopted was almost invariably a close relative, who thereby left his own family group, and was enrolled in his adoptive father's deme and phratry; he would usually marry his daughter, if there was one. If the adoption was completed in the adopter's lifetime and accepted by deme and phratry, the adoptive son entered on the property automatically at the adopter's death, in all respects like a natural son. It was also possible to adopt a son by will—and this was the only sense in which an Athenian had much testamentary freedom—but in that case the adoption had to be confirmed by the chief magistrate, the *archon*, to whose province all these family matters fell. Athenian law did, however, permit the adopted son to return eventually to his original family, provided that he left behind him in his adoptive family a legitimate son to carry on that line. If there had been no adoption, the nearest male relative inherited, from a legally defined group which extended as far as the children of first cousins, first on the paternal side and then on the maternal. The clear concern of the whole system was to ensure, as far as possible, that the family continued in direct male line and that the property went with it. The state took an interest in this through the chief archon, in whose court any of these arrangements except the straightforward inheritance of a legitimate son had to be confirmed, and who was specially charged with the care of widows and orphans and 'destitute houses', i.e. houses with no male heir. The system also tended against the accumulation of property in a single hand by inheritance, and argument in court shows that there was a strong prejudice in this direction.

It was only the male heir that counted. A woman could not inherit or hold property, or enter into any transaction that involved more than the value of a bushel of grain; any larger business which concerned her had to be dealt with by her father or guardian or husband. A daughter with no brothers 'went with the property'—that is the literal meaning of the Athenian term *epikleros* which we usually translate 'heiress'—and she married the heir unless he renounced his inheritance. If there was more than one daughter, they were assigned to the next relatives in succession. To comply with these rules, an heiress might have to leave her previous husband in order to marry, say, her uncle, and the orator Isaeus assures us that such things did occur, though we know of no instance in detail.

Other systems less imposed tight restrictions on women. At Gortyn in Crete, in the middle of the fifth century, as we see from the miscellaneous provisions which are somewhat misleadingly called the 'Gortyn Code',[1] a woman could hold property in her own right; and, though a house in town and its contents were reserved to the sons, the rest of the property was divided so as to give a daughter her share, half the amount that went to a son. The rules about remoter heirs, though different from the Athenian, proceeded on roughly the same principles, and the heiress had in some circumstances rather more freedom of

1. For the character of the Gortyn Code see pp. 177–8

choice. It has been suggested that the Cretans were in the process of evolving a more liberal system for the treament of women generally, but the new rules in the Gortyn legislation seem rather to restrict an existing freedom. If we had more examples, we should almost certainly find that the Gortyn rules fit into a more widespread pattern.

For instance, the Spartan rules appear to have been still more generous. Herodotus says that the kings decided who should marry an heiress whose father had died without disposing of her hand, and it may be that in his time the king followed a fixed rule; but, when Aristotle wrote, the father or his next male heir might marry her to whom he pleased. Women could certainly own property, indeed Aristotle complains that two-fifths of the land belonged to women. He blames the laxness of the rules, and the habit of giving large dowries, so that property became concentrated in few hands, and the gap widened between rich and poor. Bad already in the middle of the fourth century, this concentration of landed property continued till it provoked the revolutions of the late third century. No such complaint is made about Athens, which in this sphere, as in some others, was more conservative than her traditionalist rival.

*

Land as security for debt appears in all kinds of context. The main difference here between ancient and modern practice is that, in the Greek world, debt was almost always the result of mere personal emergency. The fabric of credit which holds our society together did not yet exist. Land or houses were bought for cash, and there are only the faintest hints of development towards the modern practice of buying by means of mortgage. The borrower did not intend to use the money for improvements or to set himself up in business, and lending —though, of course, the creditor entered on the transaction in the hope of gaining the interest or the security—was not, in the modern sense, an investment. (The only serious exception to this is the lending of money—never on a large scale—to merchants or shipowners for a particular voyage. The risks were great, but the possible profits high; so the interest too was high.) For citizens, the natural investment was land or a house or, in some degree, slaves. Other forms of economic activity were mostly left to the metics, who had not the right to buy land.

A Greek borrower might hand over to his creditor some object as a pledge to be redeemed when he repaid. Indeed, for the poor borrower, this might be his only resource; and a richer man might find it convenient to hand over a gold cup or jewellery for this purpose. Substantial loans were much more likely to be secured on land or houses, the most valuable things that could be offered, and not to be hidden or removed. In these transactions, the debtor normally remained in possession, losing the use of his land or house only if he failed to repay and the creditor took over the property—much as in a modern mortgage, different as the past history of that institution may be. Slaves form an intermediate category, sometimes handed over to the creditor and sometimes not. The twenty furniture-makers, whom Demosthenes included in his enumeration of his father's property, were held as pledges for a debt much less than their market value, and Demosthenes' father enjoyed the income from their work. But we also find slaves hypothecated like real property, continuing to work for the debtor during the lifetime of the loan.

No Greek state kept anything like a land register or demanded anything like the modern registration of mortgages, though Theophrastus, Aristotle's colleague and successor who made a great collection of Greek and foreign laws, at least imagines this as a theoretical possibility. Some kept, at least spasmodically, a record of land sales, and many provided for the public advertisement of sales. In all this, Greece had not moved far from the practice of small peasant communities, where the neighbours know the situation, and written record is not necessary. At Athens, we are told that notice had to be posted sixty days before the completion of a sale; and it is at Athens, a developed community far too large for general knowledge of everybody's business, that we find another form of advertisement, the stones called *horoi* which record encumbrance on land or houses. These are useful evidence, in that the surviving stones can, up to a point, be regarded as a random sample, whereas the cases which came to court and were argued by the orators naturally tend to be the exceptional and complicated instances.

The majority of *horoi* refer in condensed and simplified language to the procedure of sale *epi lysei*, that is, with the option of annulling the sale by repayment of the price. The transaction is really a kind of loan, the 'sale' becoming effective only in the case of default, and in the vast majority of known cases the nominal seller remained in possession of the property. The purpose was, no doubt, to advertise the creditor's claim on property which he did not himself occupy; the stones usually state the creditor's name, not the debtor's. They are very rough, the inscription sometimes erased to make room for another, or the amount of the debt altered to keep pace with repayment, and it could not have been difficult for a fraudulent debtor to alter the record himself or uproot it. But for some reason fourth-century Athens got the habit of this kind of record, and luckily for us on stone rather than on perishable wood. Without the *horoi*, we should not have known that the Athenians so much preferred to clothe their loans in this form. In the absence of such record from elsewhere, we have no means of knowing whether other Greek societies did the same.

Horoi concerned with orphans and dowries form a special category and introduce a different point, the fact that the conception of collateral security never took firm root in the Greek world, though Athens tentatively groped in that direction. The guardian of an orphan might be directed by the father's will, or might himself choose, to lease his ward's property to another party, who was then legally compelled to put up security for the eventual return of the property and for payment of the orphan's income meanwhile. Here, the archon was once more concerned, and sent valuers to ascertain that the security would cover the obligation. A wife's dowry had also to be formally valued, and—in the landowning class, where substantial dowries were given—the husband put up security for the return of the dowry in case the marriage were dissolved or the wife died without having borne an heir.

The distinguishing feature of these cases is the valuation, and the fact that the security was used to cover only the precise amount of the original obligation. We see from Demosthenes' dealings with his guardians—the tangled case set out in his earliest speeches, when he had just attained his majority—that if the security was worth more than the dowry the excess value returned to the 'debtor'. Two *horoi* show the excess value similarly free, and something of the same sort occurred when property was confiscated by the state: the court might allow a creditor's claim to the exact amount of his debt, the state taking the remainder of what could be got for the property. Otherwise, unless there were express agreement to the contrary, the creditor expected to take over the whole security in case of default. This has been called 'substitutive' security, the whole property taken in simple substitution for what was originally borrowed, as opposed to collateral security, which serves only to guarantee that the creditor will get his

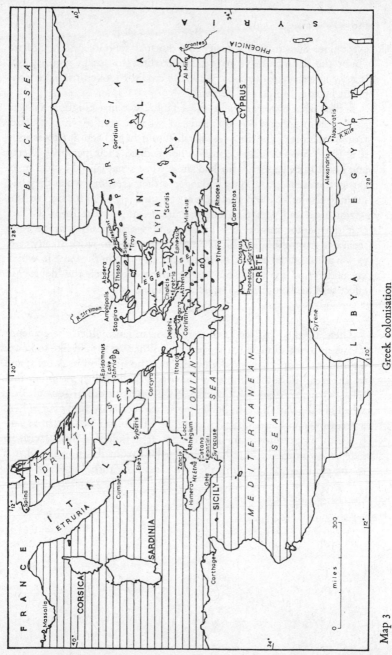

Map 3   Greek colonisation

exact due. Substitutive security was normal for Greece, though no doubt the debtor strove to get the creditor to accept security not grossly in excess of the debt, while the creditor looked to make what profit he could in case of default.

In the earlier history of debt, the defaulter was in a still more vulnerable position; there was no limit to what a creditor might seize. Commentators living in a less harsh world have been apt to assume that those pre-Solonian debtors who pledged their personal liberty and lost it must be men who had already lost what land they had in an earlier transaction, and only endangered their freedom when they had nothing else left to offer. But there are adequate parallels for the creditor seizing land and person in one operation—quite apart from the fact that the debtor might well be in a still worse position if he were separated from the land which he was accustomed to work. In any case, as was adumbrated earlier, these may not be loans in the sense in which we understand the term, but arrangements by which the 'debtor' in effect sells his labour for an indefinite future.

*

These are the main kinds of transaction in land which the evidence allows us to see. It need hardly be stressed that we should like to know a great deal more than we do, even about the situation in Athens; and in this area, more than most, we have to guard against assuming that what is true of Athens will be true of the Greek world in general. But, whatever the variations in detail, we should certainly find everywhere a predominantly agricultural society, in which land was far and away the most important form of property. It is indeed Athens, with its extensive commerce, that departed furthest from this norm, and it is to the commercial questions that we must now turn.

CHAPTER 7

Traders, craftsmen and slaves

COMMERCE AND INDUSTRY in ancient Greece were exceedingly important, but the individual operations were on a very small scale. The difficulty of keeping this continuously in mind is responsible for most of the misconceptions that arise when we try to focus on the economics of Greek society. In the total absence of statistics, ignorant as we are of the bulk of import and export of either necessities or luxuries, we are compelled to build largely on a relatively small number of instances, without being sure whether they are typical or abnormal. This means that we have to examine with special care the presuppositions we bring to these instances. Greek studies have only slowly and unevenly been liberated from their philological and literary background, and Greek history from exclusive consideration of war and politics and their moral overtones. The pioneers of the study of Greek economics inevitably thought in nineteenth-century terms, treating habits which have grown up since the Industrial Revolution as if they were immutable economic laws. Thus, they imported into the Greek world concepts which are only appropriate to a world of large and highly organised business firms. Nowhere was this more misleading than when attempts were made to estimate the effects of economic activity on political history.

Greek overseas trade was not a matter of regular shipping lines with established international ramifications. We have to think rather of separate individual voyages, in ships of very modest tonnage, made by a relatively insecure merchant, who was most unlikely to have the resources to finance the venture himself, and so depended on loans from men who were prepared to risk their money on the enterprise. The voyage might easily end in total loss, but it could make large profits if it succeeded, so interest rates were high. The lender himself was not necessarily a wealthy man: the speaker in one fourth-century case was an ex-merchant who had retired from the sea with, he claims, a modest competence, which he now used to finance the voyages of others. There were, of course, larger operators, at Athens mainly metics who were debarred from investing their money in land, men who had agents abroad who could take payment or otherwise act on their behalf. There were also some more regular runs, like the trade in grain with South Russia, where it paid a man to be on good terms with the Scythian prince concerned and to have regular representatives in a Crimean port; the rudiments of a business organisation may be found in such areas. But the unit remains small, the individual merchant, owning the cargo but probably not the ship he sailed in, not at all certain of being able to dispose of his goods at his destination, nor of being able to get a good price for his return cargo. Fluctuations in the price of grain could easily prove disastrous. But the sums of money initially laid out on these voyages were not very large either.

Of course, the parties tried in every available way to safeguard themselves, and written agreements were normal in fourth-century Athens, dealing with the varied contingencies that might arise. But, in assessing individual cases, we must remember the nature of the evidence, which consists almost entirely of the speeches composed for the cases which came into court. We must presume that, for every such case, there were many transactions which were carried through without resort to litigation. Again, in any particular case we hear only one side, and have little idea what answer could be made to the charges of unbelievable duplicity which the speaker levels against his opponent. If all traders had behaved in the manner alleged in these speeches, no one would have had enough credit to get any commerce started at all. Provided we keep this background in mind, the evidence is usable.

Industry, again, was on a scale which invalidates comparison with the large factories to which we are accustomed. Apart from the mines, a special case to be discussed later (pp. 136–7), the largest industrial unit known to us consisted of 120 slaves manufacturing shields at Athens. This was the property of a metic from Syracuse, the Cephalus who makes a brief appearance at the beginning of Plato's *Republic* and whose son Lysias wrote speeches, some of which survive, for Athenian litigants. Citizens engaged in industry in a similar way: reference has already been made to Demosthenes' father, whose estate was alleged by his son to have included two sets of specialist slave workers, thirty cutlers manufacturing knives and twenty joiners who made beds.

These were the rich operators, the exceptional establishments. The normal unit would be the individual craftsman with his slave or two, manufacturing on his own premises what he then sold in his shop. Even the larger groups did not work in factories: the word which we sometimes translate as 'factory' or 'workshop' very often refers to the group of slave workers, not to the place where they did their work. In Demosthenes' case and in others, there does not seem to be a separate building for them to work in.

Law-court speeches, written for the relatively rich, may give the wrong scale when they occasionally refer to these matters. Athenian comedy is more concerned with the common man, but the perspective of comedy is by its nature warped, and its evidence must be handled with care. Fortunately, there is more sober material in the minute accounts which Athens exacted from the magistrates who oversaw the construction of buildings and public works, and then inscribed on stone in all their detail. Here, if anywhere, one might expect to meet the large contractor employing a regular labour force, free or more likely slave. On the contrary, the work is all divided up in small parcels, let out to individual masons and carpenters, metics or citizens with their few slaves, all working side by side. If that is the pattern for great public works, it must be all the more so in the private sphere. The mason who took on a small section of a temple on the Acropolis would have done work on a similar scale for private customers at other times; and the same must be presumed for other kinds of craftsmen.

Thus, even at the top of the scale, none of this amounts to more than what is called 'cottage industry', which is indeed the form in which most industry was organised till the eighteenth century of our era. Within this range, Greek industry was on a markedly small scale and was run on slender margins. To speak of 'industry' in these circumstances is legitimate enough, provided we remember the scale, but 'mass production' is merely misleading, though the term has been used in the case of objects produced in large numbers, like those little Corinthian pots for oil or scent, so common in the archaic period, whose carelessly daubed decoration is little more than a kind of trade-mark. All these were produced individually by hand, and the economics of machine production are not relevant.

★

The first question that arises, as insistently now as it did for Minoan Crete or Mycenaean Greece, is the question what Greek traders had to offer to the outside world. The poverty of Greece, in raw materials and in cultivable land, set up steep obstacles. The olive was a solid resource, the special pride of Athens, where the prizes at the quadrennial games of the Great Panathenaea consisted of oil in jars of traditional shape and decoration (pl. 12). It was also the staple crop of many other areas; once oil export was established, it would have paid in many areas to turn the land over to olives. There was a ready market, notably in the Crimea, where the olive was not cultivated in antiquity, and in Egypt. Greek wine was also welcome in various places, including Egypt, as early as the beginning of the sixth century, when we hear of the brother of the poetess Sappho carrying wine there. (Unless the quality of unresinated Greek wine has altered radically since antiquity, this argues that the taste of the ancient Mediterranean world was different from ours.) These exports can be traced to some extent by their earthenware containers, especially in Hellenistic times, when the jars were stamped to show their origin, and these stamps have been collected and studied. In earlier times we can often recognise the containers made in particular centres, but they are naturally not the first interest of excavators and have been subjected to less intensive study than the fine pottery. The small Corinthian flasks for oil or perfume mentioned above, except for the more careful examples, must have been exported, not for their own sake but for their contents.

After that it is mostly guesswork. It is likely enough that textiles were of economic importance, as they were in Mycenaean times, but the evidence is less than we could wish. It is clear that the outside world was attracted by other manifestations of Greek craftsmanship, but for artefacts of perishable material we have not the check which archaeology can provide in the case of pottery and, to a less extent, of metalwork. Greek literature refers mainly to specialities which one Greek city imported from another, furniture and woollens from Miletus and garments of a sort of silk from the islands of Cos and Amorgos. These were the luxuries of the rich, and we hear of them, partly in the extravagances of Attic comedy, partly in that censorious and depressing later literature which denounced all deviations from bare simplicity as dangerous softness. We do not hear so much about the more humdrum products, though they were surely important as exports to the world outside. Apart from pottery and metalwork, we cannot document the objects which left the country. Metal had, in general, to be imported from outside before it could be made into anything attractive as an export. The one valuable metal that is found in Greece, silver, whose export was specially important for Athens, is a special case which must be discussed later.

Pottery, with its unique capacity for survival across so many centuries, is an exception to the complaints of the last paragraph. But it raises a related question, how much we can fairly deduce from the presence of this indestructible product on sites excavated outside Greece. We must distinguish here between fine pottery, exported for its own sake, and the coarser stuff, which was simply the container for the substantive export, the equivalent of our cans and bottles. The fine pottery, which has naturally been the object of more study, was certainly valued for its own sake as the product of a superior art. Signed Attic cups found in Etruscan tombs were not exported as containers. The presence of such cups is not, by itself, proof of an extensive trade in anything else, though it shows at least that Greek traders had access to the market in question; and the care which Attic potters took to produce shapes suitable for the Etruscan market shows that they had a direct interest in the trade. But the export of this fine pottery will not have fed many mouths. It has been calculated that, at the height of Athens' production, no more than 150 men will have been employed, and probably less, as potters and painters of these admirable vessels. The best that we can do with this evidence is to surmise that, where the fine cups went, other more perishable products of Greek craftsmanship went, also.

Between the mere containers and the fine products which might be buried in an Etruscan tomb, there is a wide range of more ordinary vessels, possibly brought in the way of trade but not self-evidently so. When we find such pottery on a foreign site, we can at least infer that Greeks had been there at the relevant date. Thus, the pottery found at Al Mina, at the mouth of the Orontes in Syria, is adequate proof that this trading-post was extensively used by Greek traders from the beginning of the eighth century—a fact which is very much worth knowing, even if we cannot from this evidence guess what the traders brought with them besides the pottery, which could have been merely for their own personal use. There has been much discussion of the question whether any of the Greek pottery found on western sites, or imitated by native communities in their neighbourhood, actually antedates the foundation of the earliest Greek colonies in Sicily and South Italy. This is a part of a burnt-out controversy about the extent to which commercial interests may have had a hand in the founding of these colonies. Few historians would now deny that the colonies themselves were planted to provide an agricultural livelihood for the colonists, or that the sites had been known to Greek traders beforehand. It seems likely that some of the pottery concerned is marginally earlier than the foundation of a neighbouring colony; but, though this may indicate the presence of traders before the colony was founded, we are again left quite uncertain about the character of the trade. Elsewhere pottery is often the most reliable index of the date at which a colony was planted. For instance, it is the pottery which fixes the foundation of the trading community at Naucratis in Egypt in the last quarter of the seventh century.

The colonies were naturally a continuing market for Greek products, especially in the early days before they had developed arts of their own. Furniture and fine clothing from the homeland no doubt had all the prestige which similar English products had in the early days of the colonisation of North America. Pottery, once more, tells us something about this. The first colonies in the west were founded at a time when Greek pottery was produced in a number of centres whose products are easily distinguishable, and in the early stages we find fabrics from a number of centres on colonial sites, as was only to be expected in view of the fact that the colonists came from very various places. The predominance of Corinthian pottery on most western sites is very noticeable, though Corinth founded only one colony in the west, the important city of Syracuse. This could perhaps be explained simply in terms of the general popularity of the Corinthian fabric in the Greek world; but, taking all the facts together, it is at least a legitimate speculation that, in the seventh century, much of the carrying trade between Greece and the west was in the hands of Corinthian merchants. The interest of the Euboean cities in the west seems to contract, after the first wave of colonisation.

It is quite another matter when, in the latter part of the sixth century, Attic pottery replaces all other fine fabrics. This was a general phenomenon, not confined to one area, and as much observable at Corinth itself as elsewhere. The virtual monopoly of Athens was achieved, to all appearance, because of the superior quality of the Attic product. Consequently, the presence of this Attic pottery in the west or elsewhere is no proof of the presence of Athenian merchants: whoever the merchants were, they had to bring Attic if they were going to bring fine pottery. If the carrying trade was previously, for the most part, in the hands of Corinthians, it may, for all we know, have remained in their hands after the time when Attic pottery achieved its predominance.

Occasionally, we get other glimpses of Greek contact with areas where they did not settle, notably two impressive finds of Greek sixth-century bronze which stimulate speculation about the artefacts that have not survived. The more recent and spectacular was found in the tomb of a Celtic princess at Vix near Chatillon, an enormous vessel over five feet high, sparely but very finely decorated, of the shape called *krater* in Greek from the deep bowls (not, of course, of these dimensions) in which they mixed their wine and water. It has two alphabets scratched on it, in lettering which is pretty certainly Laconian. Whether or not it was actually made in Laconia—this is still very much under dispute—it will be an example of the special type called by the ancients a 'Laconian *krater*', and gives us some idea of the great bronze *krater* with animals round the outside of its lip, twice mentioned by Herodotus, which the Spartans sent as a gift to king Croesus of Lydia. If it is Laconian, it does not follow that it was a Spartan who sent this as a present to the ruling family in Vix: whoever it was that was concerned to press his interests in this remote area, he could have ordered it from a Laconian workshop as a speciality suitable for a diplomatic gift. We should very much like to know who sent it and why, and by what route it travelled, perhaps up the Rhône (there were probably already Greek colonists near its mouth, and Marseilles was founded by the Phocaeans not later than 600), perhaps by some more easterly route. Either way, it is striking testimony to Greek initiative in penetrating less familiar lands, and we can reasonably guess that this was not the only Greek product that found its way to central France.

The other find was a large number of Greek bronzes, turned up in the course of operations during the 1914–18 war at Trebenishte by Lake Ochrid (in what is now Yugoslavia), almost equally distant from Greek colonies like Epidamnus on the Adriatic coast and from the ports of the Gulf of Salonica to the east. One family of native princes in the Ochrid area claimed descent from the nobility of Corinth. It may fairly be guessed that these fine works travelled up-country from the Corinthian and Corcyrean colonies on the west coast. This is less remote from the familiar centres of Greek habitation, but again an indication of wider trade: the same route could be used for things not worth burial in princely graves.

*

The export of silver from Athens is a special case which requires more comment, and it raises the whole question of Greek coinage and the part it played in Greek economy. To take this first, it has been noted already that the Mycenaean documents mention no common measure of value or medium of exchange, though there is enough silver and gold, both mentioned in the texts and recovered archaeologically. In Homer, we meet oxen as a measure of value. When Priam's ally, the Lycian, Glaucus, exchanged armour with the Greek, Diomede, the poet comments on Glaucus' folly in exchanging arms worth a hundred oxen for arms worth only nine. Again, Odysseus' father, Laertes, had bought the nurse, Eurycleia, for the worth of twenty oxen. A trace of this was apparently still to be found in the laws of the Athenian, Draco, towards the end of the seventh century: fines are expressed in numbers of oxen, though here as in Homer it will be goods to that value that change hands, not the animals themselves. In the eastern world, by that time once more familiar, the precious metals, primarily silver, had long functioned as a standard of value and means of exchange, but the silver was weighed out *ad hoc*, not counted in stamped units. On the other hand, mainland Greece, but not apparently the Greeks of Asia Minor, had by the seventh century acquired the habit of using iron objects of more or less standard size for purposes of exchange. Tripods or bowls were used in some places, but the most widespread system used iron spits, and its terminology carried over into the later coinage of the mainland: the small silver coin called *obol* took its name from the single spit, *drachma* was a 'handful' of six such spits.

Gold and silver were highly valued by the Homeric hero, but except in the somewhat stylised business of exchanging gifts he made no use of his treasure. Hesiod writes as if his world knew no common measure of value at all, and reckons wealth purely in terms of the amount of grain you can store up in your barn. But Solon at the beginning of the sixth century, and Theognis of Megara in the middle of it, complain of greedy men heaping up wealth without end; and Solon explicitly counts silver and gold in this wealth. There is no doubt that they mean the rich man's piling up of precious metal; and the gradual change from a world of barter to a monetary economy means mainly this, that wealth, matter with a steady and recognised exchange value, can now be stored indefinitely or moved from place to place in a compact and imperishable form. The next step, the minting of silver into actual coin, seems to have been taken in the third quarter of the seventh century in Lydia, where a transitional stage can be seen, flattened lumps of metal with a standard weight but no impress. The final stage follows quickly, the impress, which identifies the coin and tells the user who is supposed to have guaranteed its weight and quality.

If the first coins were struck by the kings of Lydia, the Greeks quickly made the new invention their own (and it should be remembered that Lydia itself was by this time deeply penetrated by Greek influence). Aegina, in old Greece, began to coin near the end of the century, Corinth in the first quarter of the sixth, Athens about 570. All these coined silver, but some of the earliest East Greek coins are in electrum, an alloy of gold and silver which some cities continued to use in the classical period. The coin is in principle just a guaranteed weight of metal, and the names for coins, apart from the drachma and obol mentioned above, are the names of weights. *Stater* (literally just a 'weigher') is the basic unit. In East Greece, sixty staters made up a *mina*, sixty minae a *talent*, the sexagesimal system taken direct from Babylonian practice (*mina* itself is an eastern word). Mainland systems reckoned fifty staters to the mina, and divided their stater into two or three drachmae, their drachma into six obols.

The really momentous change was to leave the world of barter and to adopt silver as a regular medium of exchange. Reference has been made already to the effects which this may have had on Athens in the late seventh century, and on other archaic regimes elsewhere. To stamp the metal and turn it into coin creates no new situation, so long as the value of the coin is simply its intrinsic silver value. The Greek coin was normally so treated, especially in the east, where it was bullion to be weighed rather than counted. The problems of coinage begin when the coin becomes a token, guaranteed by the issuing author-ity as valid payment for more than it is intrinsically worth. It is possible that some Greek cities deducted some of the nominal weight of their coins, as a mint charge or for mere profit, leaving coins to circulate within their own area at a slightly inflated value. But no state went far along this road; given the considerable irregularity of coin-weights and our general ignorance about market weights, it is not easy to be sure that they started on the road towards a token coinage at all. In these circumstances, it is something of a problem why the Greek cities began to coin in the first place.

For us, the use of coins is in daily shopping, and our larger transactions are conducted on paper; but this is nothing like the situation of Greece when coinage became general in the sixth century. By the late fifth century, Athenians certainly used coins for everyday business, but by then there were plenty of obols (pl. 13, No. 7) and still lower fractions. The early issues of most states are drachmae at the lowest, and they could only be used at all extensively in the sort of business where we should write a cheque. Clearly, then, coinage was not instituted for the sake of internal retail trade; nor for external trade either, since most coinages circulated only in a fairly circumscribed area. They were not, indeed, restricted to the issuing city. The coins of Aegina, for instance, are found all over the Aegean as far as Crete and Rhodes, but not in significant quantity outside this area. It is clear that early coins were not used systematically to purchase goods from distant markets. The fact that the first coins were struck by Lydian kings has suggested that they were struck to pay Greek mercenaries, a purpose for which small change would not be needed; but this does not explain why the cities of Greece took up coinage one after another, and persisted with it. A recent theory proposes, more generally, that coinage was originally struck for payments to and from the state treasury, and there is great attraction in this idea, which would explain why it is the state that issues the coins and not, as in some other civilisations, the private trader also. If the state was paid in coins of its own minting, it knew, apart from ingenious fraud, exactly what it was receiving. Fines were normally in whole numbers of drachmae, and most other transactions to which the state was a party would have been conducted on the scale of staters and drachmae, not involving the smaller fractions.

There are, however, two exceptions to the rule that coinage does not travel widely outside its own area: Thrace and Athens, both of which produced their own silver. The Thracian and Macedonian mints issued mainly large coins, pieces weighing four or even eight drachmae (pl. 13, No. 8). From about 525, these coins appear in fairly large numbers in hoards buried in Egypt and the Near East (pl. 12). They also spread northwards to some extent; but these issues seem to have been used primarily by merchants operating in the eastern Mediterranean (in countries which treated the coins simply as bullion), and the coinage will have started somewhat earlier than the date of deposit of the earliest hoards. There is no knowing how most of these mines in the north were owned and operated; but we know that the Athenian tyrant, Peisistratus, acquired a stake in the mining area during his second exile from Athens, and silver from the Strymon was one source of his later power. The notion of a coinage for export was almost certainly familiar in Athens in the time of Peisistratus' sons, when Athens begins to follow the Thracian lead.

Most Greek cities depended for silver on what was brought into the city in the way of trade, supplementing this by occasional booty in war. Athens was fortunate to have mines of her own in the Laurium district of south-east Attica. It is not certain how early mining began, but the really rich vein was struck round the beginning of the fifth century. It was this windfall that enabled Themistocles to expand the Athenian navy just before the Persian invasion of 480. In the fourth century, the state leased the mining rights for comparatively short periods to individual exploiters; but there is no comparable detail for the time of Themistocles or earlier, and it is possible that the Pcisistratid tyrants worked some or all of the mines on their own account. However this may be, there was a striking change in the character of Athenian coinage towards the end of the sixth century. Her earlier issues were two-drachma pieces with a variety of emblems: then, probably during the rule of Peisistratus' son Hippias, begins the familiar series of four-drachma coins with the head of Athena, and on the other side an owl with the abbreviated name of Athens (pl. 13, No. 4–5). This type quickly became known everywhere, and continued for centuries with only minor modifications. The first two issues of these coins were without small denominations, and they begin to appear in Near Eastern hoards deposited near the end of the sixth century. This appears to be another coinage for export, and it must have contributed very largely to the rise of Athenian prosperity and power at the start of the fifth century.

The absence or rarity of small denominations in these early coinages shows that most everyday transactions of the internal market were conducted by barter. In places where silver was less plentiful, this will have continued well after the time when the Athenian market relied on coined money. The freer circulation of silver cannot have failed to stimulate trade generally, all the more so because this silver circulated in units of manageable size. Athens' special advantage from her mines cannot be quantitatively measured, but Xenophon in his pamphlet on the *Revenues* had no doubt that striking her own coins was a good way to exploit it. He reckons among the attractions of their port the fact that a trader who brought a cargo there could find a great variety of possible return cargoes, or if he preferred to return empty he could take silver in a form which would be valuable everywhere; whereas the coinage of most cities was not usable (here, of course, Xenophon exaggerates) outside their own borders.

*

Xenophon's small treatise on the *Revenues* was written at the end of his life, about 355, during the financial crisis brought on by Athens' recent war with her allies. This was a time of discouraged self-questioning, when the city was offered much moral advice. Xenophon's projects are, in some ways, very revealing, though his grasp of economic theory was not profound. He believed that the value of silver was constant, though he had noticed that gold fell in value as against silver when it was plentiful. He argues that, since the silver mines showed no sign of exhaustion at that time, they never would; and so he spends most space on a proposal for the city to buy large numbers of slaves to hire out to those engaged in mining, and from this he expected large takings. But he saw correctly the advantages of Athens' geographical position for purposes of trade, the virtues of her climate, the value of her marble as well as her silver; and he realised that the essential point for solving the current crisis was to get trade moving again. When he added that Athens alienated other Greeks by her pursuit of glory and empire, that was politically tendentious; but he puts the point moderately, and it was not mere nonsense. His detailed proposals are concerned with speeding up decisions in disputes arising in the course of trade, and the building of inns and halls for commerce. He wanted the city, not only to consult the convenience of traders in ways like these, but to recognise the benefit they brought to Athens by according them official honours and an occasional dinner at public expense. Most of all, he wanted to increase the number of aliens actually resident in Athens.

This brings us back to the important question of these metics, who have several times been mentioned, non-citizens who had 'changed their homes' (the literal meaning of *metoikoi*) by formally taking up their residence in the city. Of course, any foreign trader was at liberty to bring a cargo into the port of the Peiraeus, on payment of the normal harbour dues, and to carry out whatever he took in exchange. The distinction of the metics is that they were formally registered as permanent inhabitants of Athens or the Peiraeus. They did not by this registration acquire anything like citizen rights. They had no vote in the assembly, nor the citizens' privilege of owning land, unless this was specially granted; and in the courts they could not appear personally but had to be represented by a citizen. They paid an annual tax, not specially onerous; and they were liable to military service, though probably for the most part as reserve troops for home defence. (Xenophon thought they should be allowed to build on waste land, though not to own the land, and should be excused military service.)

The number of those metics whose property was substantial enough to allow them to serve as heavy infantry, providing their own armour, was at least 3,000 at the beginning of the Peloponnesian War, out of some 30,000 active and reserve troops altogether. At another level, in the accounts of piece-work (all, as has been said, very small pieces) for the building of the Erechtheum on the Acropolis at the end of the fifth century, the metics heavily outnumber the citizens, by some three to one. The majority have good Greek names, but some clearly not; fifty years later, Xenophon was concerned that non-Greeks, Lydians and Phrygians and Syrians, should be found among the troops who fought for Athens. Many traders were certainly metics, and some prominent bankers, but we hear only of those who became in some way conspicuous. We have no statistics for the smaller fry, so that it is not easy to guess at the full proportions.

The Peiraeus was, then as now, the largest and busiest port of all Greece, and conditions in classical Athens made this status of registered foreign resident highly attractive. The fact that the metic could not buy land accentuated the gap between citizen and metic occupations. The Athenians prominent in public life were landowners, not business men. Even the men who rose to high position from business backgrounds in the late fifth century, the demagogue, Cleon, and the rest, were themselves men of inherited wealth and leisure, not active in trade or manufacture in their own persons. When we do hear of an Athenian of high position engaging in trade, that is due to special misfortune, as in the case of the very highly-born Andocides, who is found engaged in commerce during his exile from Athens. It is, on the other hand, a metic, Cephalus of Syracuse, who is found owning the largest manufacturing establishment recorded (it is to be noted that Plato treats Cephalus with respect as a social equal).

But it is important not to exaggerate here. By minimising the citizen share in trade and industry, and by extending these conditions to all other Greek cities, it is possible to give the impression that any Greek who wished to engage in trade had to leave his own city and settle elsewhere as a metic, while the conduct of the city's affairs was reserved to the uncommercial citizen. That would be misleading. It should be noted, also, that the passages from ancient authors often cited to show Greek, or rather Athenian, contempt for trade will not bear the weight that is put on them. They show, as was to be expected, some upper-class bias against the commercial life, but not that the trader was always a voteless alien—rather the reverse, that the small trader was a regular component of that democratic assembly which the wealthy and the philosophers so much distrusted. The distinction between landed citizen and metic trader or craftsman is likely to have been less marked at the lower social level. If the proportion between citizen and metic craftsmen found in the Erechtheum accounts (above) is representative—but this was in the last few years of the Peloponnesian War, which may have distorted normal proportions—the citizens formed about a quarter of the labour force at this level. That still leaves enough citizen craftsmen to be of serious weight in the assembly.

There were other commercial centres, like Miletus or Corinth, where the growth of a metic population might similarly be expected; but we have no evidence to show whether this actually took place. In many cities it must be unlikely. Nor is it certain that these conditions had always obtained at Athens, though the metic system was certainly in operation there in the early years of the fifth century. More generally, it has been debated whether the upper classes of early Greek history had the same contempt for trade and manual labour that their classical descendants show, and whether they engaged in commerce at all themselves. Going right back to the beginning, nothing could be more fierce than Odysseus' resentment at the suggestion that he could be a merchant; but in that world the gap between the hero-prince and the rest of the world was very great. Things may have been different in the late eighth or seventh centuries, in the main colonising period.

Some of the evidence alleged is very weak. When it is reported that the Bacchiadae of Corinth, the aristocracy overthrown in the middle of the seventh century, got large revenues from the Corinthian market, that is not testimony of their own concern in trade but only of their capacity to extract money from the growing class of those who did engage in trade. It is a little different when we hear of Sappho's brother, Charaxus, about whose high birth there can be no doubt, himself taking a cargo of wine to sell in Egypt, somewhere around 600. Of course, landowners at all periods must engage in commerce to the extent that they have to dispose of the surplus of the agricultural produce of their estates; but Charaxus' voyage would have been unusual in classical Athens. Similarly with another visitor to Egypt in the early sixth century, the Athenian reformer, Solon, who is said by Aristotle to have travelled 'both to trade and to learn'. These are slight indications, but it is not unreasonable to suppose that, in these early days, the metic system was not yet fully developed, and that the native rich took a more direct interest in commerce. The feeling that such occupations were unworthy of a gentleman will have been stimulated by the growth of chattel slavery after the time of Charaxus and Solon.

*

So far, the fact that much industrial work was done by slaves has been allowed to pass without comment. We must now turn to slavery, never an entirely comfortable subject for the admirer of ancient Greek civilisation. Respectable scholars have allowed themselves, a little helplessly, to feel that Greek slavery must somehow have been a more humane institution than it looks; and if that form of distortion is now less prevalent, confusion is still caused by controversy about the character of negro slavery in America, and by Marxist concentration on slavery as the basis of ancient civilisation. In the broadest terms, slavery was basic to Greek civilisation in the sense that, to abolish it and substitute free labour, if it had occurred to anyone to try this on, would have dislocated the whole society and done away with the leisure of the upper classes of Athens and Sparta. The ordinary Athenian had a very deeply ingrained feeling that it was impossible for a free man to work directly for another as his master. While it is true that free men, as well as slaves, engaged in most forms of trade and industry, the withdrawal of slaves from these tasks would have entailed a most uncomfortable reorganisation of labour and property. But the question whether it could have been otherwise must not too much preoccupy us. The first question is how the institution actually worked.

The distinction between slave and free man must have been of some importance in Mycenaean times, since the documents trouble to record the answer, but it is not possible to say what it meant to be a slave in Mycenaean Pylos till we can say in what sense the non-slave was free. Similar doubts beset attempts to sort out the Homeric position. Homer presents us, in the main, with the traditional picture, not shocking to his mind, of cities sacked and their women enslaved. Once more the world of the princes gets most of his attention—Achilles' feeling for the captive princess Briseis, and hers for him, after he had killed her father and wrecked her city; or the life Andromache may expect when her husband Hector is slain and Troy has fallen. Odysseus' faithless house-slaves, who had slept with the suitors of Penelope, were of a different class and could be hanged with less fuss and comment. Eumaeus, the faithful swineherd, kidnapped in childhood by Phoenician traders, illustrates another means of acquiring slaves, and another stereotype, the willing loyal slave who grows into a family friend; and Eurycleia, bought by barter, had been Odysseus' nurse and became the palace housekeeper, the first of a long line of foster-mothers, nurses, tutors, treasured by the family that owned them, for the most part known to us only by the genuine affection which their tombstones attest.

Again, it would be easier to analyse the condition of the slave if we could tell more clearly what it felt like to be a free man, dependent on Odysseus' palace. That palace was a close-knit and almost self-supporting unit, to which all classes were deeply committed, and for which all in their way worked—even Penelope weaves with her own hands. There were, of course, large distinctions of status and differentiations among the tasks performed—only the masters of the house and their guests were bathed and dressed by others—but the line between servile and free tasks is not very clear. The gulf between the princes and the rest is far deeper than any gulf between the different classes that serve them. If the distinction between slave and free had become the deepest and clearest of distinctions in the classical period, that is because the meaning of freedom had been clarified and its value enormously increased.

A Greek of the classical period ran the risk of slavery if he was captured in war; and there are enough instances of cities that saw their men killed and their women and children enslaved, though it is fair to remark that there was also some protest against these things. But war booty could not produce anything like the numbers required.

The main supply came from the outer world through slavedealers, that is, from the slave markets of the east; or from captives from barbarian wars sold off by their captors; or, indeed, Herodotus tells us that Thracian parents would straightforwardly sell their children. Much unskilled labour came from the north, Thracians or Phrygians (but they also produced some skilled miners); the more accomplished workers came mainly from Syria and the east. The primary fact for classical Athens is that the supply was plentiful and relatively cheap. An average slave cost not much more than might be expended on his keep for a year.

Estimates of the total slave population of Attica vary greatly, but perhaps the most probable is some 80,000–100,000 at the time of Athens' greatest prosperity and highest citizen population—an average of about one and a half slaves to every adult citizen, or about one in four of the entire population. A large part of the slave labour went in domestic service. This was not merely a matter of the gentleman keeping a proper state: it goes down to much lower levels, as in the case of the comparatively small man who appears as hero in so many of Aristophanes' comedies and constantly calls on his slave or slaves. A single family tilling a small plot of land would normally own slaves; in this typical small unit they would turn their hands to all tasks, domestic or agricultural, working alongside their masters, and the domestic tasks would include baking and weaving. (There is a large difference here from the plantation system in the southern states of America, where most of the slaves were owned by a small minority of the white population, while the remaining whites, less comfortably, managed their own concerns.) Off the land, a free man would hope to have a slave to help him in his trade, or even to take it over. A much-quoted and certainly significant instance is the cripple for whom Lysias wrote a speech, defending before the Council his right to a minute dole from the state: the cripple remarks in passing that he has difficulty in practising his trade himself, and has not yet been able to buy a slave to take it over. On public buildings, again, citizens and metics and their slaves worked side by side in small groups.

In work like this, though all were doing the same kind of job for the same wage, the slave's wage went to his master, whose profit consisted in the difference between this wage and the slave's keep. Similarly, the larger units represent an investment in a group of slaves. The income Demosthenes speaks of (p. 115) is the price obtained for their products, from which one should deduct their keep and some allowance for working off the price originally paid for them—but the group of slaves with their materials and tools were all that in the circumstances concerned Demosthenes. Another regular way of making an income was to leave the slave to work on his own at his trade, responsible for his own keep but paying in a regular sum to his master. This was especially prevalent at Athens, where 'living apart' became a technical term for slaves working on these conditions; and some of them prospered conspicuously. Another variant was the hiring out of slaves to a free employer, who again saw to the slave's keep himself and paid an agreed sum to the owner for the slave's labour. This might be done on a very small scale: indeed, we meet the case of a man setting out on a longish journey to collect the hiring-money of a single slave. But a rich man might invest heavily, as the Athenian general, Nicias, did in the late fifth century, who was said to own a thousand such slaves.

Figures like these might seem to take us back to the possibility of large contractors employing a large labour force. There is one area, the silver mines in Laurium, where slave labour was used extensively, though probably not any very large single gang in a single mine. These mines were heavily exploited from the early fifth century down to the later stages of the Peloponnesian War, and again, after a period of less activity, in the fourth century. Like other mines in the Greek world, they were somehow state property, though it is not clear whether the surface land was in private ownership or belonged to the state. The democracy, characteristically, let them out on fairly short leases to individual operators, most of them on quite a small scale, who used their own or a neighbour's surface installations and took what profit their luck gave them, after paying their royalty to the state. The records of the magistrates who sold the mining rights are partly preserved on stone, between 367 and 307, and show a large number of prominent Athenian names. The scale of their profit is not easy to calculate, but Xenophon, in his scheme for state-owned slaves to be hired out for mining, reckons, on the basis of the contracts made by Nicias and other private slaveowners, that each slave would bring in a clear obol a day. A slave force of 6,000 would thus produce an income of sixty talents a year (a sum which would, for instance, provide the pay for the rowers of a fleet of sixty ships for two months). That gives some idea of the kind of profit the hirers hoped to make. As to the scale of total exploitation of the mines, it has been estimated that, when they were most fully worked, some 30,000 slaves were employed. Many of these were Thracians or Paphlagonians, presumably men who had some experience of mining in their home countries; others, of miscellaneous origin, provided unskilled labour. Some free Athenians also worked in person.

The question is often raised, why the ancient world never developed a more efficient technology—why, for instance, the steam-engine devised by Hero of Alexandria never became anything more than an interesting toy—and whether slavery had anything to do with this apparent retardation. The same question can be asked in varying measure about any civilisation previous to our Industrial Revolution, and that is enough to show that slavery was not the only cause at work. Slavery was, no doubt, part of the cause, in that cheap imported slaves were the main means by which the upper classes of Athens had raised themselves above the necessity of devoting most of their time to subsistence agriculture, and so had gained the leisure whose fruits we still admire. Their mind and taste thus satisfactorily engaged, they were less tempted to look again at the foundation of this leisure and ask whether it might be improved. It is another aspect of the same point, that educated Athenians, the less educated inevitably following in their wake, looked with growing contempt on those mechanical occupations which kept a man from enjoying leisure. But there is less to be said for the argument, true as far as it goes, that the best minds of Greece were concentrated on theory, making great advances in mathematics and astronomy but neglecting practical improvements. After all, the technical advances of our seventeenth and later centuries were made rather in defiance of the theorists and the universities. While Plato contemplated, one of those slaves who 'lived apart' might easily have hit upon some revolutionary mechanical idea; and it need not have been difficult to finance its development. No doubt in fact all parties were concerned merely with the business in front of them, and the question is wrongly framed: we ought to be asking, not so much what prevented the ancient world from developing a steam-engine, as why it was a viable proposition in the days of Watt and Newcomen.

The low level of economic organisation helped to avoid another possible complication of slavery, the undercutting of free by slave labour. No Greek manufacturer or landowner operated on a scale where such undercutting could be effective. As has been remarked, there was no exploitation of the land by gangs of slaves in the manner of the Roman *latifundia*. Even in small-scale manufacture, the margin was too slight for anyone to offer goods or services appreciably below the market price. So near as we can calculate from dangerously insufficient information, the slave as an investment brought in a low enough return, nothing like so safe and satisfactory as land, safer but much less remunerative than lending for a merchant voyage. It was worth while, so long as the supply of slaves was plentiful and cheap, but did not lend itself to competitive exploitation of the kind that comes readily to our minds. So we find slaves and free men working together on the buildings. There is no indication that the products of slave workshops known to us were sold at a differential price, and we hear no complaints of slave competition.

*

No easy generalisation is possible about the relations between slave and master in the Greek world, since the slave's view, as usual, is not known. In the close quarters of Greek domestic life, no distance could be preserved like that which English middle-class families used to keep between themselves and their servants—and the Greek was unlikely to refrain from talking under any circumstances. The closer relation of nurse and child, tutor and pupil, easily ripened into affection, nor need we doubt stories of the loyal slave saving his master's life on the battlefield, and the like. But at its best the relationship was bound to have unhappy elements, as that when a slave was punished it was with physical blows of the kind that a free man had the right to resent. We might take an example from Aristophanes, who prided himself on his fastidiousness with regard to stock jokes. He opens the *Frogs* with Dionysus forbidding his slave, Xanthias, to make the conventional cracks about the physical hardships of the slave's life. They converse through the first half of the play with almost total freedom: the last we see of Xanthias, however, is caricature, a scene where he and another slave congratulate one another on their rascality. None of this is the authentic voice of the slave, but the free man's version of it—again, one might compare the jokes about English servants in periodicals of a generation or two ago, now happily almost unintelligible. But the blows are unmistakeably there, as fixed a feature of the scene as the free speech.

The domestic slave who was on good terms with his master stood some chance of liberation, and the slave 'living apart' and practising his trade might hope to earn enough to buy his release. Manumission was by no means uncommon, though the practice and the formalities differed a good deal from place to place. The master often retained the right to certain services for a fixed period, or for his own lifetime. Some of those 'living apart' prospered conspicuously, giving rise to disgruntled oligarchic comment that slaves in the streets of Athens might be better dressed than free men. An outstanding instance was the early fourth-century banker, Pasion, who achieved not only his freedom but Athenian citizenship. But the domestic slave with a bad master was in poor case, with little hope of redress, and the prospects were altogether bleaker for those who were hired out to the mines and other work—and we are not given even a distorted reflection of their feelings. But, after the Spartans had fortified their post outside Athens in 413, Thucydides tells us that over 20,000 slaves deserted to the enemy, the bulk of them 'craftsmen' (the word would cover any sort of skilled labour and need not be confined to the miners of Laurium, though no doubt many of the deserters were from there). We do not know what promises the invaders had held out to them, still less what eventually became of them, but the suggestion is clear that the life of even a skilled slave was one which he was ready to fly from on a very uncertain prospect.

To clarify this picture we must look at slavery outside Athens, even at the exceptional case of the Spartan helots. They were very thoroughly slaves, and are often called by the standard Greek word *douloi*. 'Serfs', or any other term drawn from a quite different context, would be misleading: and when ancient critics classify them as 'between slave and free' that cannot refer to their conditions of life, but to the fact that they were less at the disposal of individual masters than the chattels who were bought and sold freely elsewhere. The Athenian, Critias, an admirer of the Spartan system, was nearer the mark when he said that in Sparta the free were more free and the slaves more fully slaves than elsewhere. With their numbers, and the unbroken national consciousness of the Messenian helots, they were a standing danger to the Spartiate aristocracy. The brutality of their repression was notorious. Thucydides reports an occasion, at some time before 424, when the authorities proclaimed that they would set free those who could claim to have rendered particularly good service in war, and from the applicants some 2,000 were chosen out; but soon after they dis-

appeared, and no one knew how. It was said that the Spartan magistrates annually declared war on the helots, so that murders during the
year might not lie on their conscience. The institution called *crypteia*
meant, according to Aristotle, that a body of young Spartiates spent a
period of their life, hiding by day, and roaming the countryside at
night to murder helots. Whatever the truth of that,[1] there is a clear
indication of the way in which the helot danger affected normal life
when Xenophon remarks, unemphatically in passing, how the Spartans
in camp kept the slaves away from their weapons, and themselves had
spears in their hands wherever they went. Even the writers most
favourable to Sparta do not try to defend the system. Yet, even in this
grim context, there is one surprising anomaly, the fact that the Spartans
were so ready to use armed helots, or helots expressly liberated for
military service (p. 160), in their expeditions abroad. These men were
trained, in numbers not far short of the citizen body itself, and there is
no hint that they were anything but loyal. The watchful hostility which
Xenophon implies was not the whole truth about the relation between
Spartans and helots, or not the whole time.

Though it was asserted in antiquity that there was a close resemblance between the institutions of Sparta and Crete, the latter shows a
different pattern. After the Dorian conquest, a pre-Greek remnant, with
its own unintelligible speech, survived at the east end of the island:
otherwise, the surviving descendants of the Minoans were reduced
to servitude. The literary sources present us with a number of special
terms for servitude, of which it is seldom possible to say more than
that they were Cretan dialect words for some kind of slave; and with
the general statement that agriculture in Crete was in the hands of a
class resembling the helots. But the laws of Gortyn, though written
generally in dialect thick enough to defeat all but the specialist, avoid
these complications and use, quite interchangeably, two common
Greek words for slave. Their provisions relate entirely to privately
owned slaves, bought and sold on the market, though, since this is a
very miscellaneous collection of enactments, its silence about publicly
owned slaves does not prove that there were none.

In several respects, this is a more liberal slave regime than we find,
for instance, in contemporary Athens. The slave might own property,
including sheep and cattle, and his rights were carefully reserved when

1. Plato makes the life in hiding a part of the young Spartiate's training in
the endurance of hardship (see p. 208) and says nothing about the murder of
helots.

the owner died and his heirs divided up the property. Slave marriages were recognised by the law and, after provisions about the disposal of property when the marriage of free persons was terminated by divorce or death, a brief clause safeguards the property of a slave wife. The children of a slave marriage inevitably belonged to the owner of one or other parent, but a surprising provision deals with the offspring of a slave father and a free mother. The status of the child was decided according as the free woman had gone to live with the slave, or the other way round. The possible complications might tempt one to think that this was a rare situation, but the law goes on to regulate the case where a woman had both slave and free children, which suggests that the complications did arise in practice. This has some bearing on the general question of slave children, and of breeding as a source of supply of slaves—neglected above, since it does not look as if this source was of serious importance for states like Athens that had fully developed the system of chattel slavery. It may well be that, in Athens, the cost of raising and training a slave child was markedly more than the cost of buying a full-grown and trained slave; and the all-male slave population of the Athenian mines will hardly have contributed to the supply. But it must be remembered that the helot population of Laconia and Messenia, in spite of discouraging conditions of life, continued to reproduce itself, with no sign that it dwindled as time went on. The Gortyn laws suggest that in the secluded agricultural communities of Crete a substantial number of slave children was born.

But at Gortyn the slave was still an object bought and sold, incapable of acting for himself at law, mostly helpless in his owner's hands. The fact that the laws selected for public inscription make these references to the rights of slaves means, as such publication always does, that the rights were liable to be overridden. Where this happened, it cannot have been easy for the slave to obtain redress; but it is still impressive that the community should accord these rights at all. The logic of slavery is not easily applied all the time and in every respect.

At Gortyn, we also meet the man who has pledged himself to an-other, the situation which Solon forbade at Athens. The nature of this transaction is not described, since the law is only incidentally concerned with his legal position, which has some of the characteristics of slavery. For the other party, to whom the man is pledged, the text uses, not the standard word for 'master', but a participle which in effect means 'creditor'. The law contemplates that the bondsman may release himself by repayment, though we cannot tell how realistic this was. A man who had lost a case at law might be in a similar position until and unless he paid up; and one who ransomed another from captivity as a prisoner of war had extensive rights over him till he repaid the ransom. Only in the last case did Athenian law allow a private creditor such rights, though one might be imprisoned there for non-payment of a debt to the state.

From other states founded on conquest, no institutions worth long discussion are known. Corinth and Aegina, where a favourable position for trade was combined with a more restricted agricultural territory, naturally developed in a different way. They were notorious for the large number of their slaves, though the estimates recorded in antiquity are impossibly high. These must have been imported chattel slaves; the general position of these states was, presumably, more like that of Athens than that of the more purely agricultural Dorian states.

In the generation of Socrates, when everything was questioned, the justice of slavery was questioned also. Isolated voices were heard to say that all men were equally men, and that slavery was against nature. The defence of Aristotle, that some were naturally slaves, incapable of full human reason and needing the will of a master to complete their own, rings hollow to us, quite apart from the accident that 'naturally free' Greeks might be enslaved by the chances of war. But this was a world in which slavery, in some form or other, was universal, and no nation could remember a time when it had not been so. It is not surprising that there was no clamour for emancipation. It has been convincingly argued that the margin over bare subsistence in Greece was so small that the surplus which was needed to give leisure to the minority could only be achieved with artificially cheap labour. If that is right, there was not much alternative for Greece. For Athens, it had come, by the opening of the sixth century, to a choice between reducing citizens to slavery or extensive import of chattel slaves from abroad. Only a greatly improved technology, something like an industrial revolution, could effectively have altered these conditions.

*

Lastly, there is the question how far all this economic activity, distributed as it was between citizen and metic and slave, may have affected the policy of the state, and in what areas the state itself might feel called upon to intervene. The pressure that could be generated by one of these individual small businesses was, of course, negligible in comparison with what can be done by the commercial lobbying of larger interests today, though collectively the craftsmen and merchants might in more general terms affect what the state did. So, at Athens, the peasant living in one of the remoter villages might have to take two days off to come and vote in the assembly, and was clearly at a disadvantage compared with the craftsman who lived in the city; there were complaints about the extent to which the city mob controlled the destinies of Athens. But, except where their material interests were involved, in questions about food supply or jury pay or the distribution of land in cleruchies, this mob thought mostly in terms of glory and the like. The expansion of the fifth-century empire of Athens was not accomplished by pressure from businessmen.

As has been said, the state was concerned to safeguard essential imports, much the most important of which was the import of cereals. We find Athens according official honours to Crimean princes in recognition of the advantages which they granted to Athenians in their harbours. As time went on, many states, not only democracies, appointed special magistrates to look after the supply of grain: bad harvests and starvation among the poor are political events which have to be watched. In war, the enemy's supplies were naturally an objective. Thus, in 427, early in the Peloponnesian War, Athens sent a naval expedition to Sicily, among other things to explore the possibility of conquering the island and cutting off at its source a supply of food which went mainly to the Peloponnese. Shipbuilding materials were another major concern; and here the state itself was the importer, as we see from a treaty concluded in 409 with king Archelaus of Macedon for the import of timber to Athens, and from a few other treaties.

It was recognised also, and not only by Xenophon in the pamphlet discussed earlier, that the state was concerned about the general flow of commerce, from which it drew its harbour and market dues. Athens and other commercial centres, therefore, took trouble about harbour installations and other relevant buildings, and about the expeditious handling of lawsuits arising out of trade. By the fifth century, it was common for cities to make specific treaties, which gave the citizens of the one some standing in the courts of the other, an essential step if inter-city trade was to develop at all. In surviving law court speeches about commercial cases at Athens, the number of non-Athenians involved is naturally high—outright foreigners, even more than the resident metics. There was also the institution of the *proxenos*, in function something like the consuls whom we maintain abroad; but the *proxenos* of Miletus or Sparta at Athens was an Athenian citizen, who voluntarily undertook to look after the interests, public and private, of Spartans or Milesians in Athens.

But beyond this general care for the smooth workings of commerce, the state did hardly anything to promote the interests of its citizens in foreign commerce. The quest for export markets was no part at all of state policy. The Greeks knew, of course, in a general way that their necessary imports must be balanced by exports, acceptable to the other parties, but that was the affair of the individual trader; and, if Xenophon is any guide, Athens had not gone far into the theory of these matters. Besides, in the classical period, so much of the industry and trade which was centred on Athens was in the hands of non-citizens, especially of the metics; and, though their usefulness to Athens might be recognised, it was not likely that the city would make any large sacrifice, much less go to war, for their trading interests.

The question does, however, arise, whether the state had been entirely indifferent in earlier times, before the metic system was developed, and before the ideal of cultivated leisure had quite such a grip on the upper classes. The motives of the leaders of the colonial movement were, no doubt, overwhelmingly agrarian; but, as indicated earlier, it is hard not to speculate whether the state of Miletus was conscious of some commercial advantage in lining the Black Sea and its approaches with Milesian colonies, whether Chalcis had any thought of trade routes in mind when Chalcidians settled both sides of the Straits of Messina. Speculation has also been busy with the very early war between the two great cities of Euboea, Chalcis and Eretria, the conflict we call the Lelantine War, from the name of the plain in Euboea for which they fought. We know this to have been an important and remembered event, because Thucydides makes it an exception to his rule that there were no important combinations between Greek states in these early days, and says that the Greek world generally took sides. Our scraps of evidence converge on the late eighth century, and include two cases where colonists from a state on one side were expelled from a colony by men of the other. The solid block of Chalcidian colonies in north-east Sicily belongs roughly to the time of the war, whereas after the foundation of Cumae (a generation earlier) Eretria has no further part in the colonisation of the west; on the other hand, in the east, two of Eretria's allies, Miletus and Megara, proceeded in the seventh century to a near-monopoly of colonisation in the direction of the Black Sea. Whatever the result of the war at home in Euboea, it looks as if one of its results abroad was a certain division of spheres in the colonial area. We must not, however, maintain that the war was begun in order to produce these results. The Lelantine War is one of those events so remote from contemporary record that we can barely hope to ascertain the fact, and have lost the context which might explain it; and the results may be coincidental.

It is a different matter when economic causes are alleged for the Peloponnesian War at the end of the fifth century, in the fuller light of classical history. There is a certain initial plausibility here, because Athens' last action before the war looks like a stroke of economic warfare, the notorious decree which excluded Megarians from all markets and harbours in the Athenian empire; and because contemporaries speculated about the possibly discreditable and secret reasons why Pericles would not allow the quarrel to be patched up, his public explanations not being altogether convincing. But to see behind Pericles the sinister influence of a commercial party seeking to expand the trade of the Peiraeus, or even the influence of individual tycoons, would be a bad misuse of the evidence. As we have seen, Greek trade was not organised in a way that would generate such pressures, nor is it likely that a fact of this kind would wholly have escaped the attention of contemporaries. When the Spartan assembly voted for war and the Athenian assembly rejected the Spartan ultimatum, the voters were surely swayed by the kind of motives that contemporaries allege: on the one side, indignation against Athens' tyranny; on the other, impatience with political dictation from Sparta.

*

Controversy about Greek economics seems still to be in the stage of arguing about the principles on which further argument should be conducted. The first excitement of attempting economic explanation led to inappropriate modernistic interpretations, which must certainly be scrapped. It is salutary to insist that the standard categories of nineteenth-century economics are not applicable here, but the reaction may go too far, eliminating the effect of trade on Greek history altogether. It is another curiosity that Marxist interpretation of Greek history, at any rate in England, has always pursued the overt economic motive, finding comfort, for instance, in the theory that the Athenian tyrant, Peisistratus, was a mining magnate. One would have supposed that Marxists would be better employed trying to uncover the concealed economic basis of those feelings about political power and glory which on the surface moved Greek cities to what they did. The evidence for Greek economics will always remain too fragmentary for any kind of quantitative analysis: but, one way and another, there is room for a good deal more hard thinking about the place which trade and manufacture really occupied in the life of Greek society.

CHAPTER 8

Armies, navies and military leagues

THOUGH SO MUCH of their time was spent fighting one another, the Greeks did not, in general, much delight in war. It was always with them, shaping all their thoughts and policies, and the warlike virtues unavoidably took a high place in their scale of values; but few peoples have expressed more strongly, through their poets and historians and the rest, their sense of the blessings of that peace which was throughout denied to them. They were warlike by circumstance rather than militarists by inclination, and their technical contributions to the art of war were not all that many. Their most significant innovation came early, in the middle of the seventh century, the massed formation of heavy-armed infantry, those hoplites who have inevitably intruded into earlier chapters. This formation served them well at home and commanded respect abroad over several centuries. But during the classical period it gradually ceased to be effective within Greece; and when new developments were thus needed they came from the Macedonians, Philip and Alexander, not from Greek generals.

At first sight, it is surprising that a mountainous country like Greece should have depended on fighters loaded with such a weight of metal, for where there are plenty of defensible passes one might expect that light and mobile troops would have the best of it. Equipment and tactics were determined, as always, by the objective, in this case the enemy's agricultural plain, down on the level ground. Whichever side could dominate the plain could wreck the other's crops; and the narrow margin on which Greece subsisted meant that few states could survive such devastation two years running, even if the first did not bring it to capitulate. The massed formation of hoplites emerged as the most formidable instrument of this kind of war, with important social and political consequences. The needs of hoplite fighting, steady discipline and a steadfast refusal to give ground, shaped the classical Greek conception of what a good man ought to be.

*

The individual duels of the heroes of Homer are partly there to serve the story, which is interested in the doings of heroes, whereas the bulk of the army can be dismissed with a brief simile; but they are also, in a way, realistic, since pre-hoplite fighting depended much less on large formations and much more on individual prowess. The heroes' procedure was, first, to throw their spears from a distance; if the spears missed, they got to close quarters with the sword. Their defensive armour was various, a rich quarry for poetic description: the more constant items are a circular leather shield, hung by a strap round neck and shoulder, leather jerkins, and helmets of one pattern or another. Greaves to protect the legs seem, from the poet's language, to be rather a speciality of the Greek side. They used their chariots only to convey them to and from the battlefield, though the aged Nestor in one place remembers the practice of their forefathers, chariots fighting in formation. That was a method probably borrowed from abroad and not obviously appropriate to Greek terrain, but the careful listing of chariots in the Mycenaean documents would suggest that Nestor's reminiscence was founded on a genuine, if dim, memory.

Aristotle alleges that there was a period of early Greek history when cavalry dominated the battlefield, correlating this with their political dominance; and he maintains that there was a change in the basis of political power when the defence of the city fell instead on the wider body of organised hoplites. It is clear that horses, whether for fighting or racing, played an important part in the lives of the early aristocracies, but it is not easy to document a phase when cavalry were genuinely decisive in the field. In later times, they served as scouts, or could be used to harass an infantry force and restrict its free movement; but, in the stirrupless days of antiquity, a man was easily knocked off his horse, and horsemen could not charge a steady infantry formation. Perhaps the early aristocrats, like their Homeric predecessors, used their horses for transport to and from the field, but did their fighting on foot. Certainly the significant change was in the style of infantry fighting, and this had the effect which Aristotle asserts.

The hoplite's main equipment (pl. 18, 19) was a cuirass, covering most of the body, made of metal or of metal strips attached to some more flexible backing; a shield, not hung on a strap, but with a solid band inside, at the centre, through which the left arm was thrust up to the elbow, the hand holding a grip near the rim; a metal helmet, almost always with a crest; and metal greaves. The spear was not thrown, but held steady for a thrust, either from above down at the neck, or from below to reach under the lower rim of the cuirass; in reserve, the hoplite had a short sword or dagger. On present evidence, it seems that the individual items of this panoply, imported from various quarters, were adopted at first in a scattered way, beginning at the end of the eighth century. Certainly, the defensive armour would be valuable for the older style of single combat, and the introduction of these items is not evidence in itself of anything except increasing prosperity and increasing opportunity to adopt innovations from abroad.

The date at which these arms were first used in formation is less easy to determine. The archaic vase-painter naturally composed in single figures, and it is difficult to depict a massed phalanx in the kind of space allowed. Various indications do, however, converge to place the transition somewhere in the middle of the seventh century; and, once the new formation had been tried out, it spread quickly over southern Greece. It involved a line of considerable depth, eight being a common number, whose charge had thus a considerable weight behind it. If the first shock did not break one line or the other, a confused shoving—this is literally what it was called in Greek went on till something gave. Once the line broke it was not easy to re-form it, and the side which kept its formation usually routed the other. One reason was that the hoplite shield, held more firmly than the old type with its single central handgrip, was only manœuvrable within limits and could not be brought right round to cover a man's right side. This was, to some extent, covered, while the line stood firm, by the left-hand half of his neighbour's shield; but, on his own, he was unprotected on this side.

Two things were needed for the hoplite army, the economic capacity to buy the equipment, which was not provided by the state, and the capacity to act together in formation. For the first, not every farmer could afford the armour; but the numbers put into the field in the classical period are enough in themselves to show that the army included the more substantial members of what might be called a middle class, no longer just the high-born hero or the leisured noble. The social and political importance of that needs no long stressing. It is harder to get a clear picture of the way in which the ordinary city carried out any military training, apart from that year or two of initial training which youths had almost everywhere to undergo, roughly between the ages of eighteen and twenty. Yet it is hard to see how Greek armies could survive at all without some degree of peacetime practice, and one would suppose that such training in common would be an important element for the general social cohesion of the hoplite class.

We do not even hear much about the peacetime exercises of the experts of this form of war, the Spartans, whom Xenophon describes as 'technicians of war' in contrast with the improvised militia of other cities. He delighted in the technicalities of their drill—for instance, their procedure for forming up out of column of march to meet an attack from front or flank; and he points out that this drill was not, as others mistakenly assumed, a complicated matter but in principle simple, though this was a simplicity that required trained precision. He stresses, again, that other Greeks could not form up their line except with known faces on either side of them, their accustomed companions, whereas the Spartan, even if the line was broken, was able form up again, whoever was to right or left, in front or behind. This criticism rather suggests that the other Greeks did train together—at any rate, the smaller units—on a local basis. At Athens this could have been done at the level of the *trittys* (p. 83), which was in almost all cases a compact area, providing the tribal regiment with a sub-unit whose members would be neighbours to one another. But the little that we know about the system for calling up an Athenian army does not suggest that this sub-unit was likely to be called out as a whole. Thucydides accords special praise to the Spartan system for passing orders down from the commander to platoon level, a system which does not sound specially difficult as he recites it. We are left to infer that other Greek armies, the Athenian included, were somehow less well articulated and more liable to regulate their movements by mere confused shouting. It may indeed be that the general level of training was lower than we are inclined to imagine. The Spartans' technical excellence certainly derived from peacetime practice; but it could, barely, be imagined that other cities made do with the initial training period in youth, and relied thereafter on the all too frequent experience that their troops gained in actual war.

Sparta sets us other problems. Most states organised their armies in tribes in the manner described in Chapter 5, whether on a kinship or a local basis, and the subdivisions, whatever they were called, followed the same principle as the tribe. Sparta had certainly once, in the remote past, had an army based on kinship tribes and, later, one based on a territorial system. But the army familiar to Xenophon consisted of six regiments whose principle of organisation quite eludes us. Father and son might belong to different regiments, and there were men from the town of Amyclae in all regiments; so the system was not simply local or simply based on kinship, but on some other principle of selection, about which we can only say that it produced an even distribution of the various age-groups through the various units. Again, as the Spartiate aristocracy declined in numbers, the proportion of *perioikoi* in the army increased; and while it is easy to see that the Spartiates in their helot-nursed leisure had more time than other Greeks to practise for war, the same is not obviously true of the *perioikoi*. We have no idea how the *perioikoi* were selected for the units in which they served. One can only suppose that they were taken for a time away from their normal occupations and trained under Spartan leadership. With all the admiration lavished by Xenophon and others on Spartan military virtue, it is important to remember how much of it actually belongs to the *perioikoi*.

Sparta was also a model in the organisation of her military supplies. Xenophon was much impressed by a system which determined in advance the exact loads to be carried by each wagon, leaving us to infer that the baggage-train of other armies was a much more haphazard affair. Other arms than the infantry were not of great importance. The role of the cavalry, as has been said, was not large. It seems that, for some time, the principal states of southern Greece ceased even to maintain official cavalry forces; and, though there was some revival here about the middle of the fifth century, the Spartan cavalry never amounted to much, a neglect which is significant for the place of cavalry in hoplite campaigning. Archers were employed, often Cretan specialists hired for the purpose, but their chances were limited, since the arrow is not an accurate weapon beyond 200 yards and the archers did not dare to come too close. There were also slingers and other light troops, with what weapons they might have, but little defensive armour. These usually swarmed around the battlefield in large numbers, useful in preliminary skirmishes or to harass a retreat.

The Spartans gained their original ascendancy with an army of this type, in straightforward battles against neighbour enemies who fought by the familiar rules. The same arms and tactics prevailed against the invasion of the lighter-armed Persians, who relied far more on archers and cavalry, ineffective against the Greek line, if it stood firm. But, in the Peloponnesian War, the conventional strategy of devastation was no good to Sparta, for Athens was now linked to the port of the Peiraeus by a long double wall and relied on imported food. Despite angry protests against this policy of Pericles, so foreign to the whole convention of Greek warfare, the Athenian army did not come out to fight the immensely superior Peloponnesian force, which was left free to damage everything it could find in the evacuated country-side.

The set hoplite battle was ceasing to be decisive. There were only two such battles in the long Peloponnesian War, Delium in 424 and Mantineia in 418. Each was decisive in so far as it foiled an Athenian attempt to gain the initiative, but neither was of any further service to the victors, or brought them nearer to winning the war. The Corinthian War of 394 began with two outright Spartan victories on land, followed by another in 392, but the war went on as before, to be decided in the end by sea, as the Peloponnesian War had been. The only technical improvement of any significance was the Theban device, foreshadowed in the Peloponnesian War but developed mainly by Epameinondas (active from 378 to 362). This was to strengthen one wing very heavily with the toughest troops in very deep formation; then, holding back the weaker wing, to strike a decisive blow with the strengthened wing before the rest of the line was even engaged. This proved highly successful: but, though the Theban victory at Leuctra in 371 put an end to Spartan pretensions to dominate Greece, neither this nor subsequent battles enabled the Thebans to impose terms on Sparta, nor order anywhere.

In favourable circumstances, light troops might bring a hoplite column to a standstill and seriously damage it, as the Athenian general, Demosthenes, found when he marched into the mountains of Aetolia in 426—an experience which he put to good use the next year in dealing with the Spartan force, cut off on the island of Sphacteria by Pylos. Another Athenian general, Iphicrates, achieved a more spectacular success with relatively light-armed troops against a Spartan regiment on the march in 390—provoking them to charge out from their ranks, giving way to the charge, then returning to the attack, till they lost their

g of its earlier superiority, the fifth-century position
y restored.

★

sea-battle known to Thucydides was one between
orcyra, and the date, as he gives it, works out at about
varfare must, in fact, have begun long before this, for
8) and fighting are pictured on Attic Geometric pottery
ghth century; and, though most of these battles seem to be
re of opposed landings from the sea, the ships must some-
fought one another. The difficulty which the Geometric
nd in rendering anything so complex as a ship prevents us
ching any very confident conclusion about the construction of
ssels. The standard warship of the archaic period was the
nter, which takes its name from the fact that it had fifty rowers,
y-five a side, about the limit for a one-tier vessel. The classical
called the trireme, gradually came to predominate during the
century. It is evident from the name that there must be three of
ething. It has been hotly argued that there were three rowers
ling on each oar, but it seems clear by now that the trireme had,
fact, three tiers of oars, the rowers of the top bank using an out-
igger which kept their oars clear of the lower banks. This meant that
very much greater power could be developed in a ship of roughly the
same length. In the fourth century, quadriremes and quinqueremes
appear, again said to be the invention of Dionysius of Syracuse, but
not seen further east till the 330's. It is less easy to feel certain about
the construction of these; and when much higher numbers than five
are mentioned there can no longer be any question of superimposed
tiers.

The Greeks won their great victory at Salamis in 480 by enticing the
Persian fleet inside a narrow strait. This was necessary because the
Greek ships of that time were slower and less manœuvrable than their
opponents; and they were partly decked over to provide a platform
for fighting men. For his victory at the river Eurymedon, ten years
later, Cimon is said to have had his ships decked for their whole length.
Thereafter the Athenians developed their technique in another direction. They built their ships lighter, for the sake of speed and manœuvra-
bility, and they now relied, not on sinking their enemy by ramming,
but on complicated evolutions which disabled the other ship by

cohesion altogether and t...
what he could to deve...
his victory. He was remei...
equipment, but there was...
system effective on the bat...
followed. Light troops by the...

The answer, so far as there wa...
craft. The Athenians owed their i...
Peloponnesian War to the fact that i...
to take by assault a firmly defended ...
knew from early times the use of batte...
the Persians, during their sixth-century ...
shown them another method, the piling up ...
it was level with the walls; in the classical pe...
to build wooden towers and other siege-eng...
devices were all tried out, as Thucydides describ...
in the Peloponnesian attack on the small Boeotia...
429, but without effect. So the besiegers could only s...
conventional business of building their own dout...
Plataea and leaving a force there till the city was starved i...
two years later. With superior force, any city could be ...
unless, like Athens, its walls reached down to the sea and ...
mastery there. The circumvallation complete, most of the for...
had built it could go home; but still, it was a long, troubleson...
expensive process, not lightly to be undertaken.

When the change came, the chief material factor was the devel...
ment of the catapult, not so much to throw stones or other large missile...
into the besieged city as to shoot a heavier arrow with more force and
accuracy. This compelled the defenders to keep their heads down,
prevented them from wrecking the siege-engines brought against the
walls, and facilitated an assault with ladders. The catapult is said to
have been developed by the elder Dionysius of Syracuse, early in the
fourth century, but it was not commonly used further east till the time
of Philip and Alexander of Macedon. So, when Philip defeated the
conventional forces of Athens and Thebes at Chaeroneia in 338, though
the fleet of Athens was still intact she surrendered at once, as she had
not done after hoplite defeats in earlier wars. Before long, the defenders
took to mounting their own protected catapults on the walls, and the
techniques of fortification were further refined. But though the defence

regained somethin...
was never entirel...

The earliest ...
Corinth and ...
664. Naval ...
warships (pl...
of the late e...
in the natu...
times hav...
artist fou...
from rea...
these ...
pentec...
twen...
type...
sixt...
so...
pu...
in...

breaking its oars. It was these techniques that gave Athens her mastery of the seas. Thucydides, describing a sea-battle between Corinth and Corcyra just before the Peloponnesian War, allows himself to remark with an evident sense of superiority that it was fought in the old style, more like a land-battle fought from the decks of ships.

It was a commonplace, recognised alike by the friends and enemies of democracy, that the development of the fleet promoted the political dominance of the lower classes of Athens, delivering the outnumbered gentlemen into the hands of the demagogues whom they so greatly disliked and distrusted. So far as this is true, and it must be borne in mind that the gentlemen were very far from having been completely put out of action, it was a gradual process. The first expansion of the Athenian fleet by Themistocles, just before 480, to the unprecedented number of 200 ships, must have put a very great strain on the city's resources, not so much materially as in reasonably skilled manpower. The ship's captain of those days, the trierarch, was the effective commander of ship and fighting men—not, as in later usage, the man who paid for the maintenance of the ship—and it may not then have been easy to find 200 capable trierarchs. Below them, there was a heavy demand for skilled personnel, the senior members of the crew, of whom the helmsman was the most important. The rowers were not in the same way specialists, but it was advisable to have a core of really experienced men. It was noted that it was difficult to keep a ship's crew at the height of its performance for any length of time. As the empire developed, Athens drew increasingly on non-Athenian rowers, and not entirely from the inhabitants of her own subject cities. But at the beginning it was all very much an Athenian effort, from the top down. The aristocratic Cimon was the most effective and popular leader while the war against Persia continued, and in a very real sense the chief founder of the empire. It was only later, and under different conditions, that the upper classes, or some members of them, became disenchanted with the empire, linking fleet and empire with the radical democracy which they feared, in a manner slightly disconcerting to those brought up on the British association of conservatism and imperialism.

But the development did take place, and was of great importance. The Athenian fleet reached its greatest power on the resources of the empire, a concentration which no later organisation achieved, and no fleet of comparable size could be maintained anywhere in fourth-century Greece. The limiting factor was not the construction of the ships, but the payment of some 200 rowers per ship. But the revenues of the fifth-century empire supported more than just the fleet; indeed, they contributed heavily to the Parthenon and the other architectural glories of Athens. It is not true, as hostile critics alleged, that the common people of Athens were supported in idleness on the tribute of the subject cities, through the medium of state pay for juries and for other service; the system of state pay continued after the empire was gone, and at all ordinary times it was on a scale which Athens could easily afford. But it is probably true that the system would never have got started without the financial surplus which Athens drew from her empire; and it is certain that the people looked on projects for the expansion of empire, notably the Sicilian enterprise of 415, as projects which could safeguard and increase the material benefits which eased their lives. Democracy was launched before the Persian Wars and before any thought of empire, but it could hardly have been developed to its full extent had it not been for the contribution which ordinary men made to the fleet that held the empire together.

However, the precise form of naval warfare at which the Athenians excelled had no extensive future. The ships which Athenian techniques required were not very much use for any other purpose. As light as they could be made, they had no room for the crew to sleep or cook, so that a trireme had to come to land every night and could only cross a large stretch of open sea with some danger and hardship; and with their low gunwales they were very vulnerable to bad weather. Triremes could not be kept at sea to blockade an enemy port, much less a whole coast, but must have a land base nearby. In 425, the Athenians cut off a Spartan force on the island of Sphacteria, but even in summer their patrols could not entirely prevent supplies being brought over by ingenious methods from the mainland; if the Spartans could have held out till winter, no kind of blockade would then have been possible. The main use of the Athenian fleet in its great days was just to keep the enemy off the seas, and to reduce piracy, safeguarding the transport of essential supplies. But even the practised techniques of this navy were not safe against counter-strokes, especially when the Athenians had not full room to manœuvre. In 413, first a Peloponnesian fleet in the Gulf of Corinth, then the besieged Syracusans in their harbour, strengthened their prows to make ramming safer and more effective. Though this reduced the speed of their ships it was in the circumstances decisive.

The fleet could not by itself deliver any stroke that would win a war, but it could, up to a point, deliver a land force to some place which it could not have reached by marching overland. Without a very special effort, no large number could be carried. In the Peloponnesian War, this very obviously limited the value of such raids as the Athenians could make. They could never ravage the crops of Laconia or Messenia at all, where the fertile plains lie some way back from the coast. The setting up of a permanent post on enemy territory was much easier for Sparta than for Athens. Athens needed a site accessible by sea, easily defensible by a small force, and with a good supply of water, all of which limited choice. By a major effort in 415, converting a number of triremes into troop-carriers, Athens transported all the way to Sicily an armament which, at the start, in the current political situation of Sicily, was capable of dealing with any force that could be brought to oppose it. It can be argued that the expedition might have succeeded in its aims if it had wasted less time on arrival in preliminary negotiation and manoeuvre. But there were very high risks, amply foreseen, inherent in so large and distant a venture; and the deterioration of ships and crews played a large part in the final disaster, which ended Athens' unquestioned domination of the sea. No other expedition on this scale and at this distance was ever attempted. In later ages, no naval power was ever based on the trireme as the Athenians had used it.

*

If the course of Greek history produced little significant innovation in methods of fighting, the course of the Peloponnesian War caused organisational changes of some consequence. At the start of the war, the Spartan system may have been more precise and, for its own purposes, more efficient, but the Athenian was the more flexible and the better adapted for fighting the sort of war that now developed.

It is not quite clear how Athens came to possess a system so well fitted to the needs of her empire. At the start, her army was, no doubt, commanded by the king; but in the archaic period the overall command went to one of the chief magistrates, the archon called *polemarchos*, the 'commander in war', who was elected, *de facto* if not by statute, from the aristocracy, and held office for one year only. The fact that no man could be polemarch twice meant that the office rotated among the nobility and prevented the individual from aspiring to political power by way of this office. The warfare of a citizen militia with its neighbours was a relatively simple matter, and it was no doubt felt to be within the competence of any aristocrat, or at least of any aristocrat who commanded enough confidence to get himself elected. There was no reason, in principle, why the system should not have worked.

In Cleisthenes' time this, as so much else, was changed. His reform of the tribes in 507 produced ten tribal regiments, commanded in later times, and probably from the start, by officers called taxiarchs. Either Cleisthenes himself or an immediate successor a few years after 507 instituted a new board of ten 'generals' (*strategoi*). These were elected, one from each tribe, but were not tied to the command of their tribal regiment. Instead, they formed a kind of pool of military commanders, to be sent off by order of the assembly in any number, up to the full ten, that was required for the particular operation to be undertaken. (The word is not tied, as our 'general', to land operations but includes command at sea.) The original purpose of this innovation is not perfectly clear, but the reformer could hardly have hit on anything better suited to the needs of Athens in the fifty years between the Persian and Peloponnesian Wars, when the old-style militia, only able to operate in the more leisured part of the farmer's year, would have been no use at all. Instead, expeditions of varying size and composition had to be sent out in various directions. A register of hoplites was kept, in their tribes, from which the required size of contingent could be drawn, and the assembly determined the number of ships and generals to be sent out.

Generals were annually elected: not even democratic Athens, however much addicted to the lot as the proper egalitarian method of appointing magistrates, thought that this was a suitable way of selecting efficient commanders for the armed forces. Though the candidates were drawn, one from each tribe, the whole electorate voted on each candidate, so that the generals were very much city appointments, not tribal officers. The office could be repeated as long as the candidate held the confidence of the city, and Pericles is recorded as having been elected fifteen times in succession. As a natural consequence, the generalship quite quickly became the principal political prize for an ambitious Athenian, and took on executive duties which were more than merely military. The archonship, the main executive office in archaic Athens, declined in importance; the polemarch is not found on the field of battle after Marathon in 490.

The generalship remained very much the preserve of the older and wealthier families, apart from its brief tenure by the relatively low-born Cleon, which ended with his defeat and death at Amphipolis in 422. Its upper-class character increased the danger of holding it: after military failure, there is always a temptation to cast the blame on the incompetence or treachery of the commanders. The Athenians were specially liable to this temptation, since their generals were of a different social class from the mass of the voters and from most of their political leaders. Accordingly, the history of Athens in the late fifth and fourth centuries is littered with trials and condemnations of unsuccessful generals, and no doubt the condemnation was often undeserved. But, for all its risks, the career carried the kind of honour which a Greek coveted, and the tradition of state service was strong in the Athenian upper class. There are several families where we find the generalship held in successive generations over a considerable period. It might help a man, who was in court on some other charge or business, if he could claim that his father or his ancestors had held this office. Such families did not harden into an institution, like the consular families of the Roman republic, but the fact of these traditions is still important.

Sparta at the outbreak of the Peloponnesian War had nothing to match this. Almost all Spartans still thought in terms of the traditional strategy of invasion and devastation, the work of the regular army. For this army, there was a regular hierarchy of officers from platoon level up to the commanders of the six regiments called *morai*. At the apex was the king, in supreme command. It was the assembly that determined which of the two kings should lead any particular expedition; how the other officers were appointed, and for what length of time, we do not know. But, for the war against Athens, it was soon discovered that the traditional strategy of the regular army was not effective; and, worse still, that the war might require distant expeditions, occupying longer time than could be spared from the farmer's year. Although this consideration weighed less with the Spartans themselves, who could leave agriculture to their helots, it mattered a great deal to their Peloponnesian allies. The first such expedition was that of Brasidas to the north, in 424, and many more were needed before the war ended.

The answer was clear. Another kind of force must be built up, capable of providing detachments for distant and long-term service; and there must be detachable officers to command them. Sparta solved the problem with the efficiency which she usually brought to military matters. Two kinds of troops were employed. Some were paid volunteers, largely from the Peloponnese, a kind of home-grown mercenary. Unlike the Spartan aristocracy, the population generally was still increasing, and one of the old-established ways of escape from hunger at home was to hire oneself out as a mercenary abroad, where Greek soldiers had long been welcome. This was specially common among the Arcadians, who were poorer than most in agricultural land. The Sicilian tyrants were large employers of mercenaries, both in the early fifth century and in the fourth, and bodies of Greek soldiers were increasingly used, both by the Persian government and by rebels against it. Sparta's action helped to establish the habit of using mercenaries in internal Greek quarrels.

The other main source was the helots. The 700 whom Brasidas took with him to the north were still formally slaves; they were only liberated after their return home, when they were settled in a town which Sparta had recently taken over from the Eleans. It is to be noted that Brasidas' 700 must have been fully trained already when he set out from Sparta. About the same time, by what must have been a formal decision of the state, Sparta created a whole new class, called *neodamodeis* (literally 'new citizens', though it is quite certain that they received nothing like citizen rights). These were helots who were already liberated at the time when they were enrolled. For the next fifty years, they were a very important factor in Sparta's military effort. Some 3,000 of them were sent to Asia Minor in the course of the 390's, and this was certainly not the total number available. After her defeat at Leuctra in 371, when Sparta's still quite formidable power was no longer employed in distant expeditions, the *neodamodeis* disappear from the scene. The training-up of such numbers from a notoriously oppressed and ill-treated class looks like an appalling risk, though no doubt, in case of trouble, the Spartans could count on the *perioikoi* to support them. The mere prestige of the Spartans was also an important factor; maybe these privileged helots contrived to look down on their kinsmen in worse conditions.

Over these troops were set officers called harmosts, appointed *ad hoc* to lead a detached force of land troops or to command a garrison. These were evidently separate from the officers of the regular army, and it is not known how they were appointed. But already, in 424, Thucydides notes that the Spartans were concerned to see somehow

that officers of suitable calibre should be put in charge of the cities
Brasidas had taken over from Athens. Brasidas himself probably had
this title; certainly his subordinate officers did. In the later phases of
the war, and thereafter till 371, harmosts greatly multiplied in number
and function.

Beside all this Sparta had a specialised naval commander, annually
appointed. His existence, attested well before the Peloponnesian War,
shows that the Spartan fleet, while not comparable with the Athenian,
was still large enough to need regular provision for its command. In
the early years of the war, this admiral was sometimes employed to
command, not a naval squadron, but detachments of land troops; but
this unsatisfactory expedient soon gave way to the appointment of
harmosts. Towards the end of the war, when East Greece became the
main theatre of operations, the annual admiral became almost an
independent power on his own, too distant from the home authorities
to be kept under control in detail. Several of them are found playing
politics on their own account, most notably the formidable Lysander,
who for several years overshadowed all other Spartans, even the kings.

*

The main contenders in the Peloponnesian War were Athens and
Sparta, but it was formally a war between two leagues; and questions
arise about the nature of Greek leagues and alliances. The allies of
Sparta played a large part in bringing the war about in the first place;
the relations between Athens and her allies were of crucial importance
throughout, the question being whether Sparta could induce and support a large-scale revolt in the Athenian empire.

Though Sparta, no doubt, entered into alliances with other cities in
earlier times, the growth of her league may be dated from the moment
in the middle of the sixth century when she gave up the attempt to
annex and enslave Arcadian Tegea and made an alliance with her
instead. The term 'Peloponnesian League' is a modern term, the official
name of the organisation being simply and indeterminately 'the Spartans and their allies', though in literature the group is often called 'the
Peloponnesians'. It may have consisted, at the start, of a series of separate treaties with individual cities, with Sparta no doubt already the
dominant partner. But, by the end of the sixth century, probably as a
result of the difficulty Sparta had in carrying all her allies with her in

her campaign against Athens in 506, the League had acquired the rudiments of a constitution. Thucydides later refers to the 'ancient oaths' of the allies, that policy should be decided by a majority of the votes of the cities; and a clause like this presupposes some kind of general agreement. In fact, Herodotus reports, at the very end of the sixth century, a conference of the allies which actually rejected a plan put forward by the Spartans.

The procedure by which war was declared against Athens in 432 is described by Thucydides in fuller detail than we have for any other occasion. First the Corinthians, whose current grievances were the immediate cause of the proposal for war, brought a large number of allied delegations to Sparta; and they addressed the assembly, and thereafter retired while the Spartans made their own decision. Having themselves voted for war, the Spartans then summoned a formal conference of their allies and put the question to them. The effect was that neither party could commit the other to war against its will. The allies could not initiate policy except by informal representations, such as Corinth made on this occasion, but they could reject a proposition put to them by Sparta. Once war was declared, the command of the League forces and the whole strategic direction of the war devolved on Sparta. This was limited only by the extent to which the allies could offer persuasive argument to a council of war in the field, or exercise pressure by threatening to withdraw their contingent.

Sparta claimed that her allies, in contrast to those of Athens, retained their autonomy. So they did, in one sense of that much used and ambiguous word. The strength of the League depended on the military strength of its members; and, besides, Sparta had always a nervous eye on the possibility of a helot revolt in which she might need armed assistance. So she could never disarm her allies to the extent that Athens disarmed hers, and they retained that quite substantial bulwark of independence. Only a widespread revolt in favourable circumstances could enable rebels to face the technically superior Spartan army in battle. This occurred only when Sparta's prestige was for some reason at a low ebb, as for instance in the period of Sparta's comparative weakness after the Persian Wars (p. 64). Passive non-co-operation was easier, at least until Sparta was at leisure to deal with it. Thus, Elis quarrelled with Sparta in 420, stood out of the rest of the Peloponnesian War, and was brought back to obedience only after two years of war with Sparta in 402–400. But in general the allies submitted, as

Thucydides ironically puts it, to be coaxed into maintaining oligarchies of the type Sparta thought suitable. Spartan officers were appointed to oversee the mobilisation, and even the performance in the field, of the allied contingents, though these were formally under the command of their own generals.

The Athenian alliance, which we call the Confederacy of Delos, began in a quite different manner, springing suddenly into existence at the end of 478. In effect, it was a movement of revolt against Spartan leadership and the arrogance of the Spartan regent, Pausanias, though Sparta accepted the changed position and chose to regard her wartime alliance with Athens as still subsisting. In this case, we are told that the members swore 'to have the same friends and enemies', an established formula for offensive and defensive alliance, and these oaths were to last for ever, till the lumps of iron which they then dropped into the sea rose to the surface. Though the terms were thus generally expressed, it was understood that the main purpose of the association was to prosecute the war against Persia. The League had from the start at least as much of a constitution as the Peloponnesian League, and its procedure was on the same model: conferences of the allies, in which each city, large or small, had an equal vote, meeting (we do not know how regularly) on the island of Delos, where the Ionians worshipped Apollo. But the differences between the two Leagues were large, due mainly to the fact that the Athenian League was a naval organisation which needed funds to pay its rowers, and because Athens did not in the same way need the troops of its allies but rather gained strength by disarming them.

The power of Athens enormously exceeded that of any other single member. Though we have no record from the early years, it can be taken as certain that the Athenian assembly always voted separately on the issues before the League, having the same relation to the conference as Sparta to the conference of her allies. The financial contributions made by the allies were assessed, in the first instance, by the Athenian, Aristeides, to general satisfaction, and the League treasury was from the start in the hands of Athenian officials. Some cities, which had contributed their own men and ships to League campaigns, wearied of this and turned instead to paying money contributions, thereby putting themselves more into the power of Athens. Others revolted, and were forcibly brought back into the League on less favourable terms. By the middle of the fifth century, the process was far advanced, by which this League was turned into a more strictly political unit, the empire of Athens.

The Spartan and Athenian alliances were each centred on a single leader (*hegemon*) of disproportionate power, and the special position of the *hegemon* governed the whole structure of the organisation. This was not in principle resented, as was shown when Athens founded her second Confederacy in 378. That was inaugurated with a flourish of propaganda, in which Athens abjured the oppressive practices of her fifth-century empire. The second League contained an interesting constitutional innovation, in the permanent council of allied delegates which sat in Athens and presented its resolutions to the Athenian assembly in parallel with those of Athens' own Council of Five Hundred. But Athens abated nothing of her sovereignty, nor was she asked to. The members were apparently, for the time, content that the Athenian assembly should have the last word. The League of Corinth, set up by Philip after his victory in 338, was another hegemonic League, with Philip at its head, a position guaranteed to his successors and taken up by Alexander. But this was in effect simply a political organisation for the Macedonian control of Greece, with some interesting features but never willingly accepted by the member cities.

The hegemonic principle might seem a suitable means to facilitate the unification of Greece under a single leader, but in fact it did not work in this way. The Spartan League worked in reasonable harmony while it was mainly confined to its original Peloponnesian members, and while the fear of Argos within the Peloponnese, or of Athens from outside it, united the allies under Sparta's protection. When victory over Athens left most of the old Athenian empire on Sparta's hands, the old form of alliance was no longer practicable. Conferences to include all these numerous and distant cities as voting members would have been quite unmanageable. So Sparta took to commanding rather than consulting, and in the process she offended her old allies as much as her new gains. The second Athenian League similarly prospered while its members were united by common fear of Sparta and dislike of her methods of rule, but faltered when Sparta became an ally instead of a unifying enemy. The Greek cities would unite against their strongest leader, but not under the predominant city.

Meanwhile, some civilising forces were at work. It is clear from the writings of the classical period that, by the late fifth century, no state in southern Greece would openly take up arms in confessed aggression.

but needed for its own comfort some colourable pretext of self-defence. Defensive alliances for mutual protection became the rule. The aspiration of the fourth century towards a 'common peace', which should embrace all Greek cities and guarantee their autonomy, always foundered on the excessive claims of the state which found itself for the time militarily dominant. But the aspiration was there, and, if no system of sanctions was ever worked out, the need for one was in some small degree recognised. But this was a movement towards secure autonomy for the multiple, independent cities, which the Greeks saw as the only form of political organisation that suited them, not a movement towards national unification.

*

So the citizen armies of the fourth century wore themselves out to no great purpose in their indecisive wars. The Thebans, for all their victories in the decade from 371 to 362, were never widely accepted as the leaders of Greece. Militarily, they were brought to a standstill when their neighbours and enemies, the Phocians, seized Delphi and used the temple treasures to hire mercenaries at 50% over the standard rate of pay. The growth of mercenary forces was noted as one of the great evils of the time. The publicist, Isocrates, saw them mostly as a moral evil, disturbing what peace there was in Greece, to be dealt with by turning them to the east against the Persian empire. The spectacular march of Xenophon's Ten Thousand to the sea aroused large hopes by its demonstration of the vulnerability of Persia. It was almost as striking that, in the wars which Persia waged against independent Egypt from 404 to 343, both sides depended heavily on Greek troops and Greek commanders. The expense of mercenary forces was not easily borne. The Phocian windfall was an exception and did not last long; and the sacrilege of seizing temple treasures was no light matter—a little earlier, the Arcadians had drawn back from a proposal to make similar use of the treasures of Olympia. Athens, in the middle of the fourth century, had trouble enough in financing even citizen armies, and her generals only too often had to interrupt their campaigns to collect money by one means or another. Mercenaries, further, are notoriously more interested in their pay than in the causes for which they are hired to fight, though we do not hear of that evil, familiar from Italian history, the reluctance of mercenary armies to fight very strenuously against one another.

From a fairly early date in the fourth century, we find respectable Athenian generals hiring themselves out to eastern employers, when they were politically out of favour or had no satisfactory occupation at home. There was criticism of king Agesilaus of Sparta when, at the end of his life, he tried to raise money for his city by taking service with a king of Egypt, whom he then betrayed to a rival. Rootless mercenary captains built themselves small empires in the service of Thracian kings, and Demosthenes fiercely denounced the favours granted by Athens to one of these, who was made a citizen as a step to his employment by the city as a general. All this was a symptom of the fact that there was no longer any cause much worth fighting for in Greece.

Many of Demosthenes' speeches rebuke the city more generally for its reliance on mercenaries and the reluctance of the citizens to serve themselves in the city's wars. These strictures have been taken too literally by many historians, concerned about the decadence of Athens, and not recognising that Demosthenes was using all the powers of his rhetoric to persuade the city to a policy of all-out resistance to Macedon, for which the city was not yet ready. When there was a cause to fight for, the military effort was still made by the citizens themselves, Athens included, whether against Philip of Macedon or in later struggles for freedom. The loss of impetus that shows itself in the fourth-century history of Greece was primarily a political matter, not a matter of the fighting spirit of its inhabitants. Battles produced no worthwhile result. The last sentence of Xenophon's *Greek History* remarks, despairingly, that all had hoped for a clear decision from the battle of Mantineia in 362, but that after the battle there was more confusion and uncertainty than before.

CHAPTER 9

Government and law-courts

THE DOCTRINE OF the separation of powers had no place in Greek constitutional theory or practice. The councils and assemblies which passed the laws and took decisions of policy were also, for some purposes, courts of law. When at Athens separate law-courts developed, their very large juries were usually addressed as if they were themselves the assembled people; and they were, in fact, representative sections of it. The executive magistrates were usually also judges, and they had an active part in the proceedings of the legislative body. The somewhat rudimentary administration of public business was mainly in the hands of magistrates, but at Athens a very large part of this business was conducted before the council or actually by it. The evidence for the character of these institutions, for the way in which they were regarded, for the way they influenced events, is, as always, fullest for Athens; but in these spheres there is also a fair amount of information about the exceptional position of Sparta.

The character of the city's constitution was determined by, or displayed in, the composition of its assembly. In democracy, all free adult males were entitled to vote in the assembly; and though in practice, in classical Athens, it was unlikely that more than one in eight would attend any particular meeting, it was still of fundamental importance that all had the right and could on occasion attend. Oligarchies restricted their franchise by some sort of property qualification. Sparta had also a property qualification, in the sense that a citizen had to be able to pay his dues in kind to his mess; but there, there was the further restriction, that no man could become a citizen unless he had been through the very rigorous training to which the Spartan youth was subjected.

The council varied accordingly. The Athenian Council of Five Hundred, chosen annually by lot from candidates in some way preselected, was a suitable model for a democratic state. Oligarchies tended to have a smaller and stronger body, however appointed; or a board too small to be called a council at all, magistrates with a title which implied that they had the functions elsewhere discharged by a council. The most archaic type of all was the body of elderly men holding office for the remainder of their lives, like the *gerousia* of Sparta, or the venerable relic which survived beside the democratic Council at Athens, the Areopagus, into which the principal magistrates passed on completion of their year of office. By the middle of the fifth century, this last had lost all its old functions except the trial of murder cases.

How these institutions came into being is hidden in the mists of the dark age. The Spartan *gerousia* numbered thirty members, the two kings and twenty-eight others chosen by acclamation from Spartans over the age of sixty, holding office till they died. The numbers of this council, and the part which they and the people were to play in taking decisions of state, form the main subject of the archaic document called the Great Rhetra, preserved by Plutarch with some comment derived from Aristotle: the *gerousia* was to propose motions, but the decision on any proposal was to depend on the vote of the people. All this was attributed to the remote reforms of Lycurgus, and some historians maintain today that he fixed the functions of council and assembly early in the ninth century. This is a period about which it is not easy to speak with much conviction, but it would be surprising if it saw the introduction of political machinery, articulated like this. The alternative, which most historians would now prefer, is to date the relevant reforms somewhere in the seventh century. The surviving poems of Tyrtaeus, who wrote to spur the Spartan army on to greater effort during the long seventh-century revolt of Messenia, include a rendering of a Delphic oracle which, in fact, paraphrases the basic clauses of the prose Rhetra. Though the context of these verses is not certainly known and currently much disputed, they justify the belief that the reform embodied in the Rhetra is somehow connected with the Messenian revolt. Tyrtaeus evidently did not mention the name of Lycurgus, and this legendary figure may be ignored.

Though Plutarch in his interpretation of the Rhetra treats it as a document primarily concerned with the establishment of the *gerousia*, it must be assumed that for contemporaries its importance resided at least as much in the establishment of the principle that the people were to have the final decision on the proposals laid before them. It must be remembered that the Spartan 'people', though the term excluded all the numerous free *perioikoi*, was still a large body, probably not less than the 8,000 which Herodotus gives as his estimate for the year 480, and very likely more. The grant of political power to so large a body was a very wide concession for the seventh century. There are signs that Sparta suffered from unrest at the time of the Messenian revolt. Tyrtaeus' verses are evidence enough that the morale of the army was not good, and Aristotle found in his poems evidence that there was a clamour for redistribution of land at the time. Similar troubles were the cause of tyranny elsewhere at this same time, but Sparta never had a tyranny. Perhaps her answer was to give a share of power to the class which might have supported a tyrant, roughly speaking, the hoplite army.

It is not likely that so large a concession would be made without safeguards. The safeguard, embodied in the main clauses of the Rhetra, is that the initiative remains with the council, which alone has the right to put a proposal forward. This is a pattern that became very general in Greece: the preliminary deliberation of the council is called *probouleusis*, and this whole system, whereby the initiative remained with the council and the final decision lay with the assembly, has been called the probouleutic system of government. The Spartan Rhetra is the first evidence of the operation of such a system; and it is possible that it was actually invented in Sparta in the seventh century, and copied by other states from there. In Sparta itself, there was a further safeguard, in a rider said to have been added later to the Rhetra, which gave the *gerousia* power to set aside a 'crooked' decision of the people. Whatever the precise meaning of this, it was not copied outside Sparta, and indeed there is no certain evidence that it was put into practice there.

At Athens, there is no indication that any section of the citizens had ever been formally excluded from the assembly; though no doubt, in early times, the inferior members knew their place and left it to their betters to conduct the business. When Cylon tried to make himself tyrant about 632[1] and seized the Acropolis, the people were summoned to besiege him there. But when the siege prolonged itself the main body departed, leaving it to the archons to finish the matter off. This was, in a sense, an act of the assembled people, though of a people still somewhat passive in the hands of its magistrates. In 594, Solon sum-

1. The attempt was made in the year of an Olympic festival, but we do not know exactly which: 636 or 628 would also be possible dates.

moned a meeting to which he outlined his programme of reform. This was a revolutionary, rather than a regular, meeting, but its intervention was effective; and thereafter the assembly was a factor which could not be neglected. Solon set up a new probouleutic Council of Four Hundred to prepare business for the assembly. Plutarch says that he intended this as a constitutional brake, and refers to a metaphor used by Solon in which the two councils, the old Areopagus and his new Four Hundred, are the two anchors of the ship of state. This makes sense in the context. The revolutionary intervention of the people might be condoned when it led to the appointment of a reformer so consciously humane and moderate as himself, but it had its evident dangers. On another occasion, it might in its excitement force through some less suitable decision. Before Solon died, he had seen that his check was insufficient to prevent the assembly from voting Peisistratus a bodyguard, the first step towards his tyranny.

With individual variations, the probouleutic pattern spread widely in Greece. In early days, when the idea of entrusting final decision to a large assembly was new, the value of the council as a safeguard against rash decision may have been uppermost in the minds of Greek statesmen, such as the Spartan reformers or Solon. As the system established itself, this aspect of it mostly retreated into the background and other features became more prominent. There was evident technical advantage in having public business dealt with in two stages, not by one single immediate decision, and the advantage increased as public business grew more complicated. The council could also be given other functions than its share in the process of taking decisions and passing laws: at Athens, in particular, it became the main administrative body in the state.

The development naturally varied from place to place. At Athens, the council was a large body. Since Cleisthenes' reforms of 507, it consisted of 500 ordinary citizens over the age of thirty, chosen by lot and holding office for one year only; a man might serve a second term, but no more. Being a councillor took a lot of time, and, though the developed democracy paid its councillors, it did not pay them very much. No really poor man would want to serve, and it may well be that the lowest of the four Solonian income-classes, the large mass called *thetes*, was formally ineligible. With the growth of Athens' population in the later fifth century, there would have been no difficulty in finding enough councillors from the other three classes, roughly the hoplites and above; but it might have been harder when Cleisthenes first instituted his Five Hundred, and impossible without the provision for a second term. The effect would be to give a high proportion of these classes experience of service on the Council, a valuable political training.

The Council was, deliberately, not an august body of privileged persons with great prestige, but a cross-section of the assembly itself; and it was too large to transact business of any complexity except through committees. Very naturally, the assembly dominated here, coming in the course of time to amend very freely the proposals put before it, or to tack on additions unrelated to the proposal, or even, in the end, to instruct the Council to bring forward a particular proposition and lay it before the next assembly. Thus, in politics, the Council of the classical period had not retained the initiative which its formal position appears to give it. But its administrative duties multiplied, including the review of all kinds of accounts from special boards—commissioners for naval construction, officials in charge of festivals, endless others—besides what the Council administered directly itself. The press of business, especially at the height of Athens' imperial power in the late fifth century, was very great, and the congestion notorious. But what was done was done by the Council, and that was its most important task at Athens.

In oligarchies generally, so far as we can tell—oligarchies did not, like the Athenians, commit their decrees and their accounts to stone—much more political business was kept in the hands of the council or equivalent authority and there was less recourse to an assembly. Indeed, it seems likely that much more of the business was settled privately behind the scenes. Sparta is here something of an exception, in that the *gerousia* makes curiously little appearance in the narrative of political events, none at all in the history of Thucydides (432–411), and only marginally more in Xenophon's (411–362), whereas debates in the assembly are mentioned fairly often and were evidently important. The *gerousia* certainly continued to exercise its probouleutic function. Indeed, at a critical moment in the revolutionary period of the third century, it refused to put before the assembly the reforms proposed by king Agis IV. But it seems that, in general, this venerable body of very elder statesmen was not effective in its formal political function. But it was the most important law-court in Sparta, and all cases involving the more extreme penalties, death or exile or loss of civic rights, were reserved to it. The great prestige which the *gerousia* evidently continued to enjoy may be traced mainly to its judicial aspect.

*

The magistrates of the Greek states came into being as the king's original power was subdivided, or abolished altogether. Their place in the framework is basically the same everywhere, in spite of the very diverse titles which they bore. These have exercised the ingenuity of ancient and modern etymologists. There might be simple titles like *archon* at Athens and elsewhere, which means in the flattest sense 'ruler'; or more individual ones like *ephoros* at Sparta, probably an 'overseer'; down to the 'umpire' and the 'colleagues of the musicians' at Miletus, if those are fair translations. Whatever they were called, these appear all to be officers of the aristocracies which took over political power from the kings in the course of the dark age, subdividing the powers which had been united in the person of the king. Wherever we have any real information, they appear also as judicial officers.

At Athens the head of the state was simply 'the' archon, or *archon eponymos* (because he gave his name to the year).[1] The 'king' retained, with the title *basileus*, the performance of certain traditional state sacrifices and other rituals, but he was an annual officer, too, with secular duties. The polemarch commanded in war; and when he lost that function early in the fifth century, he was distinguishable as the magistrate with whom foreigners had to deal. There were six *thesmothetai*, as well, whose name ought perhaps to mean that they once created law, though tradition said that their function was to put it on record. This college of nine archons could deal with most of the political and administrative business of archaic Athens; and they divided the judicial business between their courts by categories, giving their own final verdict till Solon allowed appeal to the people.

After the reforms of Cleisthenes the archons' influence declined. By a further reform in 487, they were appointed by lot from candidates put forward from the tribes. Thereafter, though some prestige remained with the office, and it was still filled from the two richest classes, it was

1. Until the practice was established of numbering years from a fixed point, as we do, the only way of identifying a year in the past was by means of an 'eponymous' magistrate, 'the year when X was archon' (or 'ephor', etc.).

no longer the prize most sought after in politics. Instead, the general-ship described above (p. 158) became the principal vehicle for the exercise of political power. In 462, the archons lost the substance of their judicial powers as well. Besides these higher magistrates, the developed democracy of Athens proliferated minor officials with special duties, to examine the accounts of outgoing magistrates, oversee the market, and so forth.

The proceedings of oligarchies are, as usual, less easy to trace. On the political side, it may be worth mentioning the interesting federal constitution adopted by the Boeotian League in 446. The cities of Boeotia were given uniform oligarchic constitutions with a property qualification—this is, as it happens, the earliest explicit mention of property qualifications in an oligarchy. The city had four councils, of which each in turn acted as the probouleutic body; a joint meeting of the other three acted as the assembly. For federal purposes, the country was divided into eleven districts, roughly equal in population, though one might contain three or four cities while Thebes formed two districts by itself. Each district elected one of the federal magistrates, called boeotarchs, and sixty members to the federal council, sent a fixed quota of troops to the federal army, and so forth. This was a highly unusual essay in representative government, and the intention was pre-sumably to give due weight to each component part of the country and avoid mere domination by the largest city, Thebes. This intention was largely frustrated. A chance remark of Thucydides shows the weight which these arrangements gave *de facto* to the federal magis-trates. They normally expected (he says) to get their way without too much explanation with the federal council (which like the city councils was divided into four). On this occasion, in 420, the councillors for once took it into their heads to resist, but it is clear that normally the boeotarchs effectively controlled the actions of the League. Nothing is known of their judicial arrangements, except that there was a federal court to which the districts contributed judges.

Sparta, once more, is the exception. The situation there was com-plicated by the retention of hereditary kingship. Sparta had, not a single king, but two kings at once, the title descending independently in two distinct families: the origins of this unique arrangement are quite unknown. As elsewhere, the kings had lost much of their originally unrestricted power. Xenophon perhaps shows us something of the process when he describes the oath that was still, in his time, sworn every month between the kings and the powerful magistrates called ephors. The kings swore that they would keep the laws; the ephors, on behalf of the city, that they would preserve the privileges of the kings as long as they kept their oaths. Here the ephors, a magistracy set up beside the monarchy and not in replacement of it, appear as the agents of the city as against the kings. This looks to be a relic of some early bargain by which a constitution was imposed. The wholly abnormal fact about Sparta is that the kings retained, not only certain religious duties and some minor legal jurisdiction, but the effective command of the army, a sphere where it could be highly dangerous to trust to inherited talent. The assembly determined which of the two kings was to go out on any particular campaign; but, once the king was across the border in command of the army, he had complete freedom to fight, or even to negotiate, limited only by the knowledge that if he made a serious mistake he might be put on trial on his return. At home, his formal power was almost restricted to his *ex officio* membership of the *gerousia*; but, for all the restrictions, an aura of majesty still hung around the kingship, which was unusual in Greek society. These were assets which an able king could use.

The ephors were five in number, chosen annually from and by the whole citizen body. Their executive powers were unusually wide even for the magistrates of an oligarchy; and they divided judicial business between them by categories, as the archons did at Athens. They have been credited, in ancient and modern times alike, with an influence over the course of Spartan history even greater than they actually possessed. There are various causes for this—the range of their actual powers, and the fact that they were the authority with whom any foreign envoy had first to deal when he came to Sparta. Besides this, the general secretiveness of Sparta about her own concerns fostered the notion that there was some continuous and sinister influence at work all the time. In fact, it makes no sense to attribute a continuous policy to the ephorate, as such. The annual board must normally have reflected the policies dominant at the time of its election, modified for the ephors, as for the electorate, by whatever had happened in the interval before they took office or during their term. One board might noticeably differ in policy from its predecessor, nor need the board of any one year be unanimous. But the annual board itself might indeed take action, to some degree on its own initiative, which seriously affected the state's line of policy.

The ephors had extensive police powers. These looked specially formidable to outsiders, who were impressed by their right to arrest even the king in an emergency, though they could not hold him for long without trial. They were in various ways responsible for holding down the helots. They received foreign envoys in the first instance, and decided whether their requests should be forwarded to council and assembly. When an army was sent out, the ephors decided how many age-groups should be called up, and when the army should be sent out. This was a large degree of executive latitude, and it might be put to political use. Thus, in 403, when Lysander had been sent to support the oligarchy of the Thirty at Athens and was doing so with complete success, a majority of the ephors acceded to king Pausanias' request to be sent to Athens with a further army; and, once there, he acted on a policy diametrically opposed to Lysander's. The question of the final settlement with Athens was in the end remitted to the Spartan assembly (which supported Pausanias), so that the constitutional proprieties were in this sense preserved; but the initiative of the ephors certainly made a practical difference of great import to the way in which events developed. They had other powers too, as the main executive of the state, but it is not always easy to distinguish between action which they took in execution of decisions arrived at by the assembly and action which they took on their own responsibility.

They attended sessions of the *gerousia*, either of right or as a matter of habit and convenience. There is an obvious advantage in having the executive officers present at the discussion of policies which they will have to implement: for instance, the generals at Athens commonly attended meetings of the Council. The ephors also presided over meetings of the assembly, conducted its business, and put questions to the vote. That might give them a considerable advantage. Xenophon several times describes an action of the Spartan state as the action of 'the ephors and assembly'. Though that may not be formally quite correct, it probably comes nearer to reality than if he had said (as he never does) 'the *gerousia* and assembly'.

Athens, in contrast, was extravagantly careful to avoid putting such matters into the hands of a chairman with any long tenure. Originally, though no text says so, we may presume that the archon had presided over the assembly; though when Cleisthenes proposed his reforms in 507 the archon, his enemy Isagoras, was evidently unable to prevent him. The classical procedure was more complicated. The Council of

Five Hundred was broken up into ten tribal sections of fifty, and each such section had more particular charge of the state's business for one-tenth of the year. Within the section in charge, in the fifth century, a smaller committee chose every day a chairman for a single day, who presided over Council or assembly if they met on his day. In the fourth century another set of complications was evolved, not of a kind to enhance the authority of the chair. As so often, the democracy was determined to eliminate any chance of any man exercising undue influence, even at the risk that an important meeting would fall into the hands of an inexperienced, and possibly incompetent, chairman. It says much for the generally law-abiding ways of the citizen body that things did not get out of hand more often. There was a disastrous occasion, in 406, when the people's feelings erupted against the generals who had just won the victory of Arginusae over the Spartans. They shouted down all mention of constitutional safeguards and insisted on condemning to death by a single immediate vote six of these generals. But such things were rare, and this was very much the worst of them.

There are other aspects of the Athenian magistracies which demonstrate this characteristic distrust of special influence and the degree to which control was kept in the hands of Council and assembly. Any magistrate could be relieved of his office in the course of his term if his conduct was found unsatisfactory at a monthly review. There was no hierarchy of magistrates at Athens, the junior receiving his instructions from the senior and reporting to him afterwards: instead, all magistrates dealt directly with Council and assembly on their own account. This is in marked contrast with the practice of Sparta, where the ephors exercised a general authority over all other officers of the state.

*

The administration of justice developed along a similar path, by distributing functions which had originally been united in the person of the king. In the beginning, the law was what the king made of it; his judgments were the visible emanation of the wisdom implanted in him by Zeus, the king of the gods. His successors, the aristocrats, claimed a similar inspiration, or licence. Traditional custom naturally counted for much, but we know from elsewhere how very unstable that can be in the absence of a written text. Hesiod's complaints show how little the Boeotian princes of his day could be relied on. In these circumstances, any sort of certainty is an advance, and the first important stage for Greece was to get the law written down at all, even if some early Greek law was harsh enough.

The cities of Crete had a high reputation for their laws. The earliest scraps inscribed on stone come from Dreros in Crete in the late seventh century—the clearest is a brief constitutional amendment, of no great interest in itself, though it must have been controversial at the time—and there is some general probability that laws would have been written down on more tractable material before they were committed to stone. The needs of new communities, like the colonies overseas, will have encouraged codification. A community making a new start, with no tradition behind it but what the colonists brought with them from their homeland, would clearly have more need for a fixed code, especially where the colonists were not all of the same origin. Zaleucus of Locri, on the south coast of Italy, was reputed to have been one of the first to produce a written code at all, and he may really have produced his laws in the middle of the seventh century. They had the name of being both precise and very severe, as did those of his more famous successor, Charondas of Catana. It was an Athenian tradition that the lawgiver, Dracon, had codified their law in the late seventh century, but in such uncompromisingly harsh terms that Solon, a little later, repealed all but his law of murder. Some of that law remains, but otherwise nothing but a few stray words quoted, barely enough to show whether Dracon did produce a really comprehensive code. But there is no doubt about Solon, whose laws survived in full, written on great balks of wood, which were still on show in Hellenistic Athens. Commentaries were written on them by Hellenistic scholars, and the scraps that are quoted show that this was a code with a genuinely wide range. Sparta, on the other hand, had no written code at all—the revered Lycurgus was supposed to have forbidden written laws—and Aristotle, in the fourth century, complains of the danger of allowing the ephors, who might be worthless persons, to administer a traditional oral law with no check from any other authority.

Nothing like full detail is found till we reach the developed system of classical Athens, as it is revealed in law-court speeches and other sources. We may gain some insight into what preceded this from the so-called Code of Gortyn in Crete. Though this is an extensive document, carved on the curved wall of a building which still partly stands, it does not cover any single subject fully. It appears to be the result of a large-scale revision of the law of the city; amendments in a number of spheres are set out fairly systematically, but they presuppose, all through, knowledge of the existing law, which this revision only supplemented or amended. The inscription belongs to the middle of the fifth century, but the society for which it was made was less developed than contemporary Athens, and the 'Code' thus gives us a picture of a more archaic stage of the city's development.

Justice is here administered by a figure who is simply called 'the judge', with no indication what sort of person he was or how appointed —though contemporary inscriptions, here and elsewhere in Crete, show that the regular magistrates did have judicial duties. Perhaps the most striking point for us is the extent to which these laws consist of instructions to be followed mechanically by this judge. There are two distinct formulae: one tells the judge what verdict and penalty are required by particular circumstances, which may include the fact that there are witnesses available, or that the parties or their supporters are willing to swear an oath; while the other formula tells him to make his own decision after swearing an oath himself. The fixed penalties are no doubt a relic of the time, like that of which Hesiod complains, when law in the hands of the aristocracy was merely arbitrary and the prime need was to secure some kind of uniformity. The high value set on a solemn oath, usually in the name of the city's special god, calling down destruction on the swearer and his posterity if he is lying, may be regarded as another survival from primitive times. It continued to command attention, in spite of perjury, and in spite of the fact, which distressed Plato, that a case might open with two oaths, sworn by the opposing parties, one of which must be false. To challenge one's opponent to an oath could be useful to a litigant at all periods, damaging to him if he refused, not fatal to the challenger if he accepted.

In archaic Athens, the judicial machinery consisted of the Council of the Areopagus, descended from the king's council, and the courts of the archons. The first breach in this system was made by Solon, in 594, when he allowed appeal from the decision of an archon to the assembly sitting as a law-court. In this later theorists saw, with a large measure of justification, the origin of a democratic regime far beyond anything Solon can have contemplated. The full assembly was, however, a cumbrous instrument; and so, by stages that we cannot follow in detail, a court was established which was separate from the assembly, in that its members were in some way selected from the whole citizen body. Out of this, the reforms of Ephialtes in 462 created something which was essentially new. Appeal to a wider court, formerly at the discretion of the party who felt aggrieved, now became automatic, so that the appeal court became the court of first instance. The archon no longer delivered a verdict, but held only a preliminary hearing, at which the depositions of witnesses were taken and the relevant laws were cited. The whole thing was then sealed up and delivered to the court, where the archon presided but took no substantive part in the proceedings at all.

A similar procedure was followed when a case came into court as the result of dissatisfaction with an arbitrator's award. The Greeks made extensive use of arbitration, private and public. At Athens, from the end of the fifth century, there was a regular body of public arbitrators, drawn annually from the age-group at the end of their liability to military service, the men of sixty. Civil suits had to be submitted, in the first instance, to an arbitrator from this panel, presumably in order to lighten the burden on the courts. If he could bring the parties to agree, that ended the matter: if not, he heard them both and delivered his award. If either then preferred to go to court, the documents of the case were sealed up, the two sides separately, and delivered with the award to the court. There, the litigants were not allowed to depart from the case they had put to the arbitrator.

The verdict now depended on the majority vote of a large body of jurors—always to be reckoned in hundreds, and the number might rise to thousands—who also assessed the penalty where this was not fixed by law. They were selected for the particular case from a panel of 6,000, annually reviewed. The selection was by lot, and this and the large numbers were, among other things, a precaution against bribery. But the main point was to put the administration of justice into the hands of ordinary men; and the small payment of two obols, introduced by Pericles about the time of Ephialtes' reform and subsequently raised to three, was presumably meant to make it easier for the common man to serve. Democracy, as it developed, moved steadily away from the concept that public affairs of any kind needed a special expertise, and preferred to seek safety and common sense in large numbers and the use of the lot.

Athenian law made some distinction between public and private cases, but it did not make it very clearly; and the distinction is not the same as that between civil and criminal cases in modern systems. There was no public prosecutor, and for the prosecution of offences against the state Athens relied on the initiative of private persons. Patriotism might, with luck, be part of their motive; but it is was more likely that the prosecutor had some private interest, if only the satisfaction of personal or political enmity. The worst feature of the system, often seen in other systems of the same type, was the growth of a class of professional informers, called in Athens 'sycophants'—the word has changed its meaning since—who were notorious for blackmailing the rich with the threat of bringing a public charge against them. In other cases where today the police would be concerned, the matter was left to the party who had suffered injury, or to a third party acting on his behalf.

In private suits, the matter brought into court consisted in principle of the depositions made by the witnesses at the archon's preliminary hearing, or before the arbitrator; and of the relevant laws, read to the court by the official clerk, who stopped the water-clock while he read. This was a jar with a narrow spout at its base, which measured the time allowed to each litigant for his address to the jury. He was compelled to conduct the case for himself, but the practice became regular of having a speech written for one by a professional. It is these speeches, preserved as models of style and skill, that survive for our information. He might also be supported by the speeches of influential friends, according to his own importance and that of the case.

These are the outlines of the system which resulted from Ephialtes' reform. But for contemporaries its most striking feature was that it curtailed the activities of the Council of the Areopagus, leaving it only the duty of judging cases of murder, arson, and the destruction of sacred olive-stumps. It is certain that the judicial as well as the political functions of the Areopagus had once been much greater, but we do not know how the judicial duties were divided between it and the archons. But the question of murder is important, for private violence has everywhere been the toughest problem of law for societies emerging into a more stable and sophisticated civilisation. For classical Greece, it was complicated by a strong feeling about the pollution (*miasma*) created by murder, endangering anyone who received a killer into his house, and even the city which sheltered him, however unwittingly. The blood-feud flourished in early Greece. Homer provides instances enough of heroes on the run, even after accidental killing, to take refuge from the dead man's family with a king who will purify and protect them—though for Homer the purification does not take up so much emotional room as it did later. Accidental homicide remained a matter for the family to settle with the killer, but there was never a regular tariff like the *wergeld* of Germanic law, the price varying with the victim's status.

In murder, the irremediable nature of the act and the religious feeling about pollution made it both more necessary and, to that extent, easier for the state to intervene between the parties. At Athens, we have the text of part of Dracon's seventh-century law on murder, the part which deals with unpremeditated homicide, showing that by that time distinctions about the intention of the killer had already been made. The classical Areopagus met in the open air, to avoid bringing under a roof one who might prove to be a murderer; the archon called 'king' presided without his usual garland; after solemn oaths, the accuser spoke from the 'Stone of Resentment', and the accused from the 'Stone of Violence'; and so forth. Subsidiary courts show their picturesque features, like the court by the sea, where an exile might plead from a boat that his homicide was not wilful, or the court which tried inanimate objects which had caused accidental death. It was mainly religious feeling that conserved these customs, and indeed preserved the Areopagus itself at a time when its political powers could no longer be tolerated.

Already, in the archaic period, the principle was established at Athens that violence, even in less lethal forms, was an offence against the state; and, more generally, that a man who felt he had suffered injury to himself or his property must proceed duly by law, and not, as in more primitive times, take what remedy he could by his own effort. Democrats in the classical period, like the supporters of other constitutions, liked to boast that their system rested on the rule of law. The peaceful possession and transmission of property was early a concern of state. The date of the institution of the archon's oath is disputed; but in classical times his first official action was to proclaim that, whatever property a man then held, he should hold securely till the archon laid down his office.

Much less is known about the administration of justice in other cities. The Athenian jury system did not easily spread to cities without her democratic bias. Otherwise, the development through the archaic period was, no doubt, pretty much the same all over. Originally, everything was in the king's hand: the remission of some cases to his council was a natural development, easily hardening into a rule; his direct jurisdiction was as naturally inherited by his successors, the aristocratic magistrates. The distribution between kings and *gerousia* and ephors at Sparta has been mentioned already. With variations in detail, similar development may be presumed elsewhere.

But it would be a mistake to search for a coherent and unified system of Greek law. These numerous small societies had much in common, in their situation and their traditions, and some degree of generalisation is permissible about their habits of procedure or their attitude to the matters which law takes into cognisance. But they still developed in sufficient isolation to breed a whole series of different systems. To take a conspicuous instance, already mentioned, the rules about female or slave property, and about succession through an heiress, were markedly different in Athens, Gortyn and Sparta; and one is not entitled to call one variant more 'Greek' than another.

Wherever there is any large store of information, we are tempted to try to elicit general principles. But Athens is not by any means a fair sample, since its mere size and its development as a commercial centre, with the untidiness of its laws, had led by the time of the great orators to quite uncharacteristic complications. That large monument of Plato's old age, the *Laws*, which covers a wide range of human activities and professes to deal with the real, not the ideal, world, drew much of its detail from existing systems. But Plato's results are those of an imperious social reformer, not those of an enquiry into the principles which underlay the law as it stood. The mere fact that Aristotle and Theophrastus went to great lengths to assemble collections of Greek laws and customs, now almost wholly lost, shows that they expected to find an instructive diversity. Nor must help be sought from that temptingly copious source, the papyri of Hellenistic and Roman Egypt, for, though the language may be Greek, and some of the terms familiar, the underlying system was an inheritance from the Egypt of the Pharaohs, and anything but Greek.

Even the elucidation of Athenian law is hampered by the fact that law somehow failed to attract the same amount of intellectual attention that it did at Rome, and practice did not call for the formation of a body of expert lawyers. There was, indeed, one stimulus to expertise, in that respect for tradition had conserved the Solonian code of 594 as the basis of law in the fourth century, in spite of the archaic language which made much of it unintelligible to the ordinary man. We have hints in Aristophanes' comedies that a bright young man who wished to get on in public life would do well to study these hard words. But the linguistic obstacle did not here foster a class of expert interpreters, and Athens remained content with that imprecision of legal language and concepts which often makes it hard to discover what had been happening, and sometimes even what was at stake, in the more complicated property cases. The root cause is that distrust of experts, which was not by any means confined to the less educated classes in the democracy of Athens. They preferred to leave such issues to the common-sense and humanity of their juries, and legal science is perhaps one of the sacrifices which Athens made to the spirit of democracy.

*

That distrust of experts and confidence in the collective judgment of ordinary men was the essence of democracy. Its political decisions were taken after noisy debate in the primary assembly, which all could attend if they chose. That in itself meant that there could be no 'government' in our sense in Athens, no organised group to which power was delegated over long periods, as in modern systems, where the electorate is consulted only at election times, and has no control over the government in the intervals between elections. At Athens, no man exercised power longer than he could persuade the assembly that his views were right, and he had to go on convincing the same or a slightly different audience, time after time, without respite. Distrust of experts did not mean mere preference for ignorance. Xenophon, no fanatical democrat but an admirer of Sparta, ascribes to Socrates the statement that a man who wished to exert political influence at Athens must learn his trade, for the people would not listen to one who had not got the necessary facts at his fingertips. That must, in a measure, be true, or Athens could never have managed her complex public business at all. But it does not mean that the Athenians ran their affairs by the light of pure reason. The politician had to persuade ordinary men that he was right; and the medium was the spoken word, rhetoric in the full sense of the term, including a knowledge of the crowd's moods and how to influence them.

In all these circumstances, it is not altogether easy to locate the true centres of power in Athens, apart from the overriding fact that the decision of the sovereign assembly was final whenever it was invoked. The functions of government were certainly not performed by the

Council of Five Hundred, whose composition was altogether too random, its numbers too great, its mechanism too carefully tailored to democratic theory. To a limited extent, a war might be run by the generals, who had the advantage of some corporate continuity, in that the board for the year always included some who had served in previous years. They were capable, at times, of using the armed forces according to plans which the assembly knew nothing about. But their opportunities for independent action were not enormous, even in the military sphere, quite apart from the danger of prosecution if their plans went wrong. Their position gave them some initial advantage in dealing with the people, and there was no office of greater influence that a man could hold; but still they had to go on convincing the citizens that their advice was good. That was the only road to precarious success, and it was taken mainly by men without office, the quite informal group variously called the 'demagogues' (never a friendly word) or the 'orators'; or later by a descriptive participle which recognises that these men were, more than ordinary citizens, 'the politicians' of Athens.

The risks the esvolunteers took were no less than those taken by the generals, for misleading the people was a charge that could be and was formally preferred in the courts. Thucydides and others sometimes protest against the illogicality of punishing the proposer when there was no penalty for having voted for the proposal. But it was never likely to be otherwise—nor should it have been, for the professionals did claim to be wiser and to know more than the average voter, and the rewards of the career could be considerable. That, indeed, was the standard charge made by the opposition, more especially that the demagogues made money out of the war. But some of the money was legitimately earned, and public opinion did not blame the acceptance, within limits, of money for political services rendered.

To get this down to scale, it must be kept in mind that the vast bulk of the business before the assembly was neither very exciting nor concerned with high constitutional principle. Some of it, as Athens' imperial interests ramified, was complicated and not very interesting, and the ordinary man, though unwilling to relinquish the appearance of control, had here to rely on others who knew more than he did. His confidence in some spheres was still readily given to wealth and an ancient name: these were serious advantages in competing for the generalship. In matters of public policy, it naturally went in the main to those who could most convincingly claim to have the people's interests at heart. The demagogues, probably well enough off but without ancestral backing, had necessarily won support by what must be called class legislation—though most of it could be justified on social grounds, and none of it compares with the massive redistribution of income operated today in every kind of state.

The charge of electoral bribery related mainly to state pay for public service, and the payment of juries was the usual target. Ephialtes' judicial reform in 462 called for more frequent and larger juries, which might have been hard to get together without the two obols' pay introduced by Pericles, raised to three by Cleon in the 420's. The pay may possibly have worked to bring poorer men on to juries, like the elderly habitual jurors who form the chorus of Aristophanes' *Wasps*, fierce against all defendants and devoted to Cleon for raising their pay. It would be rash to suppose that all juries were composed of old brutes like these, but they could be a caricature of a real type, old men past work and dependent on their sons, with the pay for pocket-money. But there is not much other evidence to suggest that the poorest classes flocked in large numbers to serve in the courts, apart from general statements by the opponents of democracy.

Thus, Aristotle relates how Pericles was unable to compete with the generosity of his rich rival, Cimon, and accepted the advice of a friend 'to distribute their own money to the people'. More provocatively, Socrates, in Plato's *Gorgias*, says he has heard that Pericles made the Athenians idle, cowardly, talkative and greedy by instituting jury-pay. His by no means democratic interlocutor replies that he must have heard that from the men with the broken ears (that is, the boxers and pro-Spartans)—which suggests that Plato is not making the charge very solemnly. It would have been something of an achievement to become idle and greedy on two or three obols, for any labourer could earn more, and a man of moderate skill two or three times as much; and no man on the jury panel could guarantee that he would get his pay every day the courts sat. Like modern states, which compensate a man for the loss of a day's work, Athens gave the minimum sum or less. Other forms of pay caused less comment. Councillors and magistrates were in receipt of pay well before the end of the fifth century, and just after the war pay for attendance at the assembly was introduced, one obol at first, quickly raised to two and then three. In the last case, Aristotle tells us the reason, that it was impossible to raise a quorum otherwise (the payment was started at a time of acute economic distress).

It would require a fairly obstinate prejudice to see in these minimal payments a grave corruption of Athenian public morals. But the pay was appreciated by those who received it, and, in this and in other ways, Pericles and Cleon and their successors certainly legislated in favour of the poorer class, obtaining for them benefits which they would never have got without such legislation. But the demagogues were very much more than this, taking the initiative in matters of administration as well as legislation, and especially in the affairs of the empire. There was business that could not in any real sense be managed by an assembly of some thousands, or even in a full meeting of a Council of Five Hundred. Athens strove to avoid the consequences of this limitation, mainly by distributing public business among a large number of magistrates, appointed by lot. That would do for much routine business; and the numbers and the threat of strict examination of accounts to some extent neutralised the danger of corruption. But it was not a safe way of appointing military commanders, as the demo-cracy recognised by using direct election in this sphere, and it would not provide that initiative at the centre without which there would never have been any routine business to get through. Democracy, as it developed at Athens, created a kind of vacuum at the highest govern-mental level, and volunteer 'demagogues' were the answer.

*

The attempt to locate the centres of power at Sparta is a task of a different kind. The 'people', here only a fraction of the total popu-lation, claimed political equality among themselves just as much as the people of Athens; when a matter was laid before the Spartan assembly, each citizen was at least theoretically entitled to shout for the side he favoured. Over and above this, they claimed a thorough-going social equality of a kind that can never have been fully effective, and that collapsed conspicuously after Sparta's victory in the Pelopon-nesian War. They called themselves 'the Equals', avoided distinctions of dress and ate the same spare meals in their communal messes; and there were sumptuary rules, like that which restricted the kind of house a Spartan might build for himself. The fact that one category of land was legally inalienable probably represents an attempt to ensure that every citizen had the minimum holding that would enable him to keep his place within the system. Some of these features depend on legislation, and it can thus be inferred that, at some particular time, probably as a solution for the crisis which troubled Sparta in the seventh century, conscious and deliberate reform had tried to give the whole citizen body at least some substantial footing on which they could all be treated as equals.

That meant that some Spartans were given political and social privileges which they had not possessed before, or not possessed securely; but permanent real equality was too much to hope for. There is at least a suspicion that some families found it easier than others to gain admittance to the *gerousia* for their elder members. Thucydides, in the late fifth century, more than once refers to certain Spartans as being 'among the first' in the city. If one category of land was legally secured to the individual citizen, other land was the free property of an owner, even if convention frowned on the sale of it; and there were, doubtless, always inequalities here. The formal prohibition against free bequest or gift of land was repealed early in the fourth century; and by Aristotle's time, in the second half of the century, it could be complained that Spartan land was concentrated in dangerously few hands. Till late in the fifth century, there was another prohibition, against the private possession of silver or gold, which seems to have been at least partly effective. The state had always needed conventional money for its dealings abroad, which increased rapidly during the war, but internally Sparta retained a cumbrous iron coinage, a relic from the days before silver was coined in Greece, valueless outside the borders. But the ban on private silver lapsed, to general scandal, about the time of Sparta's victory over Athens, a time when service overseas had accustomed many Spartans to luxuries, forbidden at home. As time went on, Sparta was progressively transformed into an oligarchy of conventional type, where wealth was the only criterion for any sort of privilege.

Furthermore, the assembly of Sparta was, far more than other assemblies, co-terminous with the army, and the military virtues of obedience and respect for established authority had been firmly drummed into every Spartan by an elaborate system of training in youth. Some distinction could be made between the demands of discipline in the field and what was permissible in home politics. On one occasion in the summer of 418, when king Agis had made a very unpopular truce with the enemy, the army followed him home with due obedience; but then the assembly turned against him and threatened him with heavy penalties. But the habit of obedience to a superior must, one imagines, have affected the votes of these soldier-citizens, and the atmosphere of the Spartan assembly was surely very different from that of the assembly of Athens. It would help if we had any idea how the officers of the Spartan army were appointed, at every level from the commanders of the six regiments, called *morai*, down to the platoon commanders, or even how long they held their commands, but no ancient source tells us how a man made his career in the Spartan army. The only detail we know is that the commander of the navy was appointed annually and that no one might hold the office twice; but that need not be typical. We may guess that the competition was fierce enough in this essential department of Spartan life, but we do not know, and we do not know how competition here was linked with political competition.

But it is abundantly clear that the system gave special advantage to the two kings at the apex of the hierarchy, the signal exceptions to the general Spartan rule of equality. Their social privileges were extensive, and their opportunity for patronage, especially for the kind of honorific public commendation which played so large a part in Spartan society. The glamour of the office and title was something not to be found elsewhere in the Greek world. Ephors changed every year, and no one could enter the *gerousia* till he was sixty, but a king might succeed in the vigour of youth and reign for decades. Some indeed were nonentities, like Cleomenes II, who reigned for sixty years in the fourth century without once being named in historical narrative. But, till the end, the two families produced an astonishing number of able and energetic leaders, and for an active politician like Agesilaus (400–359) the kingship was a very large asset indeed.

It is in no way surprising that the kings were apt to become the foci of internal struggle at Sparta, and, from time to time, we are given instances, especially by Xenophon, who was intimate with Sparta. But the limelight does not play on the other figures in the hierarchy, except to a limited extent on the naval commanders. Brasidas, active and enterprising in the first stage of the Peloponnesian War, held a series of *ad hoc* posts. Lysander, who eventually won the war, commanded the navy in the east in 407; and, as he could not be re-appointed, Sparta had to proceed indirectly, first making him secretary to a figure-head admiral (405–4), then making his brother admiral (404–3). This ambitious man was believed to have plans to make the kingship elective instead of hereditary, and reform of the system was perhaps the only road by which such a man could attain real power. Thereafter, the *ad hoc* posts multiply, but we still do not know nearly enough about the way in which these or the regular posts were filled.

Occasional glimpses show that, below the surface, the fight for power and influence was fierce, erupting from time to time in the trial of a king or a subordinate figure. A conspicuous example was the trial of Sphodrias, the commander of a Spartan garrison in 378 at Thespiae in Boeotia, who had made an unsuccessful night march against the port of Athens, with whom Sparta was then precariously at peace. Xenophon describes the manœuvres by which king Agesilaus was induced to support his cause, the other king Cleombrotus being his patron already, and the scandalous acquittal drove Athens into alliance with Thebes against Sparta. The issue might be one of principle— Lysander's plan for a Spartan naval empire was such an issue; and Agesilaus, in a less ruthless and more diplomatic style, worked for the full exploitation of Sparta's imperial position and for the suppression of Thebes. But, for the most part, it looks more like a fight for personal power, partly concealed by Sparta's secretiveness about her internal affairs, and by the image she presented to the world of a disciplined and well-ordered state.

*

State trials give us occasional light on the noisier issues of Spartan politics; and there were, no doubt, political issues, of a less spectacular kind, in many minor trials which we do not hear of. That is the main way in which public issues would be affected by the *gerousia*, the court which tried the more serious cases, and by the ephors, whose position as judges must not be forgotten. The courts of democratic Athens played a much more visible part in the public life of that city. It is not simply a matter of spectacular trials over an openly political issue. These indeed occurred, as, for instance, the charge of embezzlement of public funds brought against Pericles in 430; or the charge of treachery brought against Callistratus in 366, which halted his career in spite of his acquittal. The most elaborate speeches extant are those made by Aeschines and Demosthenes in strictly political trials in 343 and 330. Again, it was common at Athens, as at Rome, for a young man to try to make a name for himself at the beginning of his career by bringing a charge against some prominent figure. But the real significance of the courts is found, rather, in innumerable minor cases. These might be overtly political, like the frequent charge that a proposal made in the assembly was technically illegal, or not apparently concerned with politics at all; in either case, public issues were likely to intrude, and the jury would be reminded of its duty to keep watch over the democratic constitution of the city. It clearly took its watchdog role seriously.

The juries, in fact, made little distinction between political and non-political issues, and we must not import one. By modern standards, the latitude allowed to speakers in court is unnerving. The presiding officer did not lay down the law like the judge of an English court: the litigant told the jury what the law was and what it meant, subject only to the check of the alternative interpretations his adversary would offer, and the experience of the jurors. The litigant's past services to the state, the amount he had paid out in taxes or other forms of public outlay, were all allowed their weight, as were the tears of the defendant's children and much else. The orators constantly remind the jurors that they have sworn to deliver their verdict strictly according to the law, but juries are so often implored to be lenient or rigorous for quite other reasons that we can be sure that the reminder about their oath was no mere formality. What a charitable critic might call equity had more force in an Athenian court than the strict letter of the law, and the equity had a highly political flavour.

This easy attitude was helped by a degree of uncertainty about the law itself. Solon's codification may have been adequate for the early sixth century, but detailed enactments had proliferated in the fifth century, with no central record office, at best the working records of Council, archons and the rest. The team which set to work in the last decade of the fifth century to consolidate the Athenian code had a hard task and took some ten years over it. Thereafter, Athens had a central archive in the Metroion, the temple of the Phrygian mother-goddess in the Agora; and a deliberately cumbrous procedure was established for amending and adding to the basic code, in the quite unrealistic hope of keeping this code stable. Later speeches show that the confusion continued.

In spite of all, it is likely that the Athenian judicial system worked reasonably well for its time. Sparta, without juries or written code, presents a gloomier record of injustice in those public trials which are all we know of. Athenian justice was at least more open, and access to the courts easy. It was reckoned as one of the features of Solon's reforms that most favoured the people, that he allowed to an unusual extent the intervention of a third party to start a prosecution, so that the victim of injustice was not necessarily dependent on his own efforts to resist a powerful opponent. This is another way in which the establishment of the jury-courts at Athens helped the city along its path towards democracy.

*

The question how all these mechanisms really worked was, however, less prominent in the minds of ancient writers than the strictly moral question, which was the fairest constitution, which most conduced to individual virtue. Virtue means primarily the sort of virtue that could be exercised by a man of leisure and property; the higher theorists were not much concerned with the development of virtue in the uneducated lower classes, debarred by their low employments from culture and contemplation.

Only Herodotus, writing in fresher and more expansive days before the Peloponnesian War, praises the principle of equality without reserve, usually under the name of 'freedom of speech', contrasting it with the tyranny under which an Athenian could not say, or publicly propose, what he liked. He improbably ascribes a detailed constitutional debate to the Persian conspirators, who in 522 murdered the usurper then in power and set Darius up as king. Here, the champion of democracy insists on 'the fair name' of equality, appointment by lot, magistrates responsible to the people, free discussion among equals; the oligarch stresses the irresponsibility of the uneducated; the monarchist, the internal feuds which trouble oligarchy. In the imaginary context[1] of this early essay the monarchist had to win, but the democrat gets much the best of the argument.

A much more unusual early specimen is the short pamphlet on the *Constitution of Athens*, written by an Athenian oligarch not long after the opening of the Peloponnesian War, which has come down to us because it somehow got included in the works of Xenophon. Its pur-

---

1. Herodotus himself clearly believed that he was reporting a discussion which had actually taken place. That can hardly be right, and we have to suppose that some earlier theorist had used this odd foreign setting for thoughts which are strictly Greek.

pose has been much debated—it appears to me to be addressed, with a large measure of irony, to a foreign sympathiser who does not understand the difficulty of overthrowing democracy at Athens—but for all its bias and reckless misrepresentation it has the unique merit of stating bluntly the reasons why the democratic constitution was so effectively entrenched at Athens. The people know that they are essential to the navy on which Athens depends, whereas the hoplites matter less than they did elsewhere. The assembly listens to the advice of low-born men ('madmen' is one uncharitable description) rather than to the 'good', and in this they correctly follow their own interest, for the 'good' are not well disposed to the people. Through every aspect of the subject he takes the same line, that democracy may be detestable, but the course it takes is the sensible course for its own preservation; and there is much more about the capacity of a naval power to see to its supplies, the people's enjoyment of festivals paid for by the rich, the congestion of public business, and other topics. In its odd mixture of candour and prejudice, this discussion is unique, in that it looks at the practical effect of the democratic machinery and allows for the views of the side which has not the author's sympathy.

After the oligarchic upheavals of 411 and 404, it was clear that there was no prospect of uprooting democracy except by external force; so, though the literate class was now more uniformly disenchanted with democracy, some of the heat had gone out of the controversy. For the ordinary educated man, this meant mainly that the old slogans had to be a little modified. Oligarchy had always, as in Herodotus' debate, picked on incoherence as the vulnerable feature of democratic freedom and emphasised its own ideal of 'good order'; and the oligarchs were 'the best people', or some equivalent cant term, meaning in practice the well-to-do. Now, within the democratic framework, the same distinction was made in a more muffled way, the central point still being the protection of property against possible expropriation. The preferred class were 'the well-off' or 'the notables', or more insidiously 'men of taste' or 'sensible people'; their opponents were corrupt demagogues, stirring up war to increase their opportunities of making money. Instead of advocating oligarchy, the cry was for a return to the good old days before democracy was corrupted, and the past history of Athens was dressed up to fit the thesis.

High theory could be more ruthless. Plato, drawing the outline of his ideal world, was not concerned with the lower classes of democracy, or what they could be persuaded to accept: when he talks of the democracies and oligarchies of the real world, it is in terms of gifted and graceful caricature, as only he knew how. He dodged the problem of authority, and never indicated how his ideal city was to be got going—except for his notion that it might be done by converting an already powerful tyrant. This was the basis for his unsuccessful dealings with the younger Dionysius at Syracuse. Aristotle was more concerned to describe and classify the constitutions of real cities, but his theory was based on a not very rewarding distinction between those that operated under law and those that did not. Each formal type of government, the single ruler or the few or the many, could thus be subdivided into a virtuous and a corrupt form. Tyranny, the lawless type of monarchy, was common enough in real life, and Aristotle has some interesting observations about it; but the virtuous form, the man so outstandingly good and wise that he need not be controlled by law but embodies the law in himself, is reasonably enough treated only as a limiting possibility in a theoretical scheme. Corrupt oligarchs, whose desire for wealth led to the neglect of law, were again easy enough to find; but it was not so easy to point to examples of aristocracies where law was really supreme. Neglect of law was an easy charge against democracy as it was practised in Aristotle's time; but virtue could be found in more primitive agrarian communities, where the farmers had not the leisure to attend frequent assemblies and left government to their betters. In other words, democracy might be tolerated if it was not seriously democratic. The classification fails to be fruitful, because only the lawless forms have any substance; for practical purposes, we are left with oligarchy and democracy, with tyranny as a threat in the background. Nothing much could be done with this, except to note that democracy works on a bad principle of arithmetic equality, counting votes rather than weighing the merits of the voters. But that was not much positive recommendation for oligarchy. Wealth might be defended as the capacity to contribute to the defence of a hoplite state, but the pursuit of wealth was an unattractive business and bad for the soul.

More could be done with the idealisation of Sparta as the true aristocracy devoted to the pursuit of virtue. Plato, indeed, complained that Spartan education was centred on the military virtues, to the neglect of the others, and Aristotle, writing after Sparta's defeat by Thebes, was more ready to find faults in the whole framework. But no one doubted that the Spartan lawgiver had framed his whole system for the inculcation of a special and distinctive ethos. Sparta, even in the fourth century, had numerous defenders, of whom the most persuasive was Xenophon, an exile from Athens who knew Sparta well and lived for many years on an estate granted to him by the Spartan state.[1]

The basis of the encomium was that Sparta was the ideal example of a disciplined and well-ordered state, where traditional customs were preserved, and where the young showed a proper respect for their elders, who lost no opportunity of admonishing them to virtue. The legend, as is the way of such legends, throve, quite undeterred by counter-examples from real life; and it throve especially in paradox, in the notion that at Sparta all things were done back to front, the opposite of what was done in other cities. There were some real phenomena to nourish the legend, especially the long and elaborate system of training to which the young Spartan was subjected, and the part that was played in adult life by a complex mesh of social sanctions against those who fell below the conventional standards. But very much of it was mere anti-democratic fantasy, the vision of a world consisting entirely of gentlemen, with no thought for the helots and *perioikoi* whose labours supported that world.

*

In all this, the moral issue dominates, the question what is the fair share of power for the different sections of the community, how to avoid faction and revolution, what political framework is best for the development of the individual soul. There is not much about the way in which things actually get done, what sort of people are interested in doing them, how they are to be recruited or controlled. The blind spot, throughout, is the matter of executive or administrative ability. Herodotus thought in terms of glory and patriotism and simple honesty. Thucydides in his portraits of the two statesmen he most admired, Pericles and Themistocles, concentrates on their intellectual penetration. The historians born in the fourth century thought mainly of exposing vice and encouraging virtue in their readers, and this was the declared aim of others besides the historians.

Xenophon, who had taken his part in improvising some organi-

1. But Xenophon's small treatise on Sparta is in effect an encomium on the ancient lawgiver, Lycurgus, and in the penultimate chapter he admits that the Sparta of his day no longer lived up to Lycurgus' principles.

sation for the Ten Thousand in their famous retreat to the sea, to a small extent breaks out of the pattern. When he pictures Socrates, explaining to a disappointed candidate for the generalship why it is reasonable for the Athenians to have elected a business man to a post which involved so much administration, there is some conscious paradox and exaggeration, but also a rare glimmer of realisation of what such officers had really to do. In an oblique way, Aristophanes, concerned only to mock, conveys as much information as anyone about the administrators of the Athenian empire and what was thought of them. The political work was done by the demagogues, for whom the uneducated continued to vote, and that was not merely a matter of electoral bribery. The record-keeping and much of the routine work was done by intelligent slaves, owned by the state. It was, in general, a low business, and the educated preferred more edifying topics.

CHAPTER 10

Social values and social divisions

THE SOCIAL WORLD of the Greeks was, from the start, one of fierce competition, a background fact that must be kept in sight throughout. With the clear outlines of their art and thought, with that relative absence of fumbling and indeterminacy, there goes a relish in pushing thought and action to extremes, some insensitive cruelty mixed in with the brilliance and gaiety, a need to make the most of personal power and wealth and beauty, a reluctance to compromise. It was an open-air world, with more public than private life, in which the individual felt the presence and pressure of his neighbours very heavily, and himself exerted all the pressure he could, through whatever qualities he might claim credit for.

One main indicator has rightly been found in the way they used their word for 'good'. The neuter of the adjective was mostly applied to material blessings, somewhat as we use the plural 'goods'. Things or persons were more often 'good for' something or 'good at' something. If a Greek called a person 'good' without qualification, he usually meant that he was brave, a good man in a fight; he would not be likely to mean that he was kind or helpful or disinterested. The abstract noun *aretê*, which we helplessly translate 'virtue' because we have no nearer word, implies more than usual skill at doing something, perhaps something we should recognise as virtuous, often what we should treat as, at best, morally neutral. The concern is with doing whatever it is well, and the test is success rather than good intention.

Greeks tended to see any activity as a competition or test—in their own word, an *agon*; and much has been written about the 'agonal' concept in Greek life, some of it helpful and some exaggerated. The point has also been expressed by taking up the distinction between a 'shame-culture' in which men try to avoid what will cause them disgrace in the eyes of their fellows, and a 'guilt-culture' in which they try to avoid what gives them feelings of guilt; and one can measure Greece's movement away from the world of Homer by the extent to which the former gave way to the latter. Again, a distinction has been made between the 'competitive' virtues which are summed up in the term *aretê*, and the 'co-operative' virtues which we more readily think we ought to aim at. Though the latter made some headway as Greek civilisation progressed, it is doubtful if they ever quite got the upper hand.

Homer certainly provides the extreme case of free play for the competitive virtues, the heroes before Troy proving their superiority in the most absolute way by killing their opponents. The claims of honour prevail over all other claims. They allow for retreat in face of overwhelming force, but it must be done in style, like a lion, and not like a deer. In the last resort, the hero must return to the fight, even if, like Hector, he knows he is doomed, because his situation will be intolerable if he has backed down. There are large and generous feelings at work here, and there is co-operative action—Hector must defend his city, a comrade must come to the help of another in difficulty—but the sanction is the shame of cowardice or failure. It does not fill the whole horizon, and the poet who composed the tender parting scene between Hector and his wife, Andromache, knew how much else must be lost when the hero followed the call of honour; but he treats that call as overriding all other considerations.

Courage and skill might be displayed in hunting and athletic contests, as well as in war, and more peaceful virtues were not unhonoured. Odysseus and Penelope were kind to the slave, Eumaeus, beyond the requirements of their situation. Achilles and others mourned Patroclus for his gentleness as well as his valour. But rivalry and display were never far from the surface: even hospitality was, in some degree, a competition in prodigality, and it gained a hero honour to pile up more treasure in his palace than another. The aristocratic round happily included song with its feasting: the bards were often professionals, but Achilles in his tent passed the time accompanying his own heroic lays. All the hero's activities had to be performed in the correct way. The aristocratic code was precise and elaborate, in the way that nobles have time for, to the point that a stranger must be bathed and feasted before one could think of asking his name and business.

Heroes were princes, descended from the gods, and the gulf between them and ordinary men was wide. Only once in Homer does an inferior step out of his place to argue with the kings. This was Thersites, who complained about Agamemnon's disproportionate share of the booty, and proposed that the ordinary fighters should sail away and show the king that he could not do without them. Homer weights the scales against Thersites by making him ugly and deformed, and the army extravagantly applauds Odysseus when he strikes him with the golden sceptre. No argument is deployed against him; in front of Troy, it could be taken as self-evident that there must be kings to lead and that the army must show them proper respect. The situation is a shade un-real, for the role of the army in the poem is not very like what Thersites ascribes to it. The poet was composing in a very different world, where perhaps the nobles already found it not quite so easy to chase away the equivalent of Thersites, whose subversive arguments are more co-herent than Odysseus' rough answer. Even within the world of Odysseus and the epic convention, one may legitimately wonder about the reservations of the ordinary man, or the thoughts of a slave less favoured than Eumaeus.

Hesiod, in his turn, looks at the aristocratic world from outside the charmed circle, and without much favour. This is not only because of the 'bribe-devouring princes' whose unjust judgment might favour his brother's claim against his estate. There is more than that to his fable of the nightingale, caught up by the hawk, who rebuked her for her cries, and said she must submit to her fate at the hand of the stronger. As has rightly been pointed out, that was not the end of the story: Hesiod, a singer like the nightingale, may well have won his case against his brother; in any event, the larger point remains, that his voice was heard, and his complaint against injustice survives to this day, its often grumpy quality redeemed by a gaunt dignity. He diverges still further from the heroic ideal by neglecting war as a current normal activity, even if he cannot altogether avoid speaking of fighting heroes. Hesiod stood for the same ideal, though he treats it more austerely, as the small farmer in some of Aristophanes' plays, longing to get back to the country and to leave the war to the politicians who had started it.

*

In the full aristocratic period, the gulf between the classes was no less. Indeed, the change from monarchy was a redistribution of power in the topmost class which would rather widen the distance between them and the rest. The life the nobles aimed to lead was not essentially different from that of Homer's heroes, though the isolation and self-sufficiency of the epic were a thing of the past. Horizons had widened, the modes of displaying wealth were changed. Feast and song, hunting and athletics, were their favoured occupations, and the apparatus of their lives had a new luxury.

The great athletic and musical festivals were, perhaps, the most impressive construction of the Greek aristocracies. The festival of Zeus at Olympia, held every fourth year south of Elis and under Elean supervision, was thought to have begun its formal series of numbered celebrations in 776, and that may be true. The official list of victors, compiled by Hippias early in the fourth century, may not in its earlier stages have been drawn from very reliable materials. But the picture the list gives (we have only the record of one event complete, the foot-race) is reasonable enough, of a festival which at first attracted competitors only from neighbouring areas, and then expanded in the seventh century to draw from the whole Greek world. This was a religious festival in honour of the greatest of gods, not simply a sporting event, and it was protected by a sacred truce from interruption by Greece's endless wars. An Olympic victory was always the highest prize a man could gain, though three other great meetings had international prestige: the numbered series of the games of the Pythian Apollo at Delphi starts near the beginning of the sixth century, as did Poseidon's games at the Isthmus of Corinth, and the games at Nemea, which were centred on another sanctuary of Zeus. For all these, it would be reasonable to assume that a local festival had been running some time before it was thus raised to international status. Many other local festivals acquired a wide reputation—for instance, the Great Panathenaea, celebrated every fourth year at Athens, with a lesser festival in the intervening years. There were musical as well as athletic competitions, though we know less detail of these. Peisistratus, the tyrant, is said to have introduced the recitation of Homer at the Panathenaea.

In all this, a favourite diversion of the early aristocracies was institutionalised and carried over into the classical period. The glory which attached to victory in these contests went beyond anything we can parallel from our own world, for all the value we attach to sport.[1] The poems of Pindar which survive complete are odes written for

1. This sentence was written before the international excitement of the contest for the World Cup in 1966. It may still stand: we have no Pindar, and the religious element in the Greek festival is a difference.

victors in the four great games, and they lend us some breath of the excitement which spread out beyond the athletes themselves to the city to which they belonged. When Pindar, at a time when Athens was shortly to extinguish the independence of Aegina, meditates in high style on the instability of human life and the light and comfort of the 'god-given gleam' when it comes, the victory of an Aeginetan wrestler at Delphi seems hardly enough to sustain the weight of the language. Athenian victors in the great games received free meals for life in the *prytaneion*, the town hall of Athens. Victors commonly dedicated statues at the shrine where they had won their victory, and some survive: the grave but somewhat mindless beauty of the bronze charioteer at Delphi is a powerful example, dedicated in the early fifth century by a member of the Syracusan family of tyrants. There was some protest, notably from the seventh-century Spartan poet, Tyrtaeus, who thought the defence of the city rated higher than athletic victory, and from the poet-philosopher, Xenophanes of Colophon, a puritan who thought his own wisdom more profitable. But the cult went on.

Horses were a great symbol of aristocratic pride, impossible to maintain in southern Greece unless one had land to spare or money to spend on their feed. In poetry from the *Iliad* onwards, in art from the first schematic representations of the Geometric period, the horse was a favourite element, lovingly delineated (pl. 8, 17). If cavalry achieved little on campaign, membership of the corps was a social prize. It played its part in public ceremonial, as in the procession depicted on the Parthenon frieze; and Xenophon's pamphlets on horsemanship are concerned quite as much with ceremonial as with tactics. At the great games, the important events were the chariot races, one remove further from the military sphere, for even the Homeric hero used his chariot for transport, not in the fight. This was a major opportunity for display. If victory depended on the competitor's wealth, much more than on anyone's skill, it could be argued that the display of wealth itself enhanced the city's prestige among the other Greek cities, as Thucydides makes Alcibiades say of his victory in 416. Herodotus' narrative shows how certain Athenian families of the sixth century found a victory with a chariot at Olympia a political asset within their own city. The great tyrants competed eagerly in this field, notably the Sicilian tyrants of the early fifth century, for whom Pindar wrote.

The games, as a whole, drew their competitors from the highest social class; the spectators who travelled long distances to the greater games will not have been the common people, whose turn came rather at their city's own festivals. There is this much justification for speaking of the athlete's world in classical times as an international aristocratic world. Athletes from different cities shared with one another tastes which they did not share with the lower classes of their own cities. An Aeginetan wrestler might still have an Athenian trainer, himself of the highest social class, at a time when the relations between the two states were worsening towards a war, disastrous for Aegina. But these international contacts had no perceptible effect on state policy. The social contact might encourage the Greeks to feel that they were one people, but it did nothing to stop Greek cities from fighting one another. The games continued to be an important element in Greek life as long as ancient civilisation endured; indeed, in the Hellenistic world games and gymnasia spread everywhere as one of the distinctive signs of Greek culture. But as time went on, Greek athletics became increasingly professionalised, a tendency already visible in the fifth century.

The stimulus given to poetry and art in the early aristocratic world has left a more lasting legacy. The scraps of verse we have are only a small remnant of what the ancient world possessed, but they add up to a corpus large enough for us to see that the personal poetry which succeeded the anonymous epic was written by, or occasionally for, the nobles and expressed their feelings. At the head of the series, in the middle of the seventh century, stands the bitter and powerful Archilochus of Paros, who went as a colonist to Thasos and fought against the mainland Thracians. Critics have taken him for a rebel, rather than a member of the aristocratic order, but it becomes increasingly clear that this is a misunderstanding, partly due to the fact that in much of his verse the speaker is not himself but an assumed character. The poetry of private sensibility, represented by the fragments of Sappho of Mytilene writing around 600, belongs wholly to the aristocratic world, as do the political railings of her contemporary, Alcaeus.

Choral lyric, sung by choirs on religious or other ceremonial occasions, belonged to the same world, for the singers were not the common people. Chance has preserved for us a large piece of one of the 'Maiden-songs' written by Alcman, probably himself a Lydian from Sardis, late in the seventh century, for choirs of high-born Spartan girls—together with other fragments, which show that the Sparta of his time was not a place of graceless austerity. The odes which

Pindar wrote for athletic victors were, so to speak, public poetry composed for private patrons. Beside this, we have another category of public poetry, hortatory or admonitory elegiacs. This seems to have begun in East Greece with Callinus of Ephesus, exhorting his countrymen to resist the inroads of the Cimmerians in the seventh century; it continues through the verses, in which Tyrtaeus urged the Spartans to greater effort against the Messenians; and it includes the political verses, in which Solon of Athens put his political ideas before his city and justified his reforms thereafter.

From the great funerary vases of Athens in the Geometric period, through a long series of bowls and cups and other vessels, the fine pottery of Greece was produced for upper-class users. It tells us much about their furniture and the other apparatus of their lives, as well as about their social habits (e.g. pl. 22, 26). Sculpture, for dedication in temples, was made for individual patrons, at least as much as for the city, and none of it for poor men. There was, of course, pottery of less distinction for ordinary men, and rougher stools and other furniture, just as there was certainly folk-poetry which they sang at their work or elsewhere (though it is never easy to guess the date of surviving specimens). But the art we know best is the art of the nobility, and the more diversified luxury which opened itself to them in the late eighth century and through the seventh is seen through this medium. Their new opportunities were the background to that rapacity and oppression which from the middle of the seventh century caused so many violent revolutions.

Revolution meant temporary and local dislocation; but, in general, the life of the upper classes continued along familiar lines. The games and the hunting went on, there was no abrupt change in art or poetry. The tyrants, the agents of revolution, were almost all of noble origin, with the tastes and habits of their class. With the resources of a whole city behind them, they ran to a magnificence which no single noble house could emulate. They built temples and fountains, held festivals, patronised poets and artists at their courts. But it was an important change that there should be one disproportionately rich centre of patronage overshadowing all others, and it was a small step from patronage by the city's single ruler to patronage by the city as a corporation. In many cases, the tyrants seem by deliberate policy to have fostered national festivals rather than festivals tied to a cult in the hands of a particular noble family, and the tyrant in the long run transformed the whole situation by taking the glamour to himself and eliminating competition within the city. The other main long-term change during this time of transition was a change in the composition of the upper class itself—in very general terms, a change from a society where birth was the principal criterion to a society which took more account of wealth.

*

It is not easy to follow this out in detail. For instance, we know altogether too few individuals of the eighth and seventh centuries, and we are in no position to distinguish the emergence of new names. The ancient sources were not concerned to analyse the supporters of a tyrant or to tell us about the day-to-day running of his government. They were preoccupied with his moral situation, his opportunities for sensual indulgence, his suspicion and cruelty, his reliance on money and mercenaries rather than the goodwill of his subjects—and, of course, some tyrants gave ample scope for sermons on this theme. If ancient writers speak at all of the tyrant's friends and servants, it is to dismiss them as hypocrites and flatterers. As for opposition, when it is not the grievance of an individual victim, it seems to come mainly from the resentment of surviving nobles at their exclusion from politics.

When we ask what sort of people supported a tyrant, it is unfortunate that the best-known example is untypical, the case of Peisistratus at Athens. There, so much work had been done already by Solon—the *hektemoroi* liberated, a constitution of a non-aristocratic kind established. The chief remaining problem was aristocratic faction on a regional basis, and the cure for this was the victory of Peisistratus' own party, a victory which he did not need to press too far in the way of execution and exile of opponents. He conciliated them with marriage alliances and the assignment of high office to them, and allowed the Solonian system to run on, protected by his private army from factional disturbance. Here, more than elsewhere, we can imagine the social life of the city running on unchanged.

It was otherwise where the aristocracy was violently overthrown, as at Corinth, where Cypselus killed and exiled the Bacchiadae wholesale and confiscated their property, but is said to have been personally popular with the rest of the Corinthians. The clearing-out of the Bacchiadae was probably much less complete than Herodotus makes it, and no doubt many who served them transferred their allegiance easily enough to Cypselus. That does not alter the fact that there must have been substantial change. The functions of government hitherto exercised by the Bacchiadae, together with whatever rudimentary administration Corinth needed at that time, must have been largely in new hands; and we have no direct evidence whose they were. It does not help much to look at the regime which succeeded the tyranny there. We know that there was a wealthy and successful oligarchy, with a high reputation for stability, lasting unchanged for nearly two hundred years, till it was temporarily overthrown during the war against Sparta in the 390's. But it has left us virtually no documents from the classical period, and we know nothing about it in detail.

It is clear, in general, that the revolutions which produced tyranny, coming when they did, were somehow connected with the general increase of wealth in Greece: the question is, what the precise connection was. The temptation is large, and historians have yielded to it, to speak of the rise of a commercial class in revolt against an established landed aristocracy. That is too simple, if only because great merchant families were never a feature of the social scene in Greece, the scale of commercial operation being too small, and the land dominant throughout. It is possible that some men, who had been merely traders and had prospered, found themselves in a position to buy enough land to compete with the nobles, or sought in revolution the chance to acquire land violently. In general, one should probably imagine the commercial and agricultural elements more intricately mixed. Great landowners had, of course, to become, in a measure, merchants in order to dispose of their surplus produce. Hesiod, though he hated the sea, included in his poem of advice to farmers a section on sailing in the relative safety of summer—which he would hardly have done unless it were fairly common for farmers on his scale to market some form of produce over the sea. Successful part-time commerce might enable a farmer to buy more land, or to employ more slave labour on the land he had. In ways like these, it may be imagined how men outside the original circle of nobles and larger landowners improved their position to the point where they had leisure to complain about their exclusion from political power. Where there was violence and confiscation, the supporters of a tyrant, or at least those who contributed in the longer term to the working of a tyrannical regime, are likely to have been substantial men on their way up rather than members of the poorest and most oppressed class.

For Corinth, in particular, it is easy to suspect that the commercial element was, in one way or another, stronger than in other cities. Their agricultural land comprised only a corner of that rich but narrow plain which stretches westwards towards Sicyon, and some moderately fertile inland valleys, whereas the position of Corinth on its isthmus conspicuously favoured trade. Herodotus remarks, in passing, that the Corinthians despised craftsmen less than other Greeks—not, it should be noted, that they did not despise them—and later writers credit Corinth with an unusually high number of slaves. In an ode written for a Corinthian victor, the nearest thing we have to a contemporary appraisal of Corinth, Pindar praises the justice and order of the city, remarking that these virtues foster wealth; and he picks out a few of their older technical inventions. But Pindar's Corinthian victor does not seem to differ from the well born athletes of other cities; and, for Xenophon, the oligarchs who suffered in the democratic revolution of 392 were 'the best people', a regular cant term for the upper classes anywhere. It would be rash to conclude that the oligarchs of Corinth were markedly different from oligarchs elsewhere.

But there is no doubt at all about the general effect in the long term, the emergence of wealth as the criterion for privilege. Solon's constitutional reform at Athens is symptomatic. We do not certainly know that, before his time, office was formally restricted to the aristocracy; but it must be significant that Solon's new system took no account of birth at all. He assigned privilege solely according to the extent and productivity of a man's land, grouping the citizen body into four classes, restricting high political office to the richest, while the poorest were given no rights except those of voting in the assembly and sitting on juries in the courts. The nature of the change is eloquently attested also by the nature of the complaints made by the deprived aristocrats.

Thus the rich city of Mytilene, on Lesbos, was rent at the end of the seventh century by violent quarrels inside the ruling aristocracy. These ended in the establishment of Pittacus in sole power, a man with a reputation for mildness, who ranked as one of the 'Seven Sages' of archaic Greece. That fierce partisan, the poet Alcaeus, once Pittacus' ally and then his enemy, poured out on him all the intemperate invective which enlivened Greek politics—he was fat, greedy, drunken, splay-footed, he had betrayed his comrades, and, above all, he was of low birth. Pittacus, who had earlier been numbered among the comrades of the aristocrat, Alcaeus, was certainly no man of the people, and the accusation of low birth is just the most damaging charge that Alcaeus can think of. It was alleged that Pittacus' father was Thracian, but that can hardly mean more than an element of foreign blood somewhere in the family, no crime in that world. What really troubled Alcaeus was that the Mytileneans had rejected himself and his friends— 'they have set up the low-born Pittacus as tyrant of the spiritless and ill-fated city, greatly praising him one and all', while Alcaeus in exile was left to lament, among other losses, his exclusion from the council to which he and his fathers had belonged.

More sadly and systematically, Theognis of Megara, in the middle of the sixth century, bewailed the dominance of the commoner in his city —'those who before knew no right or law, who wore out goatskins round their bodies and had their pasture like deer outside the city, they are now the great men'—and neither man nor woman shrank from marrying into a rich family of low birth. The down-to-earth eugenic opening of that poem points to the trouble we take to breed sheep and asses and horses from good stock; and it ends by complaining that 'wealth has mixed the race' of his citizens. There is a heavy emphasis in all these poems on the corrupting power of wealth. Theognis complained bitterly of his own poverty; he and Solon complained of the rapacity of the rich, who pile up wealth with no end; so also Alcaeus, who quotes as the saying of Aristodamus in Sparta 'wealth makes the man, and the poor man can be neither noble nor honoured'. These are familiar topics in any age, but it would be fair to say that the poets of these two generations were unusually preoccupied with the effect of wealth in upsetting the social and political balance.

Theognis' phrase about the men in goatskins does not mean that the very poor had as a class gained political control: that, so far as it ever happened, was the complaint of the gentleman about the fully developed democracy of the classical period. But the misery of the really poor was, certainly at Athens, and probably elsewhere, the essential background for revolution. Where the aristocrats rode highest, in Sparta and Thessaly, the agricultural labour force suffered worst, a position maintained by repression and at risk from revolt. The poems of Solon show that the poorest labourers of Attica were in the process of being ground into servitude, and it was their ferment that brought him to power. We can hardly doubt that the same development occurred elsewhere, in cities not fortunate enough to produce a Solon. But the long-term result was not to put the peasants in power. Solon went on to frame a constitution under which the poorest class had little active part, and we may assume that this peasant revolt, like others, lost impetus when the immediate grievance had been dealt with.

The long-term gainers were the class immediately below the high nobility. For a noble who believed in the value of birth, that was ample enough ground for complaint in Theognis' style. At Athens, it presumably meant that some wealthy members, not necessarily very numerous, were added to the highest classes; and that the substantial farmers who formed the hoplite army got some, though less, recognition. Where the aristocracy was violently overthrown, the effects would have been sharper, and have taken longer to digest; even at Athens, the reform of Solon was not fully accepted for a generation or so. The eventual result was a permanent enlargement of the upper class. In time to come, this wider class could unite in looking down on men of still more recent origin or on men of no substance at all.

*

The heavy infantry formation introduced in the middle of the seventh century was a stabilising factor of high importance. The hoplite line fostered an ideal very different from that of the Homeric hero, fighting his spectacular individual duels. Steadiness in charging or in standing fast became the prime military virtue, a comfort to moralists wishing to strengthen the soul against temptation. Not all went so far as Plato, who deplored the demoralising effect of naval raids, landing at an undefended spot and sailing away when resistance gathered. With conscious paradox, he professed to regret the effect of the great naval victory over the Persians at Salamis—and, for an opponent of democracy, there was something there to regret. Less radical reformers, like those who were vocal at Athens and elsewhere at the end of the fifth century, saw the mass of hoplites as a foundation on which to build a stable constitution. They were the 'men in the middle' who for Euripides and others saved the city from its extremists.

But the masters of the hoplite system were the aristocratic 'Equals' of Sparta. Ancient theorists had no doubt that the special education and physical training, which marked the Spartans off from the rest of the Greek world, had been instituted deliberately to instil the hoplite virtues into the Spartan youth. When a child was born at Sparta, the decision whether to rear it or expose it lay not with its father but with state authority. A boy was removed from his mother and began his training at the age of seven. From fourteen to twenty the young were organised, both in 'herds' under the charge of an elder youth, and in age-groups with eccentric archaic names. Hard physical training, endurance of hunger, insufficient clothing, competitive games and dances, ancestral wisdom in verse or story, made up their life. There were periods of complete retreat when the initiate had to hide up in the country and live from what he could steal; and ordeals of great severity like the famous whipping ceremony at the altar of Artemis Orthia, later an attraction maintained for Roman tourists. The Spartans also surprised the rest of Greece by the degree of athletic training their girls went through.

The initial training over, the youth who passed all tests and was admitted to the army at the age of twenty was still in the grip of the system. They ate in common, in male messes called *phiditia* to which the individual had to be co-opted; they slept in dormitories; and their very public lives were subject to advice and criticism from their elders to an extent which other Greeks found strange. Marriage, with a transvestite rite in which the bride's hair was cut short and she wore male clothing, brought no respite. After the first simulated rape, the husband might visit his wife only secretly and then return to his dormitory; it was only at a later age that the couple could set up house together and partly relax into that domestic life which not even Sparta could wholly suppress. Add to that a well-attested custom by which a wife, in certain circumstances, might be lent to another; more doubtful stories about one wife held in common among brothers; the ambiguous statement that there was no adultery in Sparta: and there was quite enough for the outside world to comment on. Any of it could be given a twist which demonstrated the high moral purpose of the legislator who invented the system, but taken together it amounts to a weakening of family life which went to dangerous lengths.

Elements of a communal male life in the same style were found in Crete, enough to start the question whether the Spartan legislator had drawn on Cretan customs. From the fact that the Cretan institution was less tightly organised, Aristotle concluded that this was the original, the Spartan version an improvement on its model. In the rest of Greece the training of the youth was confined to the indispensable minimum of preliminary military service between eighteen and twenty, and there were only vestigial remnants of the rites by which the young were admitted to the community. Enough is now known about age-groups and initiation ceremonies in the rest of the world to show that the practices of Sparta and Crete, and the attenuated vestiges found elsewhere, are relics inherited from a remoter past, not the spontaneous creation of an archaic lawgiver. But the strictness of the Spartan system, the elaboration of their age-groups and the rest, the explanations which the Spartans gave to enquirers, all suggest that these institutions at Sparta had at some time been tautened deliberately and rationalised in the interests of military efficiency, and indeed of political stability. As with so much else in Sparta, this may well be due to a reform in the seventh century, prompted by the low morale and ineffective performance of the army during the revolt of Messenia.

The formidable training programme, the military drill, the varied mechanisms of social disapproval for adult failure, contributed to make the Spartan army the steadiest and the most professional army in all Greece. Discipline was the great virtue, duly commended by Xenophon. There is much talk of self-restraint, *sophrosynê*, that characteristic oligarchic virtue of knowing one's own limits; and that contributed to political stability. The austerity which we associate with the name of Sparta seems to have been a progressive by-product, rather than an original feature of the system. It was a gay enough society at the end of the seventh century, as it is reflected in the fragments of Alcman's verse and in Laconian art, the products made by the *perioikoi* for their Spartan overlords. The quality of Laconian art does not deteriorate seriously till after the middle of the sixth century, when the pottery tails off in the way that all fine fabrics do except Attic; and the bronzework lasted longer than that. There can be no statistics, but the impression remains that there was elasticity enough down to the Persian Wars, and that it was during her troubles after that war that the notorious harshness of Spartan life got the upper hand. In the individual Spartan, it produced that commonsense wit, very brief in expression, which gave rise to the adjective 'laconic'. But there was no more native art or poetry, nor did Spartans shine in any of the activities which in general make Greece worth our study.

The system showed its weaknesses in several ways; for instance, in the frequent charges of bribery against kings and other high officials; and, most conspicuously, after the victory over Athens in 404, when the Spartan empire in Greece was found intolerable after less than ten years. The ambitious Spartan may have been manageable within the restraints of his own stiff society, but he was liable to disconcerting excesses when he went abroad; and his training made it hard for him to deal diplomatically with people who had not been habituated from infancy to the same discipline. That was Sparta's external failure. The most alarming symptom of internal trouble is the continuous fall in the birth-rate, which is not paralleled elsewhere in Greece in the classical period. The casualties of the great earthquake of 464 have been blamed; but, if the system as a whole was sound, these should not have had more than a passing effect. The development by which land fell into progressively fewer hands will also have been discouraging, but this, again, fails to account for the catastrophic rate at which numbers declined. We must assume some more deep-lying psychological effect, built into the system, an effect depending on that attenuation of family life and concentration on the service of the state which marked Sparta out as different from other places. Whatever the precise answer, it is clear that there was some fundamental deficiency in the system.

At Sparta, there were certainly social differences within the privileged citizen body, but the gulf between them and the other inhabitants of the land is far more marked. In origin, it was a gulf between hoplites and the rest, however much the line was later blurred by the drafting of *perioikoi* into the army. There were other oligarchies where service in the army, past or present, constituted the qualification for active citizenship. At Athens, that social division seems to have been of less importance, though it existed; and it might easily have been inflamed by the development of the fleet, and the political weight which that gave to the class which could not afford hoplite armour. At the end of the fifth century, in the oligarchic revolutions of 411 and 404, some attempt was made to win over the hoplite class for anti-democratic reform. Much use was made, in 411, of the slogan demanding that the franchise be restricted to 'those who can serve the state in person or with their money'. But the ordinary hoplite remained suspicious of the intentions of the extremists and, in the end, sided with the people instead. The noticeable social gulf here was rather between the middle class and the really rich, roughly the division between the hoplites and the cavalry.

*

The display made by the seventh-century aristocrats and the tyrants, and by their classical successors, depended in a large measure on the better marshalling of resources, native to Greece, and on the import of materials and finished work from the east, which gathered momentum from about the middle of the eighth century. The contrast between oriental luxury and Greek poverty set up a trouble in the Greek mind, which cannot be ignored, though its practical consequences were not of very great importance. They were both attracted and repelled by the comforts of life among their wealthier eastern neighbours; and, if argument about the moral danger of hot baths or comfortable shoes is sometimes tiresome and ludicrous, there was a genuine difference between Greek habits of life and those of Persia or Babylon, which gave the subject an air of serious moral investigation.

There could be no doubt of the wealth and luxury of the Mycenaean princes, whose bathrooms, incidentally, were superior to anything that classical Greece could show. When the palaces perished and Mycenae's channels of trade were blocked, the Greeks were thrown back, not completely but to a very large extent, on a hard life of subsistence agriculture. That hampered the development of even native resources, and there were not many superfluous comforts in the world of Hesiod. If epic allowed its heroes lavish display of treasure and finery, that was in the tradition and, in a remote way, enviable—but Homer's audience was in no danger of being corrupted by luxuries that were hardly at all accessible. The later tradition of ideal austerity had its roots in a really hard past.

No trouble could arise till trade brought in the luxuries and Greek craftsmen could imitate them. The material remains show that there was more disposition to accept than to reject, and the note of doubt was perhaps not sounded early. Painters and poets rejoiced in the decorative detail. Alcman in Sparta and Sappho in Mytilene, at the end of the seventh century, happily accepted Lydian headgear or sandals. Later, in the sixth century, Xenophanes, whose generation saw the conquest of Lydia and Ionia by the Persians, thought that his countrymen of Colophon had learnt an unprofitable softness from the Lydians. They went to the place of assembly in their purple cloaks, rejoicing in their fine hair, dripping with elaborate perfumes, and the poet disapproved. The victory of mainland Greece over the Persians in 480–479 drew attention to the comforts of Persian life, even on campaign, and bolstered the Greeks' conviction of their superiority. The Spartan regent, Pausanias, was said to have resisted the temptations of luxury found in the Persian camp at Plataea, but his later collapse was ascribed to a surrender to these same temptations. To simple minds, that was explanation enough of Sparta's failure to hold the leadership after 478. From then on, the contrast between Spartan austerity and Persian softness was very popular. Xenophon made a fine scene of the meeting between king Agesilaus of Sparta, sitting on the grass among his advisers, and the Persian, Pharnabazus, in his expensive costume, shamed by Spartan simplicity into abandoning the rugs which his attendants were ready to lay down for him. The topic was widely exploited.

For Athens, we have a simplified but useful picture from Thucydides. His countrymen, he says, were among the first to give up the practice of going about their daily business, fully armed, and to take to an easier regime; in his day, it was not long since the older men of the more prosperous class gave up wearing linen tunics and doing their hair up in buns, fastened (if that is what the word means) with golden grasshoppers; but Sparta had then led, and the rest of Greece followed, a change to a simpler costume which did not so much emphasise the difference between rich and poor. Thucydides has telescoped matters, for evidence which is more available to us than to him shows, as might be expected, several changes of fashion over the long period which his sentence should cover. He is, of course, right about the change to a simpler costume after the Persian Wars, nor is his the only reference to the grasshoppers, which became for the late fifth century a symbol of the good old times. That points up the illogic of the prejudice in favour of simplicity, for it could be pointed out, and occasionally was, that precisely these delicately dressed ancestors had faced the Persians, and beaten them, on the field of Marathon.

Persian softness was rationalised by pretending that the countrymen of the great Cyrus had been tough enough, while they stayed in their native Iranian mountains, but had been weakened after their conquest of the plains. The hardy mountaineer and the lowlander, enervated by his easy life, make a handy contrast, which has been given a fresh run in a recent history of Greece—and it is possible for muscles to grow flabby in comfort. But the lives of the Greeks were hard enough at the height of their civilisation; and it is not for us, in our time, to maintain that troops brought up on hot baths and adequate food and clothing are necessarily inferior fighters. If the mountaineer has a real advantage from his poverty, it is rather that he has less to lose and is less tied to what property he has. The Greek prejudice is betrayed, not only by its illogicality, but by the triviality of so many of its instances. In a central scene of Aeschylus' *Agamemnon*, produced in 458, the king is overpersuaded by Clytemnestra to enter his palace treading on a purple carpet; and that serves, in some degree, to put him in the wrong.

But we should do Aeschylus an injustice if we took the purple carpet too seriously as a mere material fact. The trouble is rather a religious feeling that excess of any kind is likely to trespass on the sphere which the gods reserve for their own, a sphere which might include purple carpets. Herodotus, in a famous discussion on human happiness, makes Solon tell Croesus, the Lydian, why he will call no man prosperous till he has seen how he ended: he knows that all divine power is jealous and turbulent. The concept of a jealous God is, in a sense, familiar from the Old Testament, but Solon's second adjective cannot be reconciled at all with the concept of the loving-kindness of God. 'Turbulent' is too condensed a translation; the point is that the gods are given to disturbing human affairs almost wantonly and for mischief—an extreme expression of the universal feeling of the un-certainty of human fortune, allied to all the impulses that, even in an allegedly reasonable age, make men take implausible precautions against ill luck.

Nothing can entirely guard man against divine mischief, but the jealousy might be averted by not calling too much attention to oneself, by avoiding what Greek called *hybris*, a word whose meaning ranges from 'arrogance' to 'violence':[1] in this context, it refers to any conduct by which a man might appear to lift himself above his proper level. The Greeks had a strong natural tendency to go too far—the famous Delphic maxim, 'Nothing too much', was not inscribed for a people naturally moderate—and so their literature is full of examples of excess, and cautionary tales against it. They were not, indeed, disastrously ridden by such fears; but the apprehension was there in the background and when it became active it might take strange forms.

At a more cheerful level, the excess vigour of the Greeks ran off into affectation or foppery—those irrational twists of fashion, that application of surplus energy to doing basically indifferent things in one way rather than another, which, so far as they serve any purpose, serve to mark a particular social set off from more ordinary and less sparkling mankind. There is something of this, wherever costume is not merely drab and behaviour is not repressed by rigorous convention, and one might find affectation in the more exquisite figures of several periods of

1. In Athenian law, *hybris* covers all forms of violence to the person.

Attic vase-painting and sculpture. But the lives of the upper class at the end of the fifth century, the generation of Alcibiades, give an impression of specially extravagant fantasy. I do not think this is solely because we here have Aristophanes to laugh at it all, whereas there is no such volume of comment from earlier periods.

Periods of decline may produce a stylised splendour, but a lively and varied affectation is rather a sign of vigour. There can be no doubt of the vigour of this age, intellectually as well as in art and politics. This was the time when the teachers, called sophists, travelled from city to city —not, by Plato's standard, true philosophers, but men who claimed to teach the practical art of government, which in the main meant oratory, and much else. They could charge high fees, because their teaching was fashionable, and they were welcome in the greatest houses. Plato in the opening of his *Protagoras* has left us the picture of an excited friend, waking Socrates before dawn with the news of Protagoras' arrival in Athens; and of the subsequent conversation at the house of Callias, the wealthiest noble in Athens. The parodies of the sophists, Prodicus and Hippias, which Plato has here introduced, make fun of particular intellectual quirks; but the implicit criticism does nothing to weaken the impression of a society, alert and eager for intellectual novelty. There was an opposite fashion taking Sparta for its model, running to beards and right-wing views, and charged with not washing enough; and there were the athletes and the rest, another and probably smaller minority. In between, comes the more staid and conventional dinner-party, where one would not expect too much philosophy, but moderate drinking, and songs sung by turn—either the traditional Attic drinking-songs, of which some specimens survive, religious or patriotic or faintly moralising, or the work of older poets. Aristophanes at the end of the *Frogs* remarks how agreeable it is not to sit next to Socrates, who would interrupt the flow of music with his nonsense.

Other revellers might break in, the high-spirited young, moving in a garlanded gang from one party to another—an activity with a special verb appropriated to it (pl. 23). But there would be no respectable women present, only flute-girls and others with no reputation to lose. The seclusion of Greek women may be exaggerated, if one forgets the irrepressible women of Aristophanes and looks only at Pericles in the Funeral Speech which Thucydides gives him, bleakly remarking that the best reputation a woman can achieve is that her name should not be mentioned among the men, in praise or blame. But it is a fact that a woman's place was supposed to be the home, that upper-class women were not supposed to go out unattended—the poor, who could not help it, are less often glanced at—and that they were excluded from the public activities that made up so large a part of the men's lives.

To pass over the question of male homosexuality would distort the picture of Greek society, and its special features there come easily enough under the heading of social fashion. Since our social framework makes it hard for us to look at it calmly,[1] it ought to be stated at the start that there are, and have been, many civilisations which openly tolerate homosexuality without feeling that they are doing anything remarkable, and that such civilisations are not automatically involved in immediate disaster. They have even some social compensation, in that the exclusive homosexual is not driven into hiding or subject to blackmail, while the exclusive heterosexual is no worse off, nor those who come somewhere in between. (Competent surveys put most of us into this last category, and there is no reason to think that the Greek proportions were different.) For Greece, it meant mainly that the ambiguous phase which most young males pass through was prolonged. The pursuit of boys was a young man's preoccupation; the older practitioners were liable to be found ridiculous or offensive. The average man settled down easily enough to family life; and no one, familiar with Greek art or poetry, will be disposed to underrate the strength of marital and parental affection that the ordinary Greek felt.

There were certainly disagreeable tensions involved. The boy who yielded easily was thought effeminate, a damaging charge in that war-ridden society. The reprobation of one who sold his charms was far stronger than disapproval of the female prostitute, to the extent that in Athens, if the charge were proved against him, he was excluded from public office and from speaking in the assembly. Court speeches often make this charge against the opponent, though often perfunctorily. The active partner suffered no reprobation, indeed he might be thought more virile than one who went after women; but a father was expected to protect his son against seduction. The life of the boy was complicated by pressures which, in the upper classes, might be severe. For, though the evidence does not suggest that homosexual feeling was unequally distributed between the classes, it was in the upper levels

1. This should not be so difficult by 1966, but e.g. the outburst of F. Chamoux, *The Civilisation of Greece* (English translation 1965), pp. 308–9, shows that some cautionary statement may still be needed.

that it was positively cultivated. In Aristophanes, anything but reticent on this as on other subjects, the down-to-earth hero is hardly concerned with anything but casual contacts, whereas those with leisure and money could sigh romantically and court expensively. The obstacles added to the glamour, just as with adultery among the rich, in one kind of modern novel; whereas the adultery which equally occurs among the poor lacks these adventitious charms.

It is at the high romantic level that we meet the philosophic justification—the older man guiding the boy into the paths of virtue, a spiritual relation which the physical act would only spoil—or the lover who excels on the battlefield because his beloved's eye is on him. Plato's disapproval of the physical act is unmistakably genuine, for all the use he makes of the romance in the background of his dialogues. Xenophon's high line in his description of Spartan life is belied by his narrative history. In a society where the physical act was common and not censured, it would need a high virtue to live up to the 'platonic' ideal.

At Athens, it is evident that upper-class boys were subject, as a matter of regular social practice, to something of the strain that is imposed on girls in the more permissive societies of our time. They were free, indeed, from fear of unwanted pregnancy, but surrender was compensated by no physical gratification—at best, by the social gain of having given in to a lover of high standing. It is not, however, easy to find examples of damage, caused by this strain. Alcibiades himself might seem the obvious example, spoilt in youth by universal courtship, and full of strange, fashionable affectations, but it is difficult to believe that he would have been much less troublesome in a society differently organised. His affectations were balanced by solid abilities, which led the austere Thucydides to describe him as 'the man who managed the war best for Athens' in the difficult later years of the Peloponnesian War. His chances at Athens were wrecked, not by his affectations, most of which were harmless enough, but by a deeper-seated impatience with those restraints which the current system did recognise. His personal record, in which the heterosexual escapades were the more damaging, was not so much alarming in itself, as because it seemed part of a general pattern of behaviour, which suggested to the ordinary on-looker that he meant somehow to set himself above the law. It was only for brief periods that he could win the confidence of the city.

The affectations of fifth-century Athens have their nearest parallel in those of Elizabethan England, or in the Renaissance of Western Europe generally, and Alcibiades resembles some of the wilder figures of that Renaissance. He was an extreme case of the recklessness which set in towards the end of the fifth century, which contemporaries were apt to ascribe to the unsettling doctrines of certain of the sophists, and which was certainly intensified by the strains of a long war. There were others like Critias, who went over to Sparta, led the oligarchy of the Thirty in 404 and died in battle against the democrats—for all his talents, another immoderate and uncompromising person. Things had gone more easily in the early part of the fifth century, the great, hopeful days of Athens in which the democracy matured.

*

To pick on a single moment for the birth of democracy at Athens would mislead, if the attempt were made too seriously. The reforms of Cleisthenes in 507 mark, as Herodotus noted, the formal introduction of the basic elements. But we have to allow quite as much for the effect of the tyranny, in curbing the nobles, unifying the country, and fostering the feeling that all were concerned in the state, and that it was not the property of the great families. The growth of democracy after 507 was a continuous process, a matter of increasing confidence, of a state of mind as much as of legislative enactment. Later theory held that the naval victory at Salamis had a decisive effect, the rowers being conscious that they, rather than the hoplites, had saved the city and all Greece. There can be no doubt that the new and continuing role of the fleet increased the confidence of a class, poorer than the hoplites. Ephialtes' reform of the law-courts in 462 was recognised as another landmark, and the opponents of democracy later made much of the effects on Athens of pay for jury service. So, by stages, the system reached its full development.

There is not much sign of opposition in the earlier stages, once Cleisthenes had defeated his immediate opponents in 507. At the start, all could unite in opposition to Sparta's attempts to master the city. Internal politics slumbered during the Persian Wars, when Sparta and Athens were allies; Athens was then fully occupied in the pursuit of a war against the Persians in Asia, which profited rowers and soldiers alike. The chief leader in this war was a wealthy aristocrat, Cimon, son of the Miltiades who had won the battle of Marathon in 490, a symbol in himself of the fact that as yet there was no feeling of a gulf

between the upper classes and the fleet. Internal division revived, as the
Persian War died down, and tension between Athens and Sparta increased. Ephialtes was murdered soon after the passage of his reforms,
and a small oligarchic conspiracy was discovered at Athens during the
Spartan expedition to the north in 457; but nothing more disturbed
the regime till the rise of more seriously anti-democratic organisations
in the last quarter of the century.

The democratic machinery was, in fact, easily acceptable to the
upper class so long as they themselves were visibly the governing class
still, running the machine through magistrates and generals, drawn
from their own numbers. The breach in their content came with the
death of Pericles and the rise of political leaders who did not belong to
the established families. The first, and one of the most formidable, was
the demagogue, Cleon, constantly stigmatised as a tanner, a low and
smelly trade. The demagogues are mostly made out to be tradesmen
of one kind or another, though they were men of inherited wealth,
and therefore of leisure, who by no means rose directly from the ranks
of the common people. We have long known Cleon's father as a rich
man; and even the extreme example, Cleophon, alleged to be a lyre-
maker, and fatherless, in ancient literature, now turns out to be the son
of a respectable general, active in the earlier part of the Peloponnesian
War. These were, however, families, recently risen from trade, still
perhaps drawing income from inherited workshops, with something
of a commercial tradition behind them. Their appearance at this time
reflects the increasing complexity of public business, administrative as
well as strictly political, as Athens involved herself more and more in
the management of the affairs of the whole Aegean area. The governing
class of the first half of the century was adequate for traditional needs,
but its members were not trained to these new requirements. Pericles,
himself well born, was notorious for his continuous attention to public
business and some neglect of ordinary social duty. In his footsteps
followed the professional politicians, with no family tradition behind
them, resting on the support of the mass of the people, and charged
with exploiting their prejudices and their distrust of the upper class.
But, without them, necessary business could hardly have been trans-
acted.

The old families had by no means lost their hold. Wealth and an
ancient name were still valuable assets, vaunted in law-court speeches,
and a help especially towards such posts as were still elective. The last

sphere to be invaded by the professional was the military sphere, where the well-born, like the nobility of much later nations, felt at home and claimed the right to command. Cleon's venture into the generalship, which ended with his defeat and death at Amphipolis in 422, did not encourage imitation, and the hold of the traditional governing class on military posts was broken, not by the demagogues, but by the rise of whole-time mercenary captains.

Whatever class provided the leaders, the action taken had now to be, and to be seen to be, the action of the Athenian people. This applies not only to decisions of policy but also to the construction of temples and other buildings and to the conduct of festivals. Here again, the tyranny had prepared the way, by concentrating patronage and control in a single hand. What Peisistratus and his sons built at Athens was regarded as having been their own achievement. When Cimon in the 460's repaired the south wall of the Acropolis, out of spoils won from the Persians, that may be spoken of as his doing, but it is already different; he was using public money, acquired by a victory won under his leadership. For the Parthenon, begun in 447, Pericles was in charge as an official appointed by the people. There were, similarly, overseers for the other major buildings of the time. The money spent on them was public money, and they could not have been so many or so fine without the tribute paid to Athens from her empire.

The rich were laid under contribution in other ways. Direct taxation, voted irregularly to deal with emergencies, was not in the aggregate heavy by modern standards; but it was levied on capital, not income, and levied only on men of substantial property. These men were further liable, by turns, for a wide range of public service paid for out of their own pockets, the impositions called 'liturgies'. Some of these were regular and predictable, like the training of choruses for an annual festival, for which a 'choregus' had to be found, or the festival could not be held. Others came irregularly, like the nominal command of a ship in wartime. This meant in practice its maintenance and repair, the state providing hull and rigging, and the basic pay of the crew; but the commander might find that there were deficiencies to be made up here, or the state might have its property returned the worse for wear.

The expense varied greatly from one liturgy to another. It is hard to be sure how heavily the burden fell on individuals, the more so as there is a certain ambivalence in the response. On the one hand, it was an occasion for public display of one's wealth and patriotism, to the extent that some liturgies were sometimes undertaken voluntarily; and liturgies were a form of insurance against other forms of trouble, for a rich defendant in court could point to the amount that he had paid out, and claim that the jury ought to repay the city's debt by acquitting him. On the other hand, it could certainly be a burden, sometimes falling more heavily on those less capable of sustaining it, as is shown by various attempts to redistribute the load. At need, a man could pick out another whom he believed better able to afford the expense, and challenge him to a valuation of their respective properties under the procedure called *antidosis*, literally, an exchange of property. The lamentations of the aged orator, Isocrates, under one of these challenges are not a typical response: for all the vagaries of its incidence, this was still not alarmingly heavy taxation—and, unlike the payer of modern income-tax, the rich Athenian could see, and demonstrate to others, what he was paying for.

Training in music and dance was needed for a variety of tribal competitions and other festivals, but our main interest must always be in she festivals of Dionysus, at which the tragic and comic poets competed, the entries being selected by the archon, and the production financed as a liturgy. The origins of tragedy, whatever the precise ancestry of the unique Athenian form, lie in choral singing and mime, enacted in honour of Dionysus. The main festival, the City Dionysia, was developed or enlarged in the sixth century and encouraged, though not apparently created, by the tyrants. Early in the fifth century, the plays had already taken their familiar form, with three actors and a chorus. Seven complete plays survive from Aeschylus, who fought at Marathon in 490 and was still writing in the 450's, and seven from Sophocles, whose career began in the 460's and lasted nearly to the end of the century; from Euripides, the experimentalist who shocked the devout and was endlessly teased by the comic poets down to and after his death in 406, we have, by chance, as many as nineteen. But that is all, out of a total of some 300 tragedies which survived in Hellenistic times. The music and the dancing have necessarily perished altogether, losing for us a large proportion of the effect of the original performances.

Festivals in the classical period were more fully and more consciously city festivals. In the late sixth century and the early fifth, Simonides and Pindar wrote choral lyric as often for cities as corporate bodies as they did for tyrants or private patrons. Athenian tragedy was very much a projection of the city of Athens, often glancing explicitly at the glory of the city. But, though the democracy somehow fostered it, tragedy cannot be described simply as a democratic art. The poets themselves belonged to the upper class—indeed, Sophocles was elected to the generalship in 440. The plots, with rare exceptions, were taken from the common stock of legend and concerned princes and their courts: and this meant that the outcome was known in outline before the play began, though the poet was free to improvise or alter detail. The form is curiously stiff: an introductory prologue; choral lyric of a wilful, shimmering beauty (and very complex syntax) alternating with stark argument between the actors, at a very high level of generalisation; and the catastrophe often in the form of a narrative speech by a messenger. The language is an artificially high poetic language, even in the hands of Euripides, who claimed, or was accused of claiming, that he had reduced tragedy to the level of common speech.

The whole is a compound not easily characterised in short compass, even if one foregoes any attempt to discuss the poetry as such. The contemporary world is not wholly excluded, and prehistoric kings are found remarkably respectful to the views, or even the vote, of an assembly. Aeschylus, in particular, breaks out of the heroic framework at times with topical comment: his *Eumenides*, with its account of the establishment of the Areopagus as a court to try Orestes on the charge of murder, was produced in the spring of 458, within four years of Ephialtes' controversial reform of the Areopagus, and the play is, among other things, a comment on the controversy. But these are exceptional cases. The regular concern of tragedy is with personal conflicts, issues about authority and its misuse, obedience to or defiance of the will of the gods, human passion and disaster. The persons are heroes, more than life-size, caught in difficult and sometimes atrocious situations, to which they react in heroic style, according to the code of conduct and the sense of honour inherited from the world of the epic.

Ordinary men could not live at this level; even aristocrats could only to a limited extent indulge such a sense of honour, in a world which was held together by less combative and more co-operative virtues. The ethos of the city from time to time appears through the heroic scaffolding, and the large, quotable generalisations, in which tragedy abounds, were often applicable to contemporary as well as to heroic life. But the gap remains, and tragedy was to a significant extent about a different world. These were the stories on which the audience had been brought up, and they liked both the spectacle provided, and the intransigent emotions and the formal arguments. It is, up to a point, intelligible that the democracy should have supported a competition in plays about heroes, just as it is entirely natural that it should have built a house on the Acropolis for the city's goddess, but the high quality of Attic tragedy and of the Parthenon were not predictable—a bonus we had no right to expect.

Architecture and sculpture pursue the same high heroic line. Both arts served the gods and the state: domestic architecture hardly amounted to anything before the middle of the fourth century, when Demosthenes complains that the great men of Athens were no longer satisfied with the simplicity of an earlier age; nor were statues made for the collections of private connoisseurs, as they were made or copied for wealthy Romans. These arts were not the subject of public competition as poetry and music were. In the classical period, it was the state which commissioned architect and sculptor, and laid down its conditions for the work. A few Athenian documents refer to these contracts and to the appointment of state officials to supervise their execution, and rather more of the accounts of such officials survive, inscribed on stone in all the careful detail which Athenian democracy demanded. The great sculptors were men whose names were remembered —before them, no artist had ever signed his work with his name— and they were men of some mark, who lived at least on the fringes of polite society (Daedalus, who worked for king Minos of Crete, had his established place in legend). So were the greater architects, while the fifth-century town-planner, Hippodamus of Miletus, was also a political theorist whose views Aristotle took the trouble to criticise. On the other hand, the potters and vase-painters and other small craftsmen, who did work for the private purchaser, were not remembered by name in literature. These were operators at a lower level, some of them pretty certainly slaves; but among them there were admirable artists, a fair proportion known to us by name because they, again, signed their works. It is hard to imagine that native or foreign buyers were not proud to display in use a vase, decorated by such a draughtsman as Exekias (pl. 26).

The sculpture which adorned temples and public buildings took its subjects almost entirely from the same mythological stock which provided the plots for Attic tragedy, with due regard for what was locally appropriate. The outstanding exception is the continuous frieze of the

Parthenon at Athens, which depicts the preparations for the great procession of the Panathenaea and the procession itself. It seems to be the composite work of a team of craftsmen, for whom we must suppose that a single sculptor, Pheidias or another, provided the basic drawing. It is immensely valuable to us, not only as a work of consummate art, but as a social document unique in its kind; but it was possibly alarming to Greek feeling in its emphasis on the celebrants, rather than on the gods whom they honoured.

Yet this magnificent work must have been very difficult to see in its original setting under the eaves of the great temple. We have also to remember that the buildings which partly survive on the Acropolis—Parthenon and Erechtheum and Propylaea—did not then dominate the scene quite so much as their remains do today. Isolated temples in the countryside may have made their effect in the style which we instinctively think appropriate for a monumental building: Apollo at Bassae in the mountains of western Arcadia; Artemis Aphaia on the wooded eastern headland of Aegina; perhaps, too, Poseidon on cape Sunium at the southern tip of Attica. But, on the greater sites, the long course of history and the demands of cult and dedication produced an untidy accretion of crowded building, which seriously muffled the monumental effect. Surviving foundations in the main precinct at Delphi give us the opportunity to imagine what it might be like with the buildings erect and the statues on their pedestals, though there the steep slope will always have given the great temple of Apollo its due prominence. The rock of the Athenian Acropolis, on the other hand, has been stripped to a point where it is hard to conceive what the huddle was like when one could not stand back to look at the Parthenon—when not only the numerous subsidiary temples and the free-standing statues were still there, but a mass of minor dedications, state decrees inscribed on stone stelae, and all the other apparatus which made this narrow area one of the focal points of the life of Athens.

The minor arts can bring us closer to the ordinary man, especially vase-painting. Here, the high scenes of legend and tragedy alternate with pictures of daily life, school or dinner-party or sometimes the workshop in which vase or statue was made. For the sound of contemporary social life, we can turn to Attic comedy, provided we remember its conventions and its purpose, which was not just to hold a mirror up to nature. Eleven plays of Aristophanes survive complete. The frag-

ments of other poets are enough to bring out the general similarity of
their plays, but fragments are difficult to interperet without their
contexts, and it is a risky business to try to determine how his
rivals differed from Aristophanes. Whatever its ultimate origins,
comedy in its great age, in the last third of the fifth century, was a
boisterous entertainment, full of horseplay and obscenity, much concerned with current politics, intellectually alive, and assuming that a
significant part of the audience remembered lines from the recent plays
of Euripides—though philosophic doctrines and tags from Euripides are
relevant only so far as they can be guyed, and the poet is more interested
in finding targets for political mockery than in advocating any line of
policy.

It is in the political field that Aristophanes is most easily misunder-
stood. From the gusto with which he belabours Cleon, it is all too easy
to conclude that he was an old-fashioned conservative; but those who
accept this conclusion are driven to improbable and contorted explanations of the fact that Aristophanes was so popular with audiences
which habitually voted with Cleon. There is no doubt about his
personal quarrel with Cleon, who hauled him before the Council on
the charge that his second play, produced in 426, insulted the city's
officials at a festival where foreigners were present. It does not seem
that the poet suffered any penalty, and the quarrel only added zest to
the attack he made on Cleon in the *Knights* in 424. Here Demos, the
people, is personified as a deaf and testy old man, wholly in the power
of the loudmouthed and brutal slave-steward who stands for Cleon.
The remedy is to find another who can outdo him in vulgarity, a
sausage-seller who, in unlikely alliance with the cavalry chorus, defeats
their common enemy, Cleon. In a final transformation-scene, Demos
is rejuvenated and restored to his ancestral ways by the sausage-seller,
who in some unexplained way has himself been converted to the good
old cause.

It is noticeable how Cleon is attacked mainly on social grounds, his
low birth and behaviour. His political activities, his squeezing of the
rich and financial pressure on the allies, are referred to only in reprobation. It seems the people enjoyed all this, including the personification
of themselves as an irritable old man. For one thing, comedy was
licensed buffoonery, and applause committed no one to vote against
Cleon. The social criticism was harmless as such, for no one thought
Cleon was a gentleman; the people, as so often, found no difficulty in

accepting the upper-class scale of values as valid in such a context. More important, even under the direct rule of a primary assembly, there was still a sense of distance between the ordinary voter and the self-constituted group of orators who made up the only sort of 'government' there was. They were the experts, who understood the business and proposed the motions and held the offices. There was release for quite simple and intelligible feelings in seeing them mocked and battered on the stage, where it did not matter.

Aristophanes himself was a gentleman, who could take his place in the dinner-party which forms Plato's *Symposium*; and he may have had his own political views. It would be permissible to deduce from the plays that he went further than most in his dislike of war. In the *Frogs*, in the spring before Athens' final defeat in 405, in a passage of unusual seriousness, he openly deplored the intolerance of the democracy towards some honest men in the upper classes. But his own views do not normally inhibit his fantasy, or prevent the easy identification of the ordinary man with his hero, triumphing over warmongers and politicians and anyone else who gets in the way. The level mainly aimed at seems to be that of the quite small farmer or the main rowers in the fleet, and their pantomime triumph is a crassly gluttonous feast. The small man is not spared, either. The manic stupidity and misdirected shrewdness of Aristophanes' peasant types, even if they win in the end, would allow the shopkeeper some superior laughter, just as the countryman heard the worst of city life; both might find comfort in the caricature of upper-class affectation. Add to this the often delicate and often gross play on tragic verse, which for the ordinary man demanded no more than a general acquaintance with the style, but would delight the expert by more particular allusion; and it may be seen that there was something here for everybody, apart from the bawdiness which they all enjoyed.

*

The years between the Persian and the Peloponnesian Wars saw much eager controversy, but for Athens it was by comparison with other epochs a time of social harmony. The glow lasts on into the earlier plays of Aristophanes. Thucydides ascribed the eventual defeat or Athens to internal strife; and, though his judgment presents some difficulties, there is no doubt that the strife occurred. The strain of the long war showed itself in some unpleasant outbreaks of mass hysteria.

One of the most damaging occurred in 415, just before the sailing of the great expedition to Sicily, when the square pillars with heads of Hermes, which decorated the streets of Athens, were all mutilated in the night. The further information that parodies of the Eleusinian mysteries had been perpetrated in private houses filled the people with a wild fear that these sacrilegious crimes were the prelude to oligarchic revolution or tyranny. The long investigation filled the city with panic, till in the end a confession was accepted as clearing the whole matter up. Before this, the upper class had begun to organise in retaliation; secret oligarchic clubs flourished enough to appear occasionally on the surface. Thucydides speaks of them with some contempt, and there was certainly an element of play-acting by young men pretending to more importance than they had. But the clubs helped to start an oligarchic reign of terror as a prelude to revolution in 411; and, when the revolution came, the people were scared to find how many of their nominal leaders had concealed a sympathy with the revolutionaries. The revulsion after the democratic restoration of 410 was correspondingly rancorous, with many exiles and many court sentences of partial or complete loss of civil rights. To these disqualified citizens Aristophanes refers in the *Frogs*, when he urges the city to take back into its service all who could contribute to the war.

The second oligarchy in 404 proved, if it still needed proof, that there were not enough convinced oligarchs at Athens to form an effective government. The second democratic restoration in 403, led by very moderate men, began with an amnesty which has been claimed as the first of its kind; even right-wing theorists allowed that the people had behaved better than their opponents. The immediate dislocation caused by the war passed quickly enough. Athens' economy recovered, and her port of Peiraeus was busier than ever. Politically, she was never negligible till the Macedonian conquest. But irreparable damage had been done, and some of the spring was taken out of Athens for good. The stress between rich and poor remained; Aristotle, in the second half of the fourth century, took it for granted in his political writings that every state had two main parties, divided on economic lines, and that in democracy the poor would despoil the rich as much as they could.

Though there were upheavals elsewhere, the fear of political spoliation was not realised in Athens, which, in spite of anti-democratic doubts, displayed a remarkable stability. But there was more justified fear that a man of wealth was vulnerable in the law-courts. It was alleged that, in times of stress, the prosecutor might press for conviction on the ground that the state treasury needed the fine; but times of real financial emergency were not so common. Individual danger came from the professional informers, called 'sycophants' (p. 180), who appear as a notorious evil already in the earliest of Aristophanes' extant plays in 425. There is no way of estimating the real extent of the trouble. Theophrastus in his *Characters*, a powerful collection of conversational bores, clearly finds excess complaint about sycophants ridiculous; but some complaint was justified.

The standard charges against democracy speak of corrupt demagogues, stirring up war, and malicious sycophants, blackmailing the rich. The defence is almost silent, for the theory of democracy lived rather in the minds of those who practised it than in formal expositions. Of the major writers who survive, only Herodotus endorsed it wholeheartedly, and he died in the early years of the Peloponnesian War. Thucydides, who did not long outlive the war he chronicled, was contemptuous of constitutional forms and devoted his very critical attention to the performance of politicians within their various systems. He gives only doubtful allegiance to democracy, but in his version of the Funeral Speech, delivered by Pericles over the dead of the first year of war, he has left us a bright eulogy of the freedom and ease of prewar Athenian life which weighs more heavily than constitutional analysis could do. Thereafter, the educated were united in their distrust of a system which, nevertheless, was so firmly entrenched that, after 404, no one could openly advocate oligarchy. Would-be reformers had to cloak their plans under the pretence that they wanted to return to an earlier and purer form of democracy. The prime example in this technique is that of Isocrates, an influential writer of pamphlets but no practising politician, who hankered for the ideals of a largely imaginary past. In spite of some genuine insight into the problems of his time, his plans were unrealisable except through a change of heart which would make them unnecessary, rather like those leading articles on national regeneration with which *The Times* of London at intervals delights its readers.

Neither the fears nor the hopes of Isocrates were firmly based. There was ground enough for political discouragement if one looked at intercity relations, where no combination proved stable under the insensitive rule of Sparta or the never firmly rooted supremacy of Thebes. But life within the city was anything but dead, even politically, and the intellectual ferment continued, though in different forms. Comedy died down, to be reborn in a milder and more sentimental form: a great age of poetry had ended with Euripides: much fourth-century prose fell into the easy periods of Isocrates, smoothing out what thought there was. But sculpture had not yet lost direction in its technical mastery, and painting flourished, though the painters are bare names to us, no longer given body by their reflection in vase-painting. Philosophy was greatly alive; and important advances were made in mathematics and astronomy, a prelude to the achievements of the Hellenistic age. The descriptive zoology and botany of Aristotle's school show Greek science advancing in a new direction. Their comparable collection of laws and customs and constitutions gave a fresh direction to history, which otherwise was swamped by moral enthusiasm.

Plato's brilliant near-poetic prose, with its skilful use of colloquial speech and its endless illustrations from ordinary life, is adequate consolation for the loss of Aristophanes' social comments, when they stop, early in the fourth century. Aristotle can help us too, especially in his *Ethics*, with their revealing sketches of the virtues that were applauded by the society of his time. Law-court speeches give much incidental information, provided one remembers that the standard of ingenious villainy ascribed to the speaker's opponent is hardly meant to be accepted literally, and that the cases dealt with are in the nature of things exceptional. The strictures of a Demosthenes in his public speeches may again mislead, if one forgets the latitude allowed in any age to a politician passionately advocating his preferred policy; but there is, again, important information about the ways in which the orator wanted himself or his city to be seen, and the kinds of argument that might be expected to appeal to his citizens.

Athenian society in the middle of the fourth century was more sober than it had been at the end of the fifth. There was less extravagant individualism, and the radical questioning of all accepted values which characterised the generation of Euripides and Thucydides had ended by undermining that unlimited confidence in the capacity of the individual judgment which the questioning presupposed. Speculation did not cease, but Aristotle could assume a much wider agreement among men of intelligence and good will about the goals which city or individual should pursue. His discussions of ethics and politics assume, throughout, that the city-state would continue as the dominant political form. It may be that the city could still have solved at least its internal problems, and contributed further to the stock of valuable human experience. Philip and Alexander saw to it that the further experiment was not tried.

CHAPTER 11

Gods and oracles

To UNDERSTAND THE religious feeling of an alien civilisation is never easy, and between us and the Greeks there is more ample ground for misunderstanding here than in most fields. We have been brought up, whatever our private feelings about it, in a world with a monotheistic religion, a separate and professional priesthood, a firmly asserted link between religion and morality, the concept that God loves mankind. When we turn to Greece, we are faced with all the shifting incoherence of polytheism, bound together by no organised Church or body of dogma, with stories of the conduct of the gods so scandalous that some Greeks indignantly rejected them, gods whose favour to individual men or cities might be presumed in general or secured in particular by the correct sacrifices, but whose attitude to mankind as such was by no means unequivocally friendly. Not that these gods were felt to be remote or frivolous. Greek poetry and art is full of the most solemn awe towards the divine; the bond of common worship held the Greek nation together more than any other single factor; and every Greek activity was linked with the cult of some god to an extent which makes our civilisation seem, by comparison, nakedly secular.

*

There is so much of Greek religion that it is not easy to know where to begin, but a Greek would certainly have begun with Homer. If Greece had no body of settled dogma, it had at least a book; and if the Homeric poems seem less promising religious material than the Bible, ingenuity was not wanting to wrest rules of ritual or conduct from the text of 'the poet', a title which was always sufficient to identify Homer. Herodotus had no doubt that it was Hesiod and Homer—in his opinion, some 400 years before his own time—who had given the gods their Greek names and settled their ritual; and when the philosophic poet Xenophanes in the sixth century complained that theft and adultery and deceit should be ascribed to the gods, it was Homer and Hesiod that he blamed. Homer's part was the description of the divine family in action, intervening on one side or the other on the plain of Troy, helping or hindering Odysseus' return home, with whatever else determined search could deduce from the poet's text. Hesiod's *Theogony* was a deliberate effort of systematisation, primarily the genealogy and interrelation of the gods. In its main lines, it set out the Homeric position and its background; its authority was widely accepted, but it did not efface the innumerable local variants. Hesiod claimed specific instruction from the Muses, Homer only the general inspiration common to all poets. Neither looks much like a religious prophet, as we understand the term. It is surprising that they should exercise such authority, or, perhaps we should say, surprising that so much authority was ascribed to them, though the fact that Homer was evidently the oldest text available on any subject may offer a partial explanation.

The present dynasty of gods had not always held power, and the fact that Zeus was a newcomer might be remembered in problem-pieces like Aeschylus' *Prometheus Bound*. But, practically always and for all practical purposes, Zeus was established as the incomparably powerful king of the gods, father of all, the god of the sky and the weather, whose thunderbolt was the last, unanswerable weapon. His brother, Poseidon, was another natural power, god of the sea and of horses and of earthquakes. Homer once refers to a threefold division in which the third brother, Hades, was allotted the underworld; but, though he and his house occur endlessly as synonyms for death, he hardly appears as a person. Zeus' sister and consort, Hera, goddess of marriage and childbirth, specially powerful at Argos and an embittered enemy of Troy, is rather more prominent in the *Iliad* than in the thoughts of most later Greek cities. The virgin warrior, Athena, patroness of female crafts, Hera's ally against Troy, commanded an altogether wider devotion in later times, by no means confined to her name-city, Athens. Apollo, with his bow and his music and his infallible oracles, has been taken as the embodiment of the more austere and intellectual side of Greek religion; his twin sister Artemis, a virgin huntress, who also presided over childbirth, had a well-established place. Kinder and less formidable were the deceitful Hermes, the god of

Arcadian shepherds and of travellers everywhere, messenger of the gods and conductor of souls to Hades; and another craftsman, the lame smith, Hephaestus. Ares, formally the god of war, was rather a witless and exasperating nuisance than a serious and sombre power; Homer makes his consort, Aphrodite, into a figure of fun on the battlefield, but she was dangerous in her own sphere as goddess of love. Lastly—though the catalogue could be greatly prolonged—Demeter, goddess of fertility and especially of cereal crops, and Dionysus the god of wine, play a small part in Homer, quite disproportionate to their evident weight in classical Greek life.

It may fairly be said that the epic tradition, which culminates in Homer, had given Greek religion a special twist. To an astonishing extent, with even the all-powerful Zeus only a partial exception, the gods are creatures made in the human mould and subject to strictly human passions. Though there was a wide and unbridgeable gap between man and god, the gap consisted entirely in the god's superior power and his immortality. In these aristocratic stories, the gods have gone far towards becoming super-aristocrats, playing the heroes' role at a higher level, and losing something from their own nature in the process. Homer's treatment of the gods, influential as it was, is not the whole story—the Apollo of Delphi, the Zeus of the Attic tragedians, were more than supremely powerful warriors and feasters—but the tendency displayed in the poems was a continuing tendency of the Greek mind, a kind of sterilising of the divine.

This shows itself clearly in Homer's exclusion of the irrational element, if that is a fair description of the element common to fertility rites, ecstatic cults, the cult of the gods of the underworld. All these existed in plenty in the Greek world, and can hardly have been in abeyance when the epic tradition took shape. The analogy between the earth and a human mother has formed a basis for many religions, especially in the early days of agriculture, and it was well established in the Greek peninsula before the Greek nation took shape. But the rites by which the earth-mother's fertility might be excited for the coming year were perhaps found unseemly by the epic tradition, impairing that special aristocratic dignity which it attributed to its gods. The male consort of such a goddess is apt to be quite subsidiary, where he is found at all; he may be born as a baby every year with the returning vegetation, and combine this role with his role as the earth's sexual partner. Wild music and dances are another un-Homeric element in the ritual. There were plenty of dancing priests around: the Corybantes of the Phrygian goddess Cybele; or the Couretes of Crete, whose noise was rationalised as a device to prevent the cries of the infant Zeus from being heard by his father Cronos. Crete also diverged from some common Greek notions by showing the tomb of Zeus, as well as his birthplace. Demeter herself, with her daughter, Persephone, who spent the three winter months in the underworld, was specially at home at Eleusis in Attica; the Athenians boasted that the secret of agriculture had been revealed to them first of all and then generously shared with other men. Eleusis is the scene of the seventh-century 'Homeric' hymn to Demeter, where the goddess has been tamed to a quiet stately dignity. In other corners of Greece, her worship took odder forms.

That the god of wine should run to still wilder rites is not un-expected, and Dionysus must head the list of ecstatic cults where the worshipper felt himself possessed by the god. Bands of maenads ('mad women') roamed the mountains, with ivy-wreathed sticks and snakes and fawns (pl. 29), and flesh was eaten raw, torn from the living body. It is hard to judge how far this went in the practice of a classical city. The more spectacular stories are of the first arrival of the god in Greece, and of the resistance of respectable authority, in punishment for which Dionysus sent the women mad, and horrific scenes ensued. But the possession and the mountain wandering and the raw flesh were not mere legend, though classical Greece had canalised them into ritual occasions at known intervals. The stories of Dionysus' arrival should not be interpreted as historical memory of a cult actually arriving, relatively late, on the Greek scene and being resisted by the established representatives of older cults. Many gods were thought of as having arrived at the scene of their worship at a particular point in time, not as having existed there or anywhere eternally; Apollo's first journey to Delphi forms the subject of another Homeric hymn. The resistance is, rather, a symbol of that element in the minds of so many Greeks which recoiled from the rolling eyes and the flying hair and preferred its religion more decorous. The best introduction to the whole business is Euripides' *Bacchae*, written at the end of his life, a version of the legend in which king Pentheus of Thebes was torn in pieces for his resistance. The folly of Pentheus is underlined in the scene where two old men, his father, Cadmus, and the blind seer, Teiresias, stagger out to join the maenads. Whatever else the play may contain, it has to be read as a sermon on the danger of trying to suppress the irrational altogether, a danger to which Greeks were liable.

The underworld is another matter. Its special gods were not neglected, though their worship is not specially prominent; many daylight gods had their 'chthonic' side, and some connection with the world below. There is, however, more serious concern with the dead themselves, especially the recently dead, and those who in their lives had for one reason or another made so powerful an impression as to warrant a continuing cult after their death. Greek ideas of the after-life are, by and large, properly represented in the dim Homeric picture of witless shades, very tenuously existing in the house of Hades. If Odysseus could momentarily restore their wits by letting them drink the blood of his sacrifice, that was not much of an immortality. The Thracian Getae, who did believe in the possibility of an immortal life, were reported as a curiosity: Plato's doctrine of the immortality of the soul made no progress with the ordinary man, nor did Pythagorean doctrines of transmigration. The largest hope, but we are not well informed about it, was opened up by initiation into the mysteries of Eleusis and some few other cults. In general, the Greek expected to live only in the memory of his successors, or in his own posterity; this was a large element in their urgent feeling that the family and its cult must have sons to maintain it.

However, human nature is so constituted that lack of belief in an after-life is no protection against the fear of what the dead may do to the living. The first concern was that the rites of burial should be properly carried out; Greece had its quota of ghosts haunting the survivors till they were thus laid, beginning with the dead Patroclus' appearance to Achilles in a dream. More continuous power was attributed to Agamemnon in his grave, in that impressive scene of Aeschylus' *Choephoroe* where his children, Orestes and Electra, implore his help before the murder of Clytemnestra. But this is an unfair example, in that Agamemnon was, for Aeschylus, an old-established hero with a cult in several centres. The ghosts of lesser men had their occasional day, as at the Athenian Anthesteria, the spring festival of Dionysus when the new wine was opened. The ghosts were abroad till banished by the proclamation that the feast was over, and all temples were closed till they had gone. Systematic theology might have had some trouble in accommodating all that happened in the three days of that festival.

'Hero' was not only the regular term for the leaders in the tale of Troy, it had also a religious meaning, definable in so far as the ritual for sacrifice to a hero differed from that for a god. Great achievement was one road to heroisation. The prime example, Heracles, whose labours were eventually interpreted as a clearing of monsters from the earth for the benefit of mankind, went beyond the status of hero to become a god on Olympus. At a more mundane level, the founders of colonies might receive heroic honours, like the Athenian, Hagnon, who founded Amphipolis in Thrace in 437, but lived to see his honours transferred to the Spartan, Brasidas, who took the city in 424. There were also minor heroes of another order. Some had names, though it might be that their story was little known outside the group dedicated to their worship; but when it comes to nameless heroes, like that 'hero beside the salt-pans' to whom the Athenian clan, Salaminii, sacrificed once a year, it is clear that we are no longer dealing with known mortals whose known achievements had raised them to this degree of immortality.

Various lines of explanation are possible. Local gods might fade in various ways in competition with the Olympian family, recognised by the whole nation. Some were partly or completely identified with a greater god, surviving as his satellite or in one of his local titles; this seems to have been the fate of Hyacinthus, at Amyclae, near Sparta, who finished either as a youth beloved by Apollo or in the title Apollo Hyacinthius. Some, though in the nature of things we can point to no certain instance, might live on as heroes at a lower level, or lose their names altogether. Alternatively, we may be involved here with another level of popular belief, which found divinity in local springs or trees and did not need a name for worship. All rivers were gods, the nymphs had their worship collectively or individually in small local shrines, sea and mountain had their appropriate spirits. It is only from the infrequent sacrificial calendars of local associations that we get much indication of the kind of worship that mattered here; below the level where inscription on stone begins, we know nothing at all. Again, cases are known where archaic Greeks made offerings at a Mycenaean tomb; the occupant of such a tomb, with no remembered name, would naturally be put into the category of hero.

*

Thoroughgoing polytheism, by its nature, easily tolerates and incorporates new cults as they are encountered. The classical period saw importations from Thrace and Egypt and elsewhere, and the inheritance of the dark age was already a mixed one, resisting any too simple attempt to sort it out. There is some temptation to try to distinguish the gods of the older Mediterranean substratum from those brought in by later invaders, speaking an Indo-European language. It is not hard to suppose that mother-goddess and fertility cult had existed in the south as long as agriculture; whereas Zeus, the sky-god, one of the few whose name presents no etymological puzzle, is paralleled in name and nature among the speakers of other Indo-European tongues. But this classification will not reach far. Apollo, who has been regarded as the characteristically Greek deity, has a name with no good Greek derivation; the name is probably Asiatic, whatever the Greeks may have made of the god. Worse confusion awaits those who adopt the distinction made by Nietzsche, between the rational Apollo and the irrational Dionysus, as anything but a rough, though useful, tool for the analysis of Greek religion as a whole.

Except in the rare cases where origins are known or easily deduced, they are best left alone. The right question is rather what the Greeks made of their various inheritance. Here the first issue is, what to make of the trend which Homer presents. The epic tradition rationalised, in the limited sense that it excluded some of the more obviously non-rational elements, and this may have been some help to later rationalisers. But what distinguishes the gods of the Homeric charade is not any attempt to rationalise anything, but a matter of style or social conduct. Here, a distinction has been drawn between the narrative of the poet and the speech of the characters in the story. The narrative concentrates on these very anthropomorphic deities with their clear-cut personalities and motives: the speakers habitually and very vaguely ascribe their feelings, thoughts and actions to the intervention of a god inspiring or hindering them—a mixed idea of human personality, in which will and emotion seem often to be separated from the central core of the man and treated as if they depended on these outside influences. The difference is noticeable, and may reflect two different stages of Greek thought about the gods. If so, it is the anthropomorphic elements that most call for explanation. It is these that have led critics to call the *Iliad* an entirely irreligious poem, and it is this irreligious turn that represents a deviation from the development that might have been expected.

One answer has been that the Olympian family represents the interests of the Mycenaean rulers themselves, an aristocratic minority occupied in war and feasting, which did not want to hear from its poets about religion as practised by the agricultural under-dog. But a long interval separates Homer from the Mycenaean princes. Where so much of the Mycenaean heritage had been dropped, it would be odd if the epic tradition had so exactly conserved their religious prejudices; and, though the documents show that many gods of the Olympian family were worshipped in Mycenaean times, it is by no means clear that they were worshipped in the Homeric spirit. Explanation must be sought nearer Homer's own time, in the feelings and prejudices of the aristocracies which dominated the end of the dark age. As such, the phenomenon might be expected to continue in some measure into the classical period, for the influence of other aristocratic ideals still made itself felt; it has rightly been remarked that Apollo always moved in the best society, whereas Dionysus was much more the god of the common man. Homer's treatment of the gods represents a continuing tendency in the mind of the educated and articulate upper class. The ordinary man, here as elsewhere, accepted the notions of the upper class as right and proper; but still, to some extent, he worshipped his own gods, and no doubt contrived the myth he needed for his own life.

The gods of the *Iliad* were concerned, like the heroes, with their own honour, and only in exceptional passages with human morality. That somewhat artificial gap was likely to be filled: in a sense, the simplified gods of Homer more easily became moral agents than the gods of fertility cults, which at best are morally neutral. The *Odyssey*, in general, shows more interest in morality. When Zeus is invoked as the natural protector of beggars and suppliants, that is not only a matter of manners. Hesiod and Solon were preoccupied with a classic form of the problem of evil, the question how a just and all-powerful god can allow the unjust to flourish in this life. By the fifth century, the notion of the gods, especially Zeus, as the upholders of justice was familiar, with all its problems. Some critics have made too elevated a theologian out of Aeschylus, from whom some older and rougher notes may be heard; the word which we translate justice, *dikê*, often still keeps its older sense, what is done rather than what ought to be done. But questions about the justice of the gods were certainly prominent in the great tragedies of Athens. It was sometimes denied that the gods had such moral interests, but for the philosophers it was self-evident that god's nature must be good. It was hardly more than the Epicurean sect, that maintained that the gods were not interested in mankind at all. If among them all they found no consistent and satisfying solution of the problems involved, it is not for us to complain about that.

*

In early days, what might be called public cults were naturally under the control of the aristocracy, for it was part of their general expertise that they knew the right ritual and could conduct it. In the conservative way of religion, many traces of this remained in the classical period. Cults might be taken over by the state and maintained out of state funds, but a particular ritual would still be in the hands of a particular clan. So, for instance, the rites at Eleusis were the concern of the Athenian state, which felt entirely competent to legislate about them; but the great clans, Eumolpidae and Ceryces, still provided the main officiants, and their inherited tradition was still an unwritten law which, within limits, must be respected. Again, the nobility still provided official expounders of ritual, *exegetai*, who would tell an enquirer the proper procedure in a doubtful case. In public matters of religion, however, the democracy of Athens preferred to rely on professional seers who had not this aristocratic backing.

The idea that the state was under the special protection of a particular deity, Athena at Athens, Poseidon at Corinth, Hera at Argos, was exceedingly old, and these cults were never merely the property of particular great families. It is likely that some of them were deliberately expanded during the age of tyrants. The great festival of the Panathenaea at Athens was so expanded during the sixth century; if Peisistratus did not himself initiate the change, he allowed it to develop. In the same spirit, helping to undermine the privileged position of the nobles, the tyrants encouraged the worship of Dionysus. The building of great central temples was another feature of tyrants' policy.

These temples were the houses of their gods, not places where a congregation met for worship. They were modest at first: small buildings with mud-brick walls, thatched roofs and a simple porch—the form known to us from the clay model of such a temple, dedicated to Hera at Perachora, near Corinth; or wooden buildings, with some architectural features which survived into the time of building in stone.

Stone temples began around 700, and grew to those grave and powerful forms, still in places standing as an expression of the Greek spirit (pl. 30). Worship was in the open air, sacrifices on an altar before the temple and formal processions. Priesthood, or particular ritual tasks, might be hereditary in certain clans or families, but these were part-time duties, which did not set the holder apart from the life of other men. In many cases, a man would make his own sacrifice with no priestly assistance. A meal of meat was more often than not a sacrifice; the large sacrifices at great festivals were public dinners, memorable occasions for a people who did not eat meat all that often.

In private sacrifice and prayer, a man put himself into personal relation with the deity and hoped that his offering was accepted. Most men felt their relation to some particular god to be specially close, like the grandfather of one of Isaeus' clients, who would admit only his nearest relatives when he sacrificed to the god of his favourite cult, Zeus Ctesius, who looked after household and property. Innumerable special titles of this kind brought the god nearer to the individual and his activities. The cults of close-knit groups like phratry and deme effectively involved the participant families; an occasional allusion allows us to see how strongly the individual could feel about the activities and cults of so wide a group as the Athenian tribe. The worship of Athena at Athens was almost a self-congratulatory worship of the state itself, in which each citizen felt proudly implicated. Greek religion shows profound differences of belief and form from anything our civilisation knows, especially in its lack of concern with the after-life of the individual, but it would be wrong to conclude on that account that the Greek had no personal religion.

Nor, though it easily occurs to us that this was an unsatisfying religion, is there real evidence that it had lost its hold in the enlightened times of the late fifth century and the fourth. There were, in a sense, alternatives to the orthodox worship of the Olympians, but none of them excluded orthodoxy. The Eleusinian mysteries, basically the worship of Demeter and her daughter, with Iacchus (whatever that name originally meant) as some sort of equivalent for Dionysus, offered initiation to all, free or slave. The unusual building, called the hall of initiation, was, for once, a place of assembly for the worshippers. Here, after purification and various ceremonies, something—it is no use guessing what—was shown which confirmed to the initiate, as Greek writers put it, 'better hopes after death'. That should have had great attraction if the Olympian religion left men unsatisfied. But, though many were initiated, they did not thereby separate themselves from the worship of other gods, nor does it seem that the general belief of Athenians about death and the after-life was much affected. The body of beliefs, called Orphic, is more shadowy, and was nowhere officially adopted in the way that Athens adopted the rites of Eleusis. There was a body of literature, ascribed to Orpheus or his followers, preaching an ascetic way of life, a doctrine of reincarnation which should end with the purified soul at rest in some sort of heaven, and much else. The details are confused, and difficult to disentangle from the doctrines of Pythagoras, who also believed in reincarnation. Both Orphism and Pythagoreanism seem to have been upper-class eccentricities, not a means of consoling the poor for their sufferings in this life. Plato, through the mouth of one of the characters in his *Republic*, speaks of the priests who hang round the doors of the rich, offering hope of remission of sins and a blessed life hereafter through special sacrifices and initiations.

There was no doubt an appetite for such consolations, stimulated in Plato's youth by the long strain of the Peloponnesian War, but this was a supplement to conventional religion rather than a substitute. The accusations of impiety were made, not against the adherents of these rituals and doctrines, but against intellectuals, like Socrates, who were charged with setting up gods other than those the city recognised. There was some growth of scepticism in the late fifth century, parallel with the moral relativism which some of the sophists proclaimed; but the real trouble seems to have been, partly that physical explanations of the movement of the heavenly bodies were feared as godless, partly that sophisticated doctrines about the nature of the divine were taken to be attempts to substitute a new kind of deity for the old. Xenophon and Plato were themselves men of orthodox piety; and, by their account, it seems that Socrates similarly observed the traditional rites. But, from Aristophanes' *Clouds* and other allusions, it is clear that Socrates was widely, if unjustly, regarded as a subversive astronomer. It was this, together with the not unreasonable suspicion that the young imbibed from him doctrines imperfectly compatible with democracy, that led to his condemnation in 399—a period of acute post-war depression, when Athens was not yet quite recovered from the oligarchic rule of the Thirty—and so to the execution of a death-sentence which any ordinary prisoner would have avoided by going into exile.

There remain the many private religious associations, some devoted to orthodox Greek gods, some to Thracian or Egyptian or eastern deities. There had always been private association of citizens, clubs with social purposes, which in the Greek way took some particular cult as their centre, like that association of Heracles into which the speaker in one of Isaeus' cases had been introduced in his youth 'to share their society'. This was wholly within the established framework. The cults of foreign gods were from time to time officially introduced, like that of the Thracian goddess, Bendis, referred to in the opening page of the *Republic*; or groups of foreigners, resident in Athens, might receive permission to set up a cult of their own. (Permission was necessary, because foreigners could not otherwise own land for a shrine.)

Towards the end of the fourth century, there was a large increase in the number of inscriptions on stone set up in Athens by religious associations, many of the deities being foreign. That might suggest that, in this time when the city began to lose its old importance, the city's gods were giving place to other deities, more suited to that cosmopolitan time. But many of the devotees were foreign too; the increase in the number of such inscriptions at Athens is probably only a symptom of the continuing influx of foreigners into the city, and of the increasing readiness of such bodies as these to inscribe their dedications and the rest on stone. In other parts of the Hellenistic world, private clubs, not necessarily unorthodox in their religion, show the same readiness to advertise their existence on stone. It is doubtful if the evidence from Athens would justify us in speaking of a change specifically in religious feeling.

*

Oracles were the special concern of Apollo, declaring without the possibility of error or deceit the will of his father Zeus. The most famous was that of Delphi, on its tremendously impressive site under the lower cliffs of Parnassus (pl. 31), the main recourse of mainland Greece. Its rise to panhellenic fame starts in the eighth century, and some of the oracles recorded as having been given to intending colonists in that remote time will have been advice genuinely given before they set out. It has been pointed out that, at this time, Delphi seems to have been consulted by only one group of mainland states; and the Sacred War, at the beginning of the sixth century, nominally the liberation of the holy site from the oppression of Crisa in the plain below, seems in harsher reality to have been a struggle to see that the already very influential oracle was in the right hands. But if in early days it was the object of partisan struggle, its claim to universal respect was established by the fifth century. The fact that the oracle took fright at the Persian invasion of 480, and counselled submission, was glossed over without much trouble; and, though it favoured the Peloponnesian side at the outbreak of war in 431, that did not break its ties with Athens.

Though the procedure was not secret, it so happens that no good description survives, Greek writers assuming that it was known to their readers. The oracles were delivered by a woman, the Pythia, in a state of trance, but the formal response was handed over to the enquirer, in writing, by the male priests, who may be supposed to have reduced a relatively incoherent answer to intelligible forms—in major cases, to hexameter verse. But it is worth noting that, when the Spartan king Cleomenes I bribed the oracle in 490, Herodotus names the Pythia herself as the person whom he bribed. Late sources allege that the tripod on which she sat was placed over a cleft in the ground from which intoxicating vapours issued; this physical explanation has had a surprisingly long life, though there was no cleft, and vapours are excluded by the geology of the site. Nor is there anything to be said for the view that she intoxicated herself by burning or chewing laurel leaves. The trance should be taken as genuine, in the style of a modern medium, helped out by the ritual and the Pythia's own expectation that she would be possessed by the god.

Suspicion of conscious fraud must concentrate on the possibility of editing by the male staff of the oracle. To the extent that the oracle ever followed a consistent policy, this may be partly justified. Some of the extant oracles were, no doubt, wholly or partly fabricated after the event, to the greater glory of the god, and that cannot have been done quite unconsciously. But though faith can be very accommodating it could hardly have survived large-scale conscious fraud over so many centuries, to say nothing of the feelings of the priests themselves. It is better to suppose that most answers were given in good faith, but to allow something for the influence of the priests' own wishes and knowledge in their shaping of the answer. The tradition of ambiguity helped. It is a recurrent element in stories of prophecy that the recipient should misunderstand the message and end in trouble, but that when the full facts are known the prophet's foreknowledge should be vindicated. Hence come the notorious instances of Delphic obscurity, like the case of king Croesus of Lydia, a generous benefactor whom the priests could not want to disoblige: he wanted to attack the Persians, and was told that 'if Croesus crosses the Halys he will destroy a great empire'; the oracle was vindicated in the destruction of Croesus' own kingdom, however much the priesthood might regret that event. On a smaller scale, the event foretold could be made to depend on obscure preconditions, for instance, on an omen easily mistaken; after the event, credulity could always discover that the condition had been fulfilled in some unexpected way.

Most of the oracle's business was on an unspectacular level. Response to private enquiries of a trivial nature made little impression, whatever the result. Many of the enquiries were for directions about ritual, not capable of being verified or falsified. In very many cases, the enquirer, city or individual, had worked out his own scheme beforehand and merely laid it before the oracle for approval or rejection. If approval turned out unhappily, it could easily be claimed that the enquirer had been somehow himself the cause of failure. A prophecy seriously believed may produce its own fulfilment. Nevertheless, there must have been a sizeable residue of responses where the oracle had no option but to declare the future and risk falsification. Modern scholars are very ready to treat the recorded successes as all made up after the event; but it may be doubted if the oracle could have remained in business at all, unless it had a decent record of predictions which could, without special pleading, be regarded as successful. The will to believe was, of course, an important factor throughout.

Under these limitations—and the more so, the more we are disposed to believe in the sincerity of the Delphic priesthood—it is not to be expected that Delphi would exercise a powerful influence in any special direction. Its influence on the course of political history can very easily be overrated. Its moral and civilising influence, as appraised by Greek historians out to edify, does not amount to much either. The declaration of correct ritual was naturally taken by them as an important contribution to civilisation; otherwise, we have mostly moral tales of rich and powerful enquirers being told that some virtuous and industrious peasant was better off than they. Delphi ranged itself with those forces in Greek life which counselled moderation, both in these stories, and in the two most famous of the precepts which were inscribed on the walls of the temple: 'Know thyself' and 'Nothing too much'. One may doubt if many excesses were actually warded off by these means. The mere fact of the Greeks' belief and devotion is far more important, the fact that in their shifting world Apollo's oracle could be thought of as a secure fixed point. No scientific measurement can be made of that, nor of Apollo's contribution to song and sculpture.

Delphi was under the management of a body called the Amphictiony, literally, the 'dwellers around'—there were other such bodies in Greece, less famous than this. It met originally at Thermopylae, and included all the neighbouring small tribes between Thessaly and Boeotia; these more powerful nations were themselves members, and ways were found for representing other great powers. This was a somewhat makeshift arrangement for dealing with an institution of panhellenic importance, but it worked well enough through most of the classical period; with some reshuffling, it outlasted even the seizure of the temple by the Phocians in 356. Records of their administration survive from the fourth century, particularly interesting for the lists of contributions made by the Greek states for the rebuilding of the temple, after it was destroyed in the winter of 373–2, by fire or by a landslide.

What has been said of Delphi will be true within limits of other oracles, though most of them were not subject to so great pressure. In Asia Minor, Apollo's oracle at Didyma, just south of Miletus, was available to eastern enquirers till the Persians destroyed it in 494. Further north, at Clarus, near Colophon, was another old shrine which became an oracle, where a male prophet retired into a cave to bring back the response. Zeus himself was often consulted among the oaks at Dodona, remote in the north-west of Greece, and his shrine at Olympia was also oracular; and Ammon, the god of the oracle at the oasis of Siwa in the Libyan desert, was identified with Zeus and achieved high repute in the classical period. The underground oracle of Trophonius, at Lebadeia in Boeotia, may serve as an example of an oracle, not firmly identified with any major god. The ritual of consultation was notoriously terrifying. It is described for us in some detail by the traveller Pausanias, who consulted it himself in the second century A.D.; he takes care to assure us that, in spite of report, the enquirer did eventually recover the power of laughing. There were many others; and this is the appropriate point to mention also the shrines of healing, the most notable of which was the famous temple of Asclepius at Epidaurus. The patient was laid down to sleep in the temple, and either he was cured there or he received instructions in his dreams for the treatment of his trouble.

Divination was practised, apart from the great oracles, by a variety of methods; for public purposes, the commonest was inspection of the entrails of a sacrifice. The most prominent category here is the sacrifice before battle; and the sacrifice on crossing the border for a campaign abroad constantly recurs in the Spartan record. Here again, modern critics are apt to treat the report of unfavourable omens as the device of a commander who had quite other reasons for not wanting to proceed. Sometimes they may have been a device, but the narrative of the devout Xenophon gives the clear impression that, for him at least, the inspection of these sacrifices was a serious and objective matter— Xenophon had commanded troops himself, and must have known if cheating were habitual. Still less can one question the sincerity of private divination, where no policy obscured the issue. At a lower level mere magic obtrudes, a subject which can be given some literary glamour but is unconscionably tedious in its real-life manifestations— least artificial where most malevolent, as in the curses solemnly inscribed against individual enemies, often on lead.

*

Greek art and poetry demonstrate in the most conspicuous way how life and religion were intertwined. Boxing and dance and song, mainly the last of the three, were the order of the day when the Ionians gathered at Delos to honour Apollo, in the lively description of the blind poet of Chios who wrote the Homeric hymn to Apollo, our earliest record of such a festival. The great athletic meetings were festivals in honour of their god, and there were competitions in music and song as well as horse races. Athenian tragedies and comedies were produced as entries in competitions in honour of Dionysus. Sculpture was, in the first instance, representation of a god; and the strong anthropomorphic twist given to Greek religion by the epic meant that the sculptor must idealise human form. Sacred stones of another kind survived from the dim past, when the deity might be represented by shapeless objects of the kind classified as 'aniconic', images that are 'not images', but the need to present the god in human shape set Greek sculpture moving on the path which, for good or ill, was to be its characteristic direction.

The whole development of Greek verse would have been different

if worship of the gods had not required formal song on solemn occasions
—a majestic art practised by all the major poets, with many technical
ramifications, hymns and paeans and the rest. We, unhappily, can study
only the words. The patient labour of scholars on the limited and
refractory evidence has established much about Greek music, the forms
and capacities of their instruments, the tonality of their melodies
(there was no harmony), and much else; but we have only a few specimens of musical notation, only enough to show the kind of music this
was. We know plenty of names for Greek dances, special varieties for
particular places and rites; and there are illustrations, mainly on vases,
of different types of dancer. The generalised descriptions we have do
not enable us to appreciate the total impact of any one performance;
for anything like full understanding, we should need a cinemato-
graphic record of a whole range of examples. Sparta is especially rich
in technical terms for particular kinds of dance, a lighter element in
her somewhat sombre life which we shall never be able to visualise.
From most of the Greek world we have only stray allusions.

But the words tell us a great deal. Even for Sparta, Alcman's
'Maiden-song' gives us a glimpse of the nature of the ceremonies,
dedicated there to Artemis at the end of the seventh century. The part
played by such festivals in the development of Greek civilisation
cannot easily be overestimated.

CHAPTER 12

Open speculation

THE GREEKS CHARACTERISED the outer world as 'barbarian', meaning, in the first place, only that its speech was unintelligible; though, in the fifth century, the word acquired the overtones we give it, backward and brutal as well as foreign. If a Greek were asked what distinguished his own nation from the rest, one likely reply would be that Greeks were free and barbarians were slaves. That is not a bad answer, though the sense of superiority might overflow into chauvinism, and this could be used to justify enslavement of supposedly lower races. The Greeks of the fourth century were more clearly conscious of belonging to a civilisation with certain specific characteristics, to the extent that Isocrates, in flowery praise of the intellectual achievements of Athens, declared that the definition of 'Hellene' was no longer a matter of race but of having some smattering of Athenian education. Looking back at this civilisation from our distance, one of its most remarkable features is the Greek capacity for free, general speculation, uninhibited by myth or authority.

To revert for a moment to politics, the Greeks had every right to notice and emphasise the difference between their own various regimes and the kingdoms of the East, more particularly their overwhelmingly vast neighbour, the Persian Empire. No high degree of organisation seemed possible among these barbarians, unless it was held together by the authority of a king, reinforced with an amount of pomp and ceremony which the Greeks felt to be servile and ridiculous. In the same way, it was widely felt in Western Europe, till a very late date, that society could not be held together except by that hierarchy of hereditary kings and nobles which Americans came to resent as intolerable for free men. The overthrow of monarchy in Greece, lost though it is in the mists of her early history, was a revolution as significant as the American. The Greek alternative of free discussion and majority voting had its own dangers, and historians have been ready enough to point out their mistakes, including the occasions when discussion was not free and majority decisions were not accepted; but the Greek way allowed progress as well as mistakes.

Intellectually, the habit of myth was an impediment to freedom, somewhat like royal authority in the political sphere. Myth in some form is indispensable to humanity, faced with a universe too large and various for any single man's comprehension. Each of us in our day harbours a quantity of irrational belief and prejudice about those sectors of our world for which we have not the time or will or capacity to acquire genuine information. For earlier mankind, when the stock of real information was much lower, an accepted and comprehensive framework of myth was all the more necessary, to arm the individual man with some sort of working hypothesis for action and render a probably hostile universe in some degree manageable. Greece was singularly fertile in myth: some of it trivial invention, to account for matters of no great importance; much of it highly imaginative, and the root of great poetry, in its way a vehicle for many kinds of truth. It was also the first home of the impersonal, non-mythical explanation.

*

The first name in Western science and philosophy is that of Thales of Miletus, in the early sixth century. Ionia may have been something of a backwater at the time when Euboeans and other islanders, Corinth and Crete and the rest, first renewed contact with the Eastern world; but the new impulse soon stirred the greater East Greek cities, especially Miletus. She took the lead, early in the seventh century, in establishing effective and continuous contact with Egypt. In the East, which in spite of recession at the end of the Bronze Age had never lost its literacy, curious Greeks might encounter a store of recorded experience and of techniques tested in long use, plenty which could stir an active imagination. Their adaptation of the Phoenician alphabet (p. 50), the splitting of syllables into their component vowels and consonants, is a good example of their capacity for seeing through to first principles and improving on the models they found. In Egypt and Babylon, they would find long records of astronomical observation. Thales is said to have foretold the solar eclipse of 28 May 585 which interrupted a battle between the Lydians and the Medes. With the means at his command, he could not possibly have calculated the time and area of totality, and Herodotus only credits him with the prediction that there would be an eclipse within that year. If he was using any cycle, derived from records of past eclipses, he was still uncommonly lucky to hit an eclipse that was total in his own area. This was, nevertheless, a first step towards the frame of mind in which Dion, in 357, could argue to his soldiers that an eclipse was a natural phenomenon, about which rational argument was possible, not just a dire omen.

If, in this field, Thales was dependent on luck and the records of other races, it was quite another matter when he guessed that water was the primary substance of which the whole world was composed. Mythological explanations of the origin and present state of the world were common enough, but they were conceived in the concrete terms of myth; and the agent was a divine being, whose will was accepted, by those for whom the myth was framed, as an explanation sufficient in itself. The Milesian 'physicists', of whom Thales was the first, posited instead an impersonal explanation. This was something which we can call a scientific intuition, in that it tried to account for a multiplicity of phenomena by a single, simple principle; and their belief that the underlying primordial substance persisted the same through all apparent change is in some sense still with us as the principle of the conservation of matter or of energy. This was an impressive intellectual jump, whose value lies in the fact that the question was asked at all, and not in the quality of the particular answer. Anaximander, also of Miletus, thought that the primordial substance was in itself indeterminate, without specific qualities—another remarkable jump. But the theory which mainly prevailed, in one form or another, was that of the four elements, first propounded by Empedocles, of Acragas in Sicily, in the fifth century: these were fire and air and water and earth, out of which everything else is composed, all differences being due to the different proportions of the elements involved.

The place of our earth in the universe is another subject which has always inspired myth. The early Ionians took a hand with that, too. Thales guessed that the earth floated on water, which might help to account for earthquakes. Anaximander broke more radically with conventional thought by asserting that the earth, which he took to be a disc whose diameter was three times its depth, needed no support, having no reason to move in one direction rather than another. He also introduced the notion of a rotatory movement, like that of a vortex in liquid, to account for the differentiation of elements within his indeterminate primordial substance, and so for the origin of the world as we know it. Empedocles' four elements were moved by love and strife, the more complex system of Anaxagoras (below) by what he called 'mind'. For both, these seem to have been physical substances—but if, in a sense, they look forward to the concept of force, the concept made no progress. Theories of the nature of the heavenly bodies proliferated, too, in a mechanistic way that more obviously threatened traditional religion. Anaxagoras' suggestion that the sun was a flaming stone, rather larger than the Peloponnese, is typical of the speculation that alarmed ordinary men. The Socrates of Aristophanes' *Clouds* is most unfairly credited, both with this kind of astronomy, and with introducing Vortex as chief god in place of Zeus.

All this presents a bewildering mixture. Thought that we can call scientific is here allied with procedures quite unlike those of modern science. The earliest speculators had to invent their own terminology, but that creates no serious obstacle. When Anaximander said that the elements within his system 'give justice and make reparation to one another for their injustice, according to the arrangement of time', or the notoriously obscure Heracleitus of Ephesus that 'there is an exchange of fire for all things and of all things for fire, just as of gold for goods and goods for gold', the social or economic metaphor does not obstruct understanding; nor are Empedocles' love and strife in principle less scientific terms than attraction and repulsion. Nor need the religious views of some of the speculators have created an obstacle. Empedocles was a poet and an eccentric prophet, Pythagoras a mystic whose followers were deeply embroiled in South Italian politics; but that did not mean that their successors could not build on their results. The trouble was rather the form that the follow-up took.

Logical problems began to take priority at an early stage. To go no further back, Parmenides of Elea, in Italy, early in the fifth century, denied the possibility of change and motion, appearances notwithstanding; while the famous paradoxes of his countrymen and follower, Zeno, concerned mainly with the infinite divisibility of a line, provoked active thought but diverted it in a special direction. So Anaxagoras of Clazomenae, in Ionia, who spent much of his life in Athens and was Pericles' friend, conceived a complicated pluralistic system, designed to accommodate the possibility of one substance changing into another. In this scheme, elements (or 'seeds') of every kind are to be found in every substance; the predominant element gives it its specific character, but the mixture may be varied so as to produce change. A simpler answer was given by the atomists, who began in the second half of the fifth century with Leucippus and Democritus of Abdera, on the Thracian coast. The notion that there is a limit to the division of matter disposed of some of the logical paradoxes: the specific character of a substance is due to the shape and arrangement of atoms, too small for our sight; change is possible by rearrangement of the component atoms. These speculations remained entirely theoretical. They were attempts to find a logical scheme which would account for the world being what we see, to be judged solely by their plausibility, not by the devising of experiment which might test them in practice. For another instance, the question whether a vacuum is theoretically conceivable took a high place in later discussion about the nature of the universe. Problems about matter and structure arise in still more recondite forms today, but the discussion of them does not halt experiment.

It is not that the Greeks simply renounced the empirical approach. Most conspicuously, the medical school, founded by Hippocrates of Cos in the fifth century, stressed the importance of observation as strongly as any school could; some of their case-books survive, the careful record of the symptoms of a large number of patients. This, rather than premature theory, was the right way to advance medical science in the opinion of the Hippocratics. Others besides the doctor sought, here and there, for progress on an empirical basis. At least at the start, there was some readiness for practical demonstration; for instance, both Empedocles and Anaxagoras were ready to demonstrate that air is a concrete substance. But it is certainly true that the Greeks did not undertake regular experiment in artificial laboratory conditions, the only way in which their physical theories could have been verified or serious investigation of chemistry begun. In general, they contented themselves with observing what is easily found in nature; in regard to their progress in astronomy, it has been pointed out that the heavens form a kind of natural laboratory, in which the observation of recurrent phenomena can be indefinitely repeated. The idea of using artificial means to isolate a particular phenomenon, or of repeating experiments, occurred to them only in a rudimentary way, or not at all; and their conjectures were about quality, not exact quantity.

Most of the real advances had been completed before the end of the third century. Greek science wilted for lack of practical nourishment and, though mathematics could more easily be pursued in isolation, even that study tapered off. Difficulties, arising from the lack of an adequate notation, played their part here, but a more general and pervasive cause is the scholasticism of the later Hellenistic period, its tendency to relapse on laborious criticism of the older masters. If there is a problem here, it is rather why the classical Greeks built no firmer foundation. The standard explanation is, in effect, a social one, that the educated men who used their leisure on this sort of enquiry were not prepared to dirty their hands with experiment. That is not entirely adequate: Greek craftsmanship could provide all that was needed for a start, and there were skilled slaves for technicians. Aristotle, surely, did not dirty his own hands in the dissections of animals that were carried out in his school. The trouble, somehow, goes further back, for this relentless quest for the widest form of generalisation showed itself as soon as the Greeks began thinking on these subjects at all. It pervades poetry and history as well as the scientific field. Perhaps the best we can say is that it was easy to be carried away by the excitement of these first probings, that the somewhat airy provision of general explanations was, in some sense, habit-forming. The feeling that the practical details were below the dignity of fully free men of course contributed its part.

Speculation about the reasons why Greek science got no further must not be allowed to obscure the fact that it did get started and progressed a certain distance. To try to formulate a general rule to cover a wider range of phenomena was a new activity, an exercise of the mind more testing than the creation of *ad hoc* mythological explanation, which might or might not have a poetic value of its own. Further, it was by its nature an activity which flourished in open discussion. The answers which these early enquirers sought were not to be cooked up in closed mystical hothouses, but demanded light and air. It was a help that the undogmatic nature of Greek religion left speculation almost wholly free, except for brief periods of intolerance, mainly at Athens, which did not claim many victims. But that will not account for the fact that the questioning process got started in the first place.

*

There was one partial exception to the rule that Greek speculation was not secret. That was among the followers of Pythagoras of Samos, who emigrated to South Italy and founded a mystical sect there, whose doctrines were not to be revealed to the uninitiated. Pythagoras reduced everything to number. Music played its part here, with the discovery of the mathematical relation between the simpler harmonics. So did geometry, which means literally 'measurement of land'. It is symptomatic for the whole situation that the Egyptians should long have made practical use of the fact that a triangle whose sides measure 3, 4 and 5 is right-angled; whereas it was left to the Greeks, whether or not Pythagoras himself invented the theorem which bears his name, to formulate a general rule about the squares on the sides of a right-angled triangle, and thus involve themselves in trouble with irrational numbers and incommensurate quantities. Numbers, with various mystical correlations, meant much more than this to the Pythagoreans. With their belief in the transmigration of the soul, their prohibition against the eating of beans, and much else, they formed a religious sect whose doctrines were not openly rational, in the sense of the last paragraph. As a kind of secret society with right-wing views, they played a part, which we cannot now easily unravel, in the politics of the South Italian cities. But their strictly mathematical teachings were not in the same way secret. If for nothing else, they would still be important as an influence on Plato, and as a basis for his belief that Syracuse might be transformed by instructing the younger Dionysius in geometry.

Plato was impatient of physical enquiry, just as in politics he was impatient with the priorities of the Athenian democracy, the 'harbours and dockyards and walls and tributes' which are dismissed in the *Gorgias* as worthless in comparison with the politician's true duty of trying to make his citizens better men. The Socrates of his *Phaedo* describes how he searched the physicists for a satisfying account of causation, his hopes when he heard that 'mind' was the motive force of Anaxagoras' system, his disappointment at finding that this 'mind' was a merely mechanical cause of movement. He did not want mechanics. One might account for Socrates sitting in prison in terms of the structure of his body, but that was not the reason why he awaited execution there instead of escaping over the border.

The historical Socrates remains an elusive figure, who talked to all comers and never wrote a line, and is known to us, apart from Aristophanes' caricature, only in the works of two disciples of very different temperament, Xenophon and Plato. Xenophon's Socrates has his feet very much on the ground. His paradoxes are mainly the application of a robust commonsense in unexpected directions—as in the case of one Aristarchus, who emerged from the Peloponnesian War with his income diminished and a large number of female relatives to support. So Socrates, in defiance of normal prejudice, advised him to set them spinning and weaving for the market, and they were all happy. It is Xenophon again who describes a scene with the Thirty, whose attempt to silence Socrates was met with ironical questions, what he was or was not allowed to say; Critias adds that he must keep away from 'the cobblers and carpenters and smiths' he is always chattering about. Plato's constant use of the craftsman's skill as an analogy for the skill required in politicians and others looks like a genuine legacy from the teacher he so greatly admired.

Xenophon's account of Socrates took the form of an attempt to reconstruct his conversations. Plato's dialogues are a very individual form of art, sustained and elaborately organised conversation-pieces, mostly centred on Socrates. The setting is the high society of Athens in the late fifth century, admirably observed and beautifully conveyed, more by implication than by direct description; and Plato's gift of characterisation overflows into very happy parody. He was never the prisoner of his dramatic dates, so that the Athens of his maturity in the first half of the fourth century slips into the picture, too. The lively form reflects his known dislike of the rigidity of straightforward exposition; so does the indirect approach through the allegories or 'myths' sometimes told at the end of a dialogue. There are stretches which approximate to treatise form, when the interlocutors decline into puppets, merely assenting to Socrates' propositions; but then the puppets come to life again, to remind us that real argument continues, and will continue, though the particular conversation must somewhere end. Plato's Socrates is very different from the practical moralist, delineated by Xenophon—an individual figure, drawn with more subtlety, but certainly no less affection, who questions doctrine at a deeper level and more pertinaciously. If the argument sometimes draws him into regions where the historical Socrates did not much venture, he loses nothing of his special flavour.

There is no doubt about the affection and loyalty which Socrates inspired among his followers, or the great influence that he exercised. Nor, uncertain as we may be about his doctrines, is there any doubt that he spent his time trying to clarify such concepts as justice by that persistent and rigorous method of question and answer which has earned the name of the Socratic method. Greek enquiry in the fields of morals and politics, and into the theory of knowledge, did not begin with

Socrates; but his influence surely deepened those enquiries and stimulated a certain reaction away from the questions about the structure of
the physical world which the Milesians had started. Plato's testimony
about the effect of Socrates on his own development cannot be over-
looked. I can make no technical assessment of his achievement in logic,
but his concern with the betterment of the human soul overrides everything else: theoretically, in careful analysis of the language we use about
the soul and its qualities; practically, in his passionate desire for a
political system which would allow it its full development, not warped
by the strains of Greek life as he knew it. He was no cold or detached
theorist. He knew that the ideal city of his *Republic* was a dream, and
would probably have allowed that there was much fantasy still in the
second-best city whose institutions he elaborated so carefully in the
Laws. But all his work flames with longing for real change.

There are some forbidding features in Plato's dream of a world where
everyone knew his place and confined himself to his own proper
business. One of the less attractive is the way he concentrates on the
training and perfection of an élite and leaves the rest of the population
out in the cold. For all his observant interest in the whole of humanity,
he was ruthless in pursuit of an absolute and immutable ideal. For him,
the objects of experience were imperfect approximations to the 'idea'
or 'form' perceived by the philosopher's understanding. These forms
are the only objects of true knowledge, whereas in the shifting world of
experience nothing but 'opinion' is possible. Contemplation of the
highest of the forms is the ultimate task of the perfected philosopher;
to tear him away from it, to deal with the affairs of this world, is to
deprive him of his due felicity. Nevertheless, he must be torn away, for
only he knows the true nature of the goals to which political activity
ought to be directed. They are of supreme importance, as absolute as
the forms, and as unattainable, but the world will go wrong if it aims
at anything else.

The *Republic* starts as an attempt by Socrates and his friends to define
the nature of justice. The construction of the ideal city is, formally,
an incident of this quest, as are all the other tremendous topics, the
tripartite division of the soul and its immortality, the communism of
the upper class, the equality of the sexes, the censorship of poetry, and
the rest. The basic 'justice' of the system is that every element should
attend to its own proper function and to nothing else. In the individual
soul, the rational part must control and organise the passions and the

irrational 'spirited' part of the soul (Plato's *thymoeides* is not readily translated by any standard modern term). In the city, the cobblers and all must stick to their own tasks and not intervene in areas beyond the scope of their talents, especially not in government. Detailed prescription is given only for the ruling class, a stern education in mathematics and philosophy; thereafter, notably in the *Laws*, unrelenting supervision of all the activities of their lives. The influence both of Pythagoras and of Sparta is clear. To this extent, Plato thought extensively about the perpetuation of his system, once it was started; but he devoted little serious thought to the question how much a system, or any part of it, was to be set up in the first place. For a man who understood his own world so well, he was dishearteningly abstracted from the real world in his speculations.

For Aristotle, on the other hand, the correct starting-point was description of the world as it is. Drastic, systematic reform was not, in the same way, the breath of his life. He began, indeed, in the school called the Academy, the gymnasium outside Athens where Plato taught; and, like other disciples, he began by imitating the master's form and wrote numerous dialogues, all now lost. The voluminous surviving works, more than mere lecture notes, but not all of them finished treatises, were not meant for general literary circulation. Their preservation, and their eventual publication in Roman times, must count among the most influential accidents in the history of western thought. A substantial part of his effort was given to the formulation of a viable system of logic, and still more to the descriptive sciences. Here, he himself worked mainly on the animal world; his pupil and successor, Theophrastus, among the plants. The same energetic drive towards system and classification informs his moral and political works, where his astonishingly capacious mind fastened, first, on human behaviour as it is actually observed. He and his school collected up constitutions and laws and customs from the Greek and barbarian world as a basis for further study. If these had come down to us, along with the *Politics*, we should be far better informed about all aspects of Greek society.

Though holes can be picked in detail, and sometimes in principle, over all Aristotle's massive common sense is as remarkable as his range. It is mainly from this ground that he criticises Plato's proposals, not only as impracticable, but as undesirable as well; the criticism makes Plato appear even more rigid in principle than his dialogues show him. From this distance, it is clear that the gulf between the two men was less wide, their area of agreement more extensive, than Aristotle thought. For both, the given context is the Greek city, and a city small enough for that political and social intimacy in which Greek institutions might flourish, in a stricter and tidier form than they did at Athens—though, while Aristotle taught, Alexander was conquering Asia and wrestling with problems of another order. For both, the highest good was the life of contemplation, unattainable except by the man of independent means; if the craftsmen's souls were stunted by their low work, that was a fact of life which was merely accepted, though Aristotle was more explicitly conscious that the lower classes must somehow be kept contented. His thought in all this is very much teleological, that is, he believed that every organism at every level has its own natural purpose or end towards which it works or should work, and that it can only be happy in achieving that end. In terms of social or political organisation, the effect is not very different from Plato's conception of justice.

When Aristotle died in 322, the Greek city had already suffered that curtailment of its political freedom which was to render most of his *Politics* irrelevant, though for a generation or two the old cities intermittently struggled against recognition of their new position. His school—located in another gymnasium whose name lives on, the Lyceum—went on beside Plato's Academy; and both of them flourished, alongside others less rooted in the city idiom and better adapted to the needs of Hellenistic society. 'Epicurean' has come to mean a man who lives for pleasure alone, but that caricatures the doctrines of the Athenian, Epicurus. He accepted the atomists' picture of the universe, taught that the gods existed but were not interested in the fate of man, and hoped to induce in his followers a composure of mind which would neutralise the fear of death. These were doctrines which attracted some tough minds, like that of the Roman poet, Lucretius, but were hardly calculated to inspire wide masses. Epicurus opened his school about 310, while Zeno—from Citium in Cyprus, possibly Phoenician by blood—began his own teaching some few years later, in the public colonnade at Athens called the Stoa Poikile, a school with wider influence and a more varied future. The Stoics, closer in their doctrine to the sense of our adjective 'stoic', taught that the virtue of the individual soul was paramount, irrespective of a man's material conditions and status. They, too, had their physical theory, interesting to us in that they exploited the notion of a continuum, the *pneuma* ('breath' or 'spirit' originally), which in their speculation permeated all matter; and that they made large use of the observed behaviour of waves in liquid in an enclosed space—not that there is any direct connection between their unverified theory and modern wave mechanics. Their moral teaching underwent various changes of direction, playing down the founder's insistence on the importance of knowledge for true virtue, turning the 'stoic' disregard of outward circumstances into mere acceptance of existing status, and much more. With the other schools, this one died away in the end. Its regard for the individual soul was overtaken by Christian doctrine, while the mighty corpus of Aristotle's work survived, despite some zealous opposition, under the wing of the Church.

The relevance of Greek thought for our world is more often indirect than direct. The observed affinities between ancient and modern scientific thought do not document a direct connection; when men once begin to think scientifically at all, there is bound to be some measure of coincidence in the type of answers that they give. But Plato stimulated the age of Galileo, and there is some direct debt to Aristotle in the descriptive sciences. Their moral and political thought is bound to strike us as, in some degree, alien. It is not so much that the theories of the classical period were built into a city framework then in the process of dissolution, and that they cannot always be stretched to fit our larger units, which are incapable of direct government in the ancient style. It is more important that these theories are based on the premise that men are irredeemably unequal, to a degree which makes them unmanageable, even for the least egalitarian of today's theorists. They were, indeed, wholly unacceptable to the democratic Athens in which they were formulated. Plato did not expect to appeal to the masses; the rule of Demetrius of Phalerum (317–307), Aristotle's pupil and the agent of Macedon, was not endeared to the Athenians by his faint attempt to put some of his master's principles into practice.

That is not the end of the matter. The values which a Platonic or Aristotelian élite might pursue are not at all negligible, then or now. If I have dwelt on the repressive features in Plato's vision, that was necessary to bring out some important differences. It must not obscure the fact that Greek theorists continually capture our minds with genuine insights, as valid now as then. Plato's foundations are not often of the kind that we can build upon directly; but there is much to be learnt, even from following out the direct line of his or Aristotle's argument, and still more from following out implications with which they were not directly concerned.

Once more, the point lies not so much in the particular answers given, valuable and powerful as they often are, but in the fact that the questions were asked at all, and asked in this way. There was never any shortage of beliefs about the nature and status of the human soul, but these had been instinctive beliefs, religious creeds, mythical explanations, which asked for acceptance and perhaps for the performance of ritual, not for rational argument. It was a new thing, at any rate in the area west of India, that a man should set his mind to examining his own mental and spiritual make-up and the concepts which regulated his behaviour, without reference to outside authority. It was perhaps more revolutionary that he should initiate open rational argument about his own place in society, and ask what kind of society can be justified by reason. The first burst of questioning produced some slap-dash answers, and the activities of the sophists in the second half of the fifth century were really unsettling, as their critics claimed. With Socrates and Plato, the questioning manifestly reached a deeper and more serious level; and the effects have been felt ever since in Western European society. Here there is real continuity, mainly through Aristotle. His canonisation as the ultimate authority in so many fields came, in time, to provoke impatient and necessary revolt; but without the revered *maestro di color che sanno* we should have begun our inquiries at an altogether lower level and spent more time fumbling.

*

This eager, abstract questioning was not manifested only among the professed philosophers, but shows itself readily in poetry, more particularly in Attic tragedy. Most Greek poets are prolific in general statement—witness the lines of Simonides on the instability of human virtue, discussed at length in Plato's *Protagoras*, or the abrupt generalisations which Pindar injects into his praise of athletic victors. The Athenian tragic poets of the fifth century blossom into abstraction to a degree hard to parallel. This was a very argumentative art, breaking out at every turn into formal contests of words, set speeches or alternating single lines. The speaker is never content to take his situation on its merits as it stands, but must always treat his opponent as the example of some general principle of vice or folly; the comments of the chorus are mostly complex comments on the human condition at large, as exemplified in this particular phase of the main characters' troubles. A general theme is often very near the surface: the three plays of

Aeschylus' *Oresteia* are not only the rich poetic treatment of a traditional story, but a discussion of the blood-feud; Sophocles' *Antigone* takes to pieces the conflict of conscience and authority, the unwritten law against the positive enactment of the king. The state which subsidised and organised this highly intellectual art was staking an unusual amount on open argument about first principles, not for a small group of dedicated intellectuals, but before a wide audience of ordinary citizens who were under no compulsion to attend.

Greek historical writing, which, at any rate in Thucydides' hands, gained scope enough for generalisation, took its origin partly from seamen's handbooks which listed the harbours and peoples of the Mediterranean coasts, with notes on local customs and local history; and partly from epic and from the attempt, which began early, to reduce the varied personnel of Greek legend to intelligible order. Hecataeus of Miletus, who played a part in the Ionian Revolt against Persia of 499–494, composed both a geographical *Circuit of the World* and voluminous *Genealogies* (only minute fragments remain), which he prefaced by saying that he wrote 'as the truth seems to me to be; for the stories of the Greeks are many and, as I think, absurd'. That was a large step towards a rational conception of history, which was realised in the next generation by Herodotus. His work included extensive description of the customs and history of the Persians and the many peoples with whom they came into contact, leading up to an account of the wars between Greek and Persian which came to a head, during his boyhood, with Xerxes' invasion of Greece in 480. This last was in the strict and narrow sense a historical subject. It was a new phenomenon that such a thing should be described and analysed by a private individual, not logged in a bare chronicle or boasted of in royal monuments.

It is significant that Greek historiography begins, not with limited chronicles, but with the full-scale 'histories' of Herodotus. *Historiai* means literally 'inquiries', and the original meaning fits that wide-ranging and inquisitive traveller, though the word soon acquired the more restricted meaning of our 'history'. He is, in a sense, a deceptive writer: his easy, flowing style and apparently loose arrangement of his material conceal his skill, while his infinite candour is easily mistaken for simplicity. His declared purpose was to save great works and deeds from oblivion, Greek and barbarian alike; and, among the things he aimed to set down, he singled out 'the reason why they fought with one another'. Yet this regard for glory, with its epic overtones, might seem to conflict with his conviction that the war was a mere evil; his readiness to defend oracles or to recognise a divine plan do not combine comfortably with his flashes of up-to-date rationalism. Nor does the programmatic statement cover anything like all he offers. It is not easy to formulate, or even to be very certain about, the basis from which he starts—his contemporary and friend, Sophocles, puzzles the mind in a fashion not too dissimilar—and it may be that we try to categorise too closely, that we should merely be grateful for his honesty, for the wide range of sympathy that led later and more foolish men to charge him with favouring the barbarian, for the boldness of his great design.

No one who has read Thucydides would want to call him easy, but, up to a point, his general intention is more explicitly stated and more detectable in the result. Herodotus set himself to recover the course of a war, fought by the previous generation—and the fact that the battles of the Persian Wars remain largely unintelligible is due partly to the date at which he began his investigation, partly to a certain lack of military realism in his own mind. Thucydides aimed to describe the contemporary Peloponnesian War, in which he himself had played some part. He laid down for himself a formidably high standard of factual accuracy, by oral questioning of as wide a range of informants as he could reach; and his exile from Athens in 424, on the charge that, as one of Athens' generals in the north, he had failed to save Amphipolis from Brasidas, gave him the opportunity of using Peloponnesian as well as Athenian sources. The resultant narrative is a finished work of painful art, which does not much reveal the nature of its sources or offer us the chance of checking him by outside evidence. But it has always carried conviction, and what it reveals of the writer's character suggests that he was as careful as he claimed. It is a singularly bare narrative, especially in the earlier books. He seems curiously reluctant to tell us even about the strictly military thoughts of his actors. Analysis of motive and character is largely confined to the highly-charged speeches which make up a substantial part of the work: shorter addresses by generals to their troops; longer political debates, often summarised as a pair of opposed speeches. Their difficult style packs the maximum of meaning and overtone into a compact phrase, the concentration of which cannot be conveyed in translation into a less inflected language. They also generalise, almost more rapidly than tragedy, turning our attention to the overall character of Athenians or Spartans, the norms of behaviour of oligarchs or democrats, the limits of deterrent punish-

ment, the compulsions of imperialism, and whatever else stretched
Thucydides' powerful mind.

He knew, and often stressed, the limited extent to which events can
be predicted or controlled; but he valued, above all other qualities of a
statesman, correct analysis and foresight—for him, a very intellectual
conception. He claimed that his work was not mere entertainment, but
would be useful to those to whom it fell to analyse similar situations in
the future. The whole tenor of the work shows that he had in mind,
primarily, political lessons. Paradoxically, the military narrative of
marches and battles is exceedingly full (and not deeply instructive):
the political narrative is hardly at all continuous, consisting rather of a
selection of episodes, fiercely and often obliquely illuminated by
the speeches, as if the intention were to highlight the elements he
thought significant and avoid repeating his themes. Thus, in spite of
his evident familiarity with the language and methods of fifth-century
medicine, which has led some critics to suggest that he was trying to
apply Hippocratic analysis to political behaviour, what he gives us is
very far from being a Hippocratic case-book; his affinities with the
sophists and tragedians are more important. His instinct for generalisation does not formally conflict with his demand for accuracy, but it
drove him in a direction which no other historian has followed. His
masterpiece was unfinished, both in the sense that it stops in the summer
of 411, nearly seven years before the surrender of Athens, and in that he
clearly spent part of his later years revising what he had written and
adding to it. Maybe he had set himself a task beyond the possibility of
completion.

Thucydides may be charged with narrowing the scope of history to
the field of war and politics, though wider curiosity in Herodotus'
manner continued in descriptive works and in the Aristotelian collections. The fourth century narrowed its vision further by its preoccupation with moral education. Plato, anxiously determined to
protect the children of his imagined élite from contact with false
doctrine, and Isocrates, smoothly claiming to be the true philosopher
and moralist, are in their different ways both symptoms of a general
tendency. This shows itself in history in a professed intention to provide
examples for the encouragement of virtue and to deter the young from
vice. The professions must not be taken too solemnly, and the real
historians were not inhibited. Even Plutarch, in the second century A.D.,
a man whose preoccupation with moral questions was no matter of

fashion but deeply embedded in his nature, was seduced away from it, time and again, by the genuine historical curiosity which he shows in his *Lives*. But, where the profession was taken seriously by its author, it tended to inhibit thought. This seems to have happened with Ephorus whose lost universal history exerted great influence: to judge by the traces, he thought he had done justice to the events which led up to the foundation of the Delian Confederacy in 478, when he had condemned the conduct of the Spartan regent, Pausanias, and commended the Athenian, Aristeides.

*

The facile moralising was, at least in part, a legacy from the publicist, Isocrates, whose rhetorical style did further damage. Rhetoric for the Greeks was both an essential part of their lives and a serious obstacle to progress. In public life, a man must make his way at every step by the immediate persuasion of the spoken word. Whether he was addressing assembly or law-court or a more restricted body, he would be speaking to a public meeting rather than to a quiet committee, without the support of circulated documents, and with no backcloth of daily journalism, to make his own or others' views familiar to his hearers. The immediate effect was all-important; it would be naive to expect that mere reasonableness or a good case would be enough. It was early realised that persuasion was an art, up to a point teachable, and professional teaching was well established in the second half of the fifth century. When the sophists claimed to teach their pupils how to succeed in public life, rhetoric was a large part of what they meant, though, to do them justice, it was not the whole. The contests of Attic tragedy exhibit all the tricks of this trade, as well as the art of the poets; and the private life of the Greeks was lived so much in public that the pervasive rhetorical manner crept in here too.

Skill naturally bred mistrust. If a man of good will needed to learn how to present his argument effectively, the selfish or malicious could be taught to dress their case in well-seeming guise. It was a standing charge against the sophists that they 'made the worse appear the better cause', and it was this immoral lesson which the hero of Aristophanes' *Clouds* went to learn from, of all people, Socrates. Again, the charge is often made in court that the opponent is a skilful speaker and the jury must beware of being deceived by him. From the frequency with which this crops up, it is clear that the accusation of cleverness might damage

a man. Juries, of course, were familiar with the style, and would recognise the more obvious artifices, but it was worth a litigant's while to
get his speech written for him by an expert. Persuasive oratory was
certainly one of the pressures that would be effective in an Athenian
law-court.

A more insidious danger was the inevitable desire to display this art
as an art. It is not easy to define the point at which a legitimate concern
with style shades off into preoccupation with manner at the expense of
matter; but it is easy to perceive that many Greek writers of the
fourth and later centuries passed that danger-point. The most influential
was again Isocrates, who polished for long years his pamplets, written
in the form of speeches, and taught to many pupils the smooth and easy
periods he had perfected. This was a style of only limited use in the
abrupt vicissitudes of politics. Isocrates took to the written word in
compensation for his inadequacy in live oratory; the tough and nervous
tones of a Demosthenes were far removed from his, though they, too,
were based on study and practice. The exaltation of virtuosity did
palpable harm, as in the already mentioned case of the historian,
Ephorus. This was not due mainly to the influence of Isocrates: public
display was normal and inevitable for a world which talked and
listened far more than it read. Already, in the fifth century, Herodotus
had recited parts of his *Histories* in Athens, and it is alleged that he received a substantial reward from the state. But Herodotus had much to
communicate, and no one who reads him can doubt that the uppermost motive with him was the urge to make known the results of his
enquiries. The balance was always delicate, between style as a vehicle
and style as an end in itself. We must not try to pinpoint a specific
moment when it, once for all, tipped over; but certainly, as time went
on, virtuosity weighed heavier.

Rhetoric was a major element in what may be called secondary
education. The elementary education of the upper classes was entrusted
to skilled slaves, of whom there was no lack, the *paidagogoi* who have
given us the word 'pedagogue'; and to schoolmasters, who taught singing as well as letters (pl. 32). Physical training was amply catered for in
the gymnasia, to which the *paidagogos* accompanied his charge. Further
education was a more random business, with enough experts willing
to teach for their fees, and rhetoric was a ware much in demand. While
Greek freedom lasted, and it mattered what a Greek city decided to do,
this was a necessary preparation for public life, whatever its side

effects. When the study became, in the gloomiest sense of the word, academic, only the side effects remained, and they were not such as to encourage depth of thought. It had been a source of strength for Greek civilisation that its problems, of all kinds, were thrashed out very much in public. The shallowness which the study of rhetoric might (not must) encourage was the corresponding weakness.

*

If many Greeks thought that the characteristic virtue of their civilisation was its freedom, we need not shrink from agreement, nor confine the freedom to the political sphere which the Greek would have intended. The openness of mind and readiness to discuss, which have been the main subject of this chapter, must take pride of place among the claims which the Greeks have on our attention, along with the clear vision of their artists and the vigorous beauty of their poetry and the best of their prose. Their contemporaries, the barbarians, from whom at the start they learnt so much, achieved many things, but not this freedom. The monumental rigour of Egypt stiffened thought as well as art, priestly authority weighed heavily, and the insidious influence of magic wrecked much, including the empirical advances of their medicine. Babylon is still with us in the 360 degrees of our circles; but their mathematics and astronomy, like their law, served practical ends which have merely perished. The imagination of the Scythians, and later of the Celts, made fascinating abstract patterns out of living forms, but did not nourish an organised body of knowledge. Of all the various cultures which the Romans met in their career of conquest, it was Greece that took them captive, and that was no accident. Hence the large Greek component in our inheritance, with which no other compares except the Jewish contribution to the Christian tradition.

Our grasp of this culture is a precarious one. Of all that the Greeks made, only their pottery, their engraved gems and some of their bronze present to our eye the same image that they saw; and we set these things apart in museums for study and pleasure, where they spent them in use or dedicated them to a god. If we saw the sculpture and architecture in its first gaudy colour, most of us would have to make large adjustments. Large-scale painting is virtually lost, and so is their music and dancing. We do not know with certainty how the language sounded, nor can we hope to gather all the overtones a phrase would have for contemporary ears.

Nevertheless, the literature lives, in quantity enough for devoted philologists to make out very much more than the bare meaning. The language is unusually expressive and flexible, the poetry, even at this distance, has an unusual power and grace, and current experience shows that, even when diluted in translation, it still makes its impact. In the visual arts, enough remains, not only to move us, but to stimulate current argument; and scholarship can fill in some of the gaps in the series from late copies. This is a world whose air we can breathe. It is different enough from our own to force us to look at it attentively, not only at the high masterpieces, but at ordinary things; and like enough, for us to feel that the issues which moved the Greeks are substantially of the same kind that move us. The study of it is not just antiquarian study of our origins. Homer and Herodotus, Euripides and Plato, have still the power to surprise us and to sharpen our vision of the world we live in.

Table of dates

466	Democracy at Syracuse
465	Revolt of Thasos from Athens
464	Earthquake at Sparta. Messenian revolt
462/1	Reforms of Ephialtes at Athens. Murder of Ephialtes. Exile of Cimon
460–454	Athenian expedition to Egypt
459–454	Fighting in Greece (First Peloponnesian War)
455	Euripides' first play. Approximate date of Thucydides' birth
454	Treasury of Confederacy moved from Delos to Athens
451	Pericles' law restricting Athenian citizenship
449	Peace between Athens and Persia
447	Parthenon begun
446	Boeotia and Megara revolt from Athenian control. Federal constitution of Boeotia. Spartan invasion of Attica. Thirty Years' Peace between Athens and Sparta
440	Revolt of Samos against Athens
437	Athens founds Amphipolis in Thrace
436	Birth of Isocrates
431	Outbreak of Peloponnesian War
429–427	Peloponnesian siege of Plataea
429	Death of Pericles. Birth of Plato
427	Aristophanes' first play
427–424	First Athenian expedition to Sicily
425	Spartan detachment cut off on Sphacteria near Pylos and forced to surrender
424	Expedition of Brasidas to Thrace. Athenian defeat at Delium in Boeotia. Brasidas captures Amphipolis. Thucydides exiled from Athens
422	Battle outside Amphipolis, Cleon and Brasidas killed
421	Peace of Nicias
420 onwards	Sporadic fighting in Peloponnese
418	Sparta defeats Athens and Argos at Mantineia
415	Athenian expedition against Syracuse
413	Sparta formally resumes war against Athens, and fortifies Deceleia in Attica. Destruction of Athenian force in Sicily

Bibliography

The unevenness of this bibliography is inevitable. For some aspects of Greek civilisation it is possible to direct the reader to a modern summary with a good bibliography; for many, the information is scattered through periodicals or concealed in books mainly concerned with other subjects. I have, as a rule, both referred to comprehensive surveys, even if they are out of date, and tried to show where one might make a start in looking for more recent literature, but it is not easy to follow this policy consistently. Where I have referred in the text to current controversy, I have sometimes gone into more detail, including reference to articles in the more accessible technical periodicals.

Translations happily multiply, and a detailed list would take up too much space. The most comprehensive series is the *Loeb Classical Library* (Cambridge: Harvard University Press); many important works are now available in recent Penguin translations (Baltimore: Penguin Books). Older and more stilted versions are sometimes, but by no means always, more faithful to the Greek than those in an acceptable modern idiom. The verse translations of Richmond Lattimore deserve special mention.

Chapter I Geography and climate

Murray's Classical Atlas (London: G. B. Grundy; second edition, 1917) shows physical features better than the otherwise fuller and often more accurate atlases of H. Kiepert; A. A. M. van der Heyden and H. H. Scullard's *Atlas of the Classical World* (London: Nelson; 1959), not quite an atlas in the ordinary sense of the word, has some useful photographs of the countryside; see also M. Cary, *The Geographic Background of Greek and Roman History* (New York: Oxford University Press; 1949). Full treatment of climate in A. Philippson, *Das griechisches Klima* (Bonn: Dümmler; 1948). For the special problems of Mediterranean agriculture, C. E. Stevens in *Cambridge Economic History of Europe*, Vol. I, chapter 2 (London: Cambridge University Press; second edition 1966); detail about cereals, A. Jardé, *Les céréales dans l'antiquité grecque* (only Vol. I published, Paris: Bibliothèque des Ecoles françaises d'Athènes et de Rome; 1925); L. A. Moritz, *Grain-mills and Flour in Classical Antiquity* (New York: Oxford University Press; 1958). Survey of mineral resources: O. Davies,

Roman Mines in Europe (London: Oxford University Press; 1935). On the social effects of the climate, Virginia Woolf's "On Not Knowing Greek" in *The Common Reader* (New York: Harcourt; 1940) is as rewarding as any academic treatise.

Chapters II and III   Mycenaean Greece; The dark ages and Homer

Vols. I and II of the *Cambridge Ancient History* are in process of revision (I. E. S. Edwards, C. J. Gadd, N. G. L. Hammond), and the consolidated Vol. I is expected shortly. Meanwhile, the various chapters are issued as separate fascicles (New York: Cambridge University Press) and offer a short cut to modern views and bibliography; for instance, C. Blegen's chapter on *Troy* (1961) offers a digestible introduction, whereas the four splendid volumes of his definitive report of the excavations would not be a sensible starting-point. Other specially useful chapters are: J. L. Caskey, *Greece, Crete, and the Aegean Islands in the Early Bronze Age* (1966); F. Matz, *Minoan Civilisation: Maturity and Zenith* (1962); J. Chadwick, *The Prehistory of the Greek Language* (1963); G. S. Kirk, *The Homeric Poems as History* (1964); V. R. d'A. Desborough and N. G. L. Hammond, *The End of Mycenaean Civilisation and the Dark Age* (1962); J. M. Cook, *Greek Settlements in the Eastern Aegean and Asia Minor* (1961). Some useful essays are collected in G. S. Kirk (editor), *The Language and Background of Homer* (New York: Barnes & Noble; 1964), including: S. Dow, "The Greeks in the Bronze Age"; J. Chadwick, "The Greek Dialects and Greek Pre-history"; and M. I. Finley, "Homer and Mycenae: Property and Tenure".

E. T. Vermeule, *Greece in the Bronze Age* (Chicago University Press; 1964) gives a balanced and discerning survey at full length; C. G. Starr, *The Origins of Greek Civilization, 1100–650 B.C.* (New York: Knopf; 1961) covers a longer period, with full use of the archaeological material and sound warnings about the pitfalls; for the Mycenaean breakdown, I have drawn heavily on the historical conclusions of V. R. d'A. Desborough, *The Last Mycenaeans and Their Successors* (New York: Oxford University Press; 1964). C. D. Buck, *The Greek Dialects* (Chicago University Press; 1955), the standard work in English, still posits separate migration for each major dialect; on the other side, J. Chadwick (above). M. Ventris and J. Chadwick, *Documents in Mycenaean Greek* (New York: Cambridge University Press; 1956), remains the basic work for "Linear B", though much has been added and corrected in later technical discussion. Homer's technique and oral tradition: C. M. Bowra, *Heroic Poetry* (New York: St. Martin's; 1952), with a balanced statement on heroic poetry and history in chapter 15; G. S. Kirk, *The Songs of Homer* (New York: Cambridge University Press; 1962); A. Lesky, *A History of Greek Literature* (English translation of the second edition of 1963, New York: Crowell; 1966), should be consulted on this as on all literary questions; and the relevant works cited in the last paragraph. Homeric society: M. I. Finley, *The World of Odysseus* (New York: Viking; 1954).

On Geometric pottery, the forthcoming work of J. N. Coldstream (London: Methuen). Renewal of contact with the East: T. J. Dunbabin, *The Greeks and Their Eastern Neighbors* (London: Hellenic Society; 1957); J. Boardman, *The Greeks Overseas* (Gloucester: Peter Smith; 1964) gives an admirable general survey, especially good on Al Mina. The alphabet: L. H. Jeffery, *The Local Scripts of Archaic Greece* (New York: Oxford University Press; 1961), part one.

Page 17: C. Renfrew, J. R. Cann, J. E. Dixon, "Obsidian in the Aegean", in *Annual of the British School at Athens* No. 60 (1965), pp. 223–247, now find that obsidian from Melos was used very early in the Greek Neolithic period, but that there was no Neolithic settlement on the island.

Pages 23–24: on this very involved question, see L. R. Palmer and J. Boardman, *On the Knossos Tablets* (New York: Oxford University Press; 1963).

Page 27: J. T. Killen, "The Wool Industry of Crete in the Late Bronze Age", in *Annual of the British School at Athens* No. 59 (1964), pp. 1–15.

Page 39: Lesky (above), 19 ff.; recent discussion, M. I. Finley and others, in *Journal of Hellenic Studies* No. 84 (1964), pp. 1–20.

Chapter IV   Outlines of political history

The *Cambridge Ancient History,* Vols. III–VI (1925–1927) is dated in its general conception and in many details, but still useful; so is G. Glotz and R. Cohen, *Histoire grecque,* Vols. I–III (Paris: Presses universitaires; 1938–1941). One-volume histories: J. B. Bury, *History of Greece to the Death of Alexander the Great* (London: Macmillan; third edition revised by R. Meiggs, 1959), whose style (unrevised) deters some readers; N. G. L. Hammond, *History of Greece to 322 B.C.* (New York: Oxford University Press; 1959), at its best on topography and military history; A. R. Burn, *Pelican History of Greece* (Baltimore: Penguin Books; 1965) is more lively reading. So are his *The Lyric Age of Greece* (New York: St. Martin's; 1961), for the seventh and sixth centuries, and *Persia and Greece* (New York: St. Martin's; 1962), for the period 546–478 B.C. On the archaic period, see also A. Andrewes, *The Greek Tyrants* (New York: Harper; 1956). There are no similar general studies for the classical period, but some of the works cited for Chapter IX are relevant; for Alexander, see note at end.

T. J. Dunbabin, *The Western Greeks* (London: Oxford University Press; 1948), deals in detail with the period down to 480 B.C., using archaeological material not available to E. A. Freeman, whose four-volume *History of Sicily* (New York: Burt Franklin; published originally in England 1891–1894) is still the best detailed guide thereafter; for a shorter survey, A. G. Woodhead, *The*

Greeks in the West (New York: Praeger; 1962). For the East, J. M. Cook, *The Greeks in Ionia and the East* (New York; Praeger; 1962).

Chapter V   Tribes and kinship groups

There is no good survey of Greek kinship institutions, but G. Glotz, *La solidarité de la famille dans le droit criminel en Grèce* (Paris: Bibliothèque des Ecoles françaises d'Athènes et de Rome; 1904), runs over much of the ground at considerable length. The evidence on phratries was assembled by M. Guarducci, "L'istituzione della fratria", in *Memorie de Lincei*, Vol. 6, 1937. For the view taken of them in the text (page 80), see "Phratries in Homer", in *Hermes* No. 89 (1961), pp. 129–140; "Philochoros on Phratries", in *Journal of Hellenic Studies* No. 81 (1961), pp. 1–15.

On the organizational framework in general, the two volumes of G. Busolt and H. Swoboda, *Griechische Staatskunde* (Munich: Beck; 1920, 1926) are a mine of information, as they are on many topics besides the strictly constitutional ones. For Athens: C. Hignett (Chapter IX below); H. T. Wade-Gery, *Essays in Greek History* (London: Oxford University Press; 1958), especially pp. 150–154.

Chapter VI   Landowners, peasants and colonists

No comprehensive survey since P. Guiraud, *La propriété foncière en Grèce* (Paris: Hachette; 1893); and no recent special study of the particular areas discussed here, except for Athens (below).

Colonization: Dunbabin, *Western Greeks* (Chapter IV above); Boardman, *Greeks Overseas* (Chapters II–III above); J. Bérard, *La colonisation grecque de l'Italie méridionale et de la Sicile dans l'antiquité: l'histoire et la légende* (Paris; second edition, 1957). For Cyrene: F. Chamoux, *Cyrène sous la monarchie des Battiades* (Paris: Bibliothèque des Ecoles françaises d'Athènes et de Rome; 1953); the inscription referred to on page 99 is fully discussed by A. J. Graham, in *Journal of Hellenic Studies* No. 80 (1960), pp. 94–111.

W. J. Woodhouse, *Solon the Liberator* (New York: Octagon Books; originally published in England in 1938) based his analysis on the view that land was inalienable in archaic Greece (chapter 8); N. G. L. Hammond, "Land Tenure in Athens and Solon's *Seisachtheia*", in *Journal of Hellenic Studies* No. 81 (1961), pp. 76–98, refining on J. V. A. Fine, *Horoi* (*Hesperia*, supplement 9, 1951), maintained that land in the plain of Attica was inalienable till the late fifth century; no detailed refutation has been published, but some counter-arguments are given in the text. Literature on Solon is apt to be extravagant; the recent tendency has been—e.g. A. Masaracchia, *Solone* (Florence: La nuove Italia; 1958)—to stress his moderation so far that his reforms almost vanish. Debt-bondage: M. I. Finley, "La servitude pour dettes", in *Rev. hist. de droit français et étranger*, 4.43 (1965), pp. 159–184.

Inheritance: W. R. W. Harrison, *Athenian Law*, Vol. I (London: Oxford University Press; forthcoming). Security: M. I. Finley, *Land and Credit in Ancient Athens* (New Brunswick: Rutgers University Press; 1952).

Chapter VII   Traders, craftsmen and slaves

The basic work of A. Boeckh, *Die Staatshaushaltung der Athener* (Berlin; third edition edited by M. Fränkel, 1886; and English translation published London; 1842), still needs to be consulted on many topics; F. W. Heichelheim, *An Economic History of the Ancient World*, Vol. I (Leiden: Sijthoff; English translation 1958), p. 193 ff., and Vol. II (1964), is a survey with extensive bibliography; H. Michell, *The Economics of Ancient Greece* (New York: Barnes & Noble; second edition, 1963), mainly collects technical detail. On the scale of commerce and industry: J. Hasebroek, *Trade and Politics in Ancient Greece* (New York: Biblo & Tannen; English translation 1933), makes valuable criticisms but is sometimes rough with the archaeological evidence; E. Will, "Trois quarts de siècle de recherches sur l'économie grecque antique", in *Annales* 9 (1954), pp. 7–22.

Coinage: the basic handbook, B. V. Head, *Historia Numorum* (London: Oxford University Press; 1911), is in process of revision, by now a long and difficult business; the most reliable approach currently available is in Dr. Kraay's introduction and notes to C. M. Kraay and Max Hirmer, *Greek Coins* (New York: Abrams; 1966), a magnificent collection of photographs. Metics: the standard work is still M. Clerc, *Les métèques athéniens* (Paris: Bibliothèque des Ecoles françaises d'Athènes et de Rome; 1893). Slavery: W. L. Westermann, *The Slave Systems of Greek and Roman Antiquity* (Philadelphia: American Philosophical Society; 1955), has serious defects; see G. E. M. de Ste. Croix in *Classical Review* n.s. 7 (1957), pp. 54–59, a serious contribution in its own right; the best modern introduction and bibliography is the volume of essays in M. I. Finley (editor), *Slavery in Classical Antiquity* (Cambridge, England: Heffer; 1960). Athenian silver mines: E. Ardaillon, *Les mines du Laurion dans l'antiquité* (Paris: Bibliothèque des Ecoles françaises d'Athènes et de Rome; 1897); R. J. Hopper, "The Mines and Miners of Ancient Athens", *Greece and Rome* 2.8 (1961), pp. 138–151.

Page 123: numbers in the pottery industry: R. M. Cook, "Archaeological Argument: Some Principles", in *Antiquity*, 34 (1960), pp. 177–179; full detail, "Die Bedeutung der bemalten Keramik für den griechischen Handel", in

Jahrbuch des deutschen archäologischen Instituts 74 (1959), pp. 114–123.

Page 125: R. Joffroy, *Le trésor de Vix*, *Côte d'Or* (*Mon. et Mém. Fond. E. Piot*, 48 i; Paris: Presses universitaires; 1954); Laconian alphabet; Jeffery, *Local Scripts* (Chapters II–III above), pp. 191–2; M. Gjodesen, *American Journal of Archaeology* No. 67 (1963), pp. 335–346, argues for an early date (*c.* 575 B.C.), and less persuasively for Corinthian manufacture.

Page 127: P. Jacobsthal, in *Journal of Hellenic Studies* No. 71 (1951), pp. 85–95, and E. S. G. Robinson, *ibid.* pp. 156–167, demolished older theories which placed the beginnings of coinage at a much earlier date, but these still appear; for Athens, C. M. Kraay in *Numismatic Chronicle* 6.16 (1956), pp. 43–68.

Page 128: coinage to pay mercenaries: R. M. Cook, in *Historia* No. 7 (1958), pp. 259–261; for transactions with the state, C. M. Kraay, *Journal of Hellenic Studies* No. 84 (1964), pp. 76–91.

Page 145: commercial reasons for the Peloponnesian War were hotly argued by F. M. Cornford, *Thucydides Mythistoricus* (New York: Humanities Press; 1907), chapter one.

Page 145–146: Marxists on Greek history: e.g. G. Thomson, *Aeschylus and Athens* (London: Lawrence and Wishart; 1941).

Chapter VIII Armies, navies and milita. y leagues

General survey: F. E. Adcock, *The Greek and Macedonian Art of War* (Berkeley: University of California Press; 1957). Armour: A. Snodgrass, *Early Greek Armour and Weapons* (Chicago: Aldine; 1964). Introduction of hoplites: H. L. Lorimer, "The Hoplite Phalanx", in *Annual of the British School at Athens* No. 42 (1947), pp. 76–138, followed in *Greek Tyrants* (above, Chapter IV), chapter 3; but A. Snodgrass, "The Hoplite Reform and History", in *Journal of Hellenic Studies* No. 85 (1965), pp. 110–122, argues for a different sequence.

Ships: A. Momigliano, "Sea-power in Greek Thought", in *Classical Review* No. 58 (1944), pp. 1–7 (reprinted in *Secondo contributo all storia degli studi classici;* Rome: Ediz. di storia e lett.; 1960), pp. 57–67. A. W. Gomme, "A Forgotten Factor in Greek Naval Strategy", in *Essays in Greek History and Literature* (London: Oxford University Press; 1937), pp. 190–203. Construction of the trireme (page 154): J. S. Morrison, in *Mariner's Mirror* No. 27 (1941), pp. 14–44; *Classical Quarterly* No. 41 (1947), pp. 122–135.

Peloponnesian League: J. A. O. Larsen, "Sparta and the Ionian Revolt", in *Classical Philology* No. 27 (1932), pp. 136–150; "The Constitution of the Peloponnesian League", *ibid.* 28 (1933), pp. 257–276; 29 (1934), pp. 1–19. Delian League: massive but uneven treatment in B. D. Meritt, H. T. Wade-Gery, M. F. McGregor, *The Athenian Tribute Lists*, Vol. III (Princeton: American School of Classical Studies; 1950); a fresh study is expected from

R. Meiggs. On relations between Athens and her subjects, G. E. M. de Ste. Croix, "The Character of the Athenian Empire", in *Historia* No. 3 (1954), pp. 1-41.

Mercenaries: H. W. Parke, *Greek Mercenary Soldiers from the Earliest Times to the Battle of Ipsus* (London: Oxford University Press; 1933).

Chapter IX   Government and lawcourts

General: G. Glotz, *The Greek City* (New York: Barnes & Noble; English translation 1965); V. Ehrenberg, *The Greek State* (New York: Barnes & Noble; 1960); Busolt and Swoboda, *Griechische Staatskunde* (above, Chapter V). Law: J. W. Jones, *The Law and Legal Theory of the Greeks* (London: Oxford University Press; 1956); R. J. Bonner and G. Smith, *The Administration of Justice from Homer to Aristotle* (Chicago University Press; two volumes, 1930, 1938).

Athens: H. T. Wade-Gery, *Essays in Greek History* (London: Oxford University Press; 1958); C. Hignett, *History of the Athenian Constitution* (New York: Oxford University Press; 1952), full coverage, excessive scepticism about the evidence for the early stages, unfortunately stops at the end of the fifth century; A. H. M. Jones, *Athenian Democracy* (New York: Barnes & Noble; 1957), is more concerned with the way the constitution actually worked; C. Mossé, *La fin de la démocratie athénienne* (Paris: Presses universitaires; 1962). See also G. M. Calhoun, *Athenian Clubs in Politics and Legislation* (Austin: University of Texas; 1913); M. I. Finley, "Athenian Demagogues", in *Past and Present* No. 21 (1962), pp. 3-24.

The literature on Sparta is more excitable: P. Roussel, *Sparte* (Paris: de Boccard; second edition, 1962), a brief and sensible introduction; H. Michell, *Sparta* (New York: Cambridge University Press; 1952), covers more ground but does not dig deep; G. L. Huxley, *Early Sparta* (Cambridge: Harvard University Press; 1962), offers bolder speculations. The Great Rhetra (page 168): H. T. Wade-Gery, *Essays* (above), pp. 37-85; N. G. L. Hammond, in *Journal of Hellenic Studies* No. 70 (1950), pp. 42-64, holds out for a very early date.

T. A. Sinclair, *History of Greek Political Thought* (London: Routledge & Kegan Paul; 1952), surveys the whole field. On the character of the pamphlet of the "Pseudo-Xenophon" (pages 191-192), A. W Gomme, *More Essays in Greek History and Literature* (London: Oxford University Press; 1962), pp. 38-69 (but his late date for it is not generally accepted). On the idealization of Sparta, F. Ollier: *Le mirage spartiate* (Paris: de Boccard; Vol. I, 1933).

Chapter X   Social values and social divisions

On the competitive character of Greek society: E. R. Dodds, *The Greeks and the Irrational* (Berkeley: University of California Press; 1951), especially chapter 2; C. M. Bowra, *The Greek Experience* (New York: World; 1957), especially chapter 2; A. W. H. Adkins, *Merit and Responsibility: A Study in Greek Values* (New York: Oxford University Press; 1960). On athletics and Greek feeling about them: E. N. Gardiner, *Greek Athletic Sports and Festivals* (London: Macmillan; 1910); C. M. Bowra, *Pindar* (New York: Oxford University Press; 1964), chapter 4.

Page 198: on Hesiod's fable of the nightingale, see H. T. Wade-Gery, *Essays* (above), chapter 9, pp. 10–12.

On all the literature referred to, Lesky's survey (above), chapters 2–3, makes far the best starting-point. Particular writers, etc.: *Fondation Hardt, Entretiens, tome x: Archiloque* (Geneva: 1964); C. M. Bowra, *Early Greek Elegists* (New York: Barnes & Noble; 1960), and *Greek Lyric Poetry* (New York: Oxford University Press; second edition, 1961); D. L. Page, *Alcman: The Partheneion* (London: Oxford University Press; 1951), and *Sappho and Alcaeus* (New York: Oxford University Press; 1955). Attic tragedy: W. W. Pickard-Cambridge, *Dithyramb, Tragedy and Comedy* (New York: Oxford University Press; second edition, revised by T. B. L. Webster, 1962), and *The Attic Theatre* (London: Oxford University Press; third edition, 1907; revised edition, J. P. A. Gould and D. M. Lewis, forthcoming); J. Jones, *On Aristotle and Greek Tragedy* (New York: Oxford University Press; 1962); T. B. L. Webster, *Greek Theatre Production* (New York: Hillary House; 1956). Comedy: K. J. Dover, in M. Platnauer (editor), *Fifty Years of Classical Scholarship* (London: Oxford University Press; 1954), chapter 4; A. W. Gomme, "Aristophanes and Politics", in *More Essays* (above), chapter 9, pp. 70–91, a spirited attack on older views which detaches Aristophanes almost too completely from current politics.

J. Boardman, *Greek Art* (New York: Praeger; 1964) is the best recent survey. In more detail: C. M. Robertson, *Greek Painting* (New York: Skira; 1959); R. M. Cook, *Greek Painted Pottery* (London: Methuen; 1960); J. D. Beazley, *Potter and Painter in Ancient Athens* (London: Proceedings of the British Academy; 1946); Rhys Carpenter, *Greek Sculpture* (University of Chicago Press; 1960); *id., The Esthetic Basis of Greek Art* (Bloomington: University of Indiana Press; 1959); G. M. A. Richter, *Kouroi* (New York: Oxford University Press; 1942); J. Charbonneaux, *Greek Bronzes* (London: Elek; English translation, 1961); R. A. Higgins, *Greek and Roman Jewellery* (New York: Humanities Press; 1961); A. W. Lawrence, *Greek Architecture* (Baltimore: Penguin Books, 1957); R. E. Wycherley, *How the Greeks Built Cities* (New York: St. Martin's; second edition, 1962).

Spartan social system: H. Jeanmaire, *Couroi et courètes: essai sur l'éducation spartiate etc.* (Lille: 1939); W. Den Boer, *Laconian Studies* (Amsterdam; 1954), part three. J. Hatzfeld, *Alcibiade* (Paris: Presses universitaires; 1951), is the calmest study available on that controversial figure. On male homosexuality, I have mostly followed the sober statement of K. J. Dover, "Eros and Nomos", in *Bulletin of the London Institute of Classical Studies* No. 11 (1964), pp. 31–42.

Chapter XI   Gods and oracles

H. J. Rose, *Handbook of Greek Mythology* (New York: Dutton; sixth edition, 1960); W. K. C. Guthrie, *The Greeks and Their Gods* (Boston: Beacon; 1965); J. Harrison, *Prolegomena to the Study of Greek Religion* (New York: Meridian Books; 1955, originally published in England 1903); E. Rohde, *Psyche* (New York: Harper's; English translation, 1925); M. Nilsson, *Greek Popular Religion* (New York: Columbia University Press; 1940). For the wilder manifestations, see E. R. Dodds' edition of Euripides' *Bacchae* (New York: Oxford University Press; second edition, 1960), and his *Greeks and the Irrational* (above), chapter 10. On heroes: A. D. Nock, "The Cult of Heroes", in *Harvard Theological Review* No. 37 (1944), pp. 141–174.

H. W. Parke and D. E. W. Wormell, *The Delphic Oracle* (New York: Humanities Press; 1956); P. Amandry, *La mantique apollinienne à Delphes* (Paris: Bibliothèque des Ecoles françaises d'Athènes et de Rome; 1950); C. R. Whittaker, "The Delphic Oracle: Belief and Behaviour in Ancient Greece—and Africa," in *Harvard Theological Review* No. 58 (1965), pp. 21–47; H. W. Parke, *The Oracles of Zeus* (London: Oxford University Press; 1967).

Chapter XII   Open speculation

On the Greek attitude to other nations, H. C. Baldry, *The Unity of Mankind in Greek Thought* (New York: Cambridge University Press; 1965).

G. S. Kirk and J. E. Raven, *The Pre-Socratic Philosophers: A Critical History with a Collection of Texts* (New York: Cambridge University Press; 1957); B. Farrington, *Greek Science* (Baltimore: Penguin Books; 1953); S. Sambursky, *The Physical World of the Greeks* (New York: Humanities Press; 1956).

W. K. C. Guthrie, *A History of Greek Philosophy* (New York: Cambridge University Press; Vol. I 1962; in progress). The literature on Plato is immense: to give one older and one recent example, A. E. Taylor, *Plato: The Man and His Work* (New York: Humanities Press; third edition, originally published in England 1929); J. E. Raven, *Plato's Thought in the Making* (New York: Cambridge University Press; 1966). D. J. Allan, *The Philosophy of Aristotle* (New York: Oxford University Press; 1952); J. H. Randall, *Aristotle* (New York:

Columbia University Press; 1960). E. R. Bevan, *Stoics and Sceptics* (London: Oxford University Press; 1913, reprinted New York: Barnes & Noble; 1959).

G. T. Griffith, "The Greek Historians", in M. Platnauer (editor), *Fifty Years* (above), chapter 10. J. L. Myres, *Herodotus: Father of History* (London: Oxford University Press; 1953), is wayward and interesting, but more critical attention is needed for Herodotus; plenty has been devoted to Thucydides, e.g. J. H. Finley, *Thucydides* (Ann Arbor: University of Michigan Press; 1963); see the good brief introduction by P. A. Brunt to an abridged translation in the series *The Great Histories* (New York: Washington Square Press; 1963). Rhetoric: G. Kennedy, *The Art of Persuasion in Greece* (Princeton University Press; 1963). Education: H. I. Marrou, *History of Education in Antiquity* (New York: Sheed & Ward; English translation, 1956).

From the voluminous literature on Alexander and Hellenistic period, only a very brief selection can be given. U. Wilcken, *Alexander the Great* (London: Chatto and Windus; English translation, 1932), is still the best one-volume history; W. W. Tarn, *Alexander the Great* (London: Cambridge University Press; two volumes, 1948), discusses the problems in full in his second volume, *Sources and Studies;* see further, G. T. Griffith (editor), *Alexander the Great: The Main Problems* (New York: Barnes & Noble; 1966), essays from a variety of viewpoints. The Hellenistic narrative in *Cambridge Ancient History,* Vols. VI–VII (1927–1928) is mostly by Tarn with chapters on Egypt and Syria by M. Rostovtzeff. W. W. Tarn and G. T. Griffith, *Hellenistic Civilization* (New York: St. Martin's; third edition, 1952), a one-volume survey with a brief historical outline; M. Rostovtzeff, *Social and Economic History of the Hellenistic World* (New York: Oxford University Press; three volumes, 1953), stands out as one of the major works of our time on ancient history.

Index